Growing a Healthy Children's Ministry

*a step-by-step handbook
to cultivating Christian kids
in any environment*

steve alley

Standard
PUBLISHING
CINCINNATI, OHIO

Growing a Healthy Children's Ministry
by Steve Alley

Published by Standard Publishing, Cincinnati, Ohio
A division of Standex International Corporation

Credits
Cover design by Joel Armstrong
Interior design by Joel Armstrong
Cover and inside illustrations by Paula Becker
Project editor: Bruce E. Stoker

08 07 06 05 04 03 02   5 4 3 2 1
ISBN 0-7847-1390-1
Printed in the United States of America

Dedication

I offer this book into God's hands, for His use. It is dedicated to Him, and to my ministry partner since 1972, my wife, Cora. Without her wisdom, organization, editing skills and consistent encouragement, I could not have accomplished this work. Thanks for being my closest friend and fan.

Acknowledgments

I believe we are who we know. God has used many people in my life to make me who I am today. This book is the product of the wisdom of hundreds of people throughout my ministry years. I want to specifically thank my assistant, Tracy Carpenter, and her husband, Mike, for their role in the creation of this book. You've been my mentors. Thank you both for your creativity and passion for children.

Table of Contents

*I*f you have ever taken on the task of creating and caring for a garden, you know the joys and frustrations of coaxing life from dirt. You may have experienced a little glimpse of God's character as your dreams of "enjoying the fruit" were threatened by worms, gophers, mold, or aphids. You might have felt a bit of godly joy when you discovered the first squash under a leaf after weeks of labor and patient care. You might remember the deep satisfaction of sharing the produce of your garden with your family or friends around the dinner table as you told endless stories of the work of your hands. All it takes is one garden, in your whole lifetime, to affect your views of God, faith, work, and faithfulness.

God likes gardening. He made a garden to be the first home for his most precious creation: humans. He put Adam in the garden to work it and take care of it. God called his creation of the garden "good." The purpose of the garden was to be an environment in which humans could enjoy the presence of God and learn about life. Throughout the Bible, God continues to connect the truths of life to the principles of gardening. Jesus often referred to farming and keeping a vineyard as examples of God's work and care for us.

Ministry is also like a garden. We, in children's ministry, are caretakers of the most critical "gardens" in all of life: the souls of children. Jesus gave us the frightfully exhilarating honor of coaxing spiritual life from the "dirt" of human nature. God has given us the tools, and his calloused hands are gently guiding ours as we cultivate, plant, and nurture the tender shoots of children's formative views of life and God. There are weeds, pests, and diseases for which to watch out; but in our minds we are driven on by the hope of the "fruit" of our labor: children who have intimate relationships with God and who are willing to sacrificially serve him at home, at school, in the community, and in the world.

The book you have in your hands is meant to be a reference book for *the "garden" of your children's ministry.* It is not meant to be read once and then put back on your shelf as a symbol of your knowledge. It is my hope that it will serve you as my own copy of *The New Western Garden Book* by Sunset Books has helped me in my gardening endeavors. My copy of *The New Western Garden Book* gathers no dust. Its pages are worn and decorated with muddy fingerprints that prove my regular use of its information in the real life encounters I face in my own garden. I could never fully know all that is in the garden book; I simply refer to its information, as I need it. It is my hope that the Lord will use this book in the same way. I hope you will find guidance in these pages as you seek God's leading in growing the garden of your children's ministry.

I realize that there is a high potential for a book being outdated weeks after it is produced in today's busy, fast-moving world. I have put much effort into giving you tools to stay current with the world in which you are called to minister. The principles of ministry today are the same as when Jesus first referred to them, and the same as when Noah finished building the ark. The foundations of caring for people and following God are unaffected by time in the same way that the principles of pruning rose bushes never change. It is my hope that, in the pages that follow, you will find assistance in learning how to evaluate the "soil" of your community, recognize the "climate" of your church, choose the best "seeds" to plant, become actively aware of the threats to your plants, discover how to care for the requirements of your garden, and ultimately enjoy a rich, fruitful harvest of powerful, world-changing children!

Gardening today is not like it used to be. Advancements in technology and biology have helped us create plants that are resistant to diseases, grow faster, and produce more. In many ways, ministry in today's world reflects those improvements as well. The increase in technology, information, and the general pace of life greatly affects all of us, especially our children.

Today's society has produced people who are hesitant to commit to anything that may require inconvenience or sacrifice on their part. Instant results and thrilling experiences are what people are looking for today. It is unfortunate that the children are learning these patterns earlier than ever before.

Churches must keep up with the trends and pace of society while still remaining true to the calling we all share to carry out the Great Commission. Being aware of the conditions of today's busy world is vital, but even more critical is our ability to consistently connect children to the One who faithfully offers hope, security, purpose, and peace no matter how busy we become.

The weather is good! This is the season for planting! Put on your work clothes, roll up your sleeves, get your gloves on, and let's go to work. What you're about to encounter in the garden of your ministry will not only change your life, but will also potentially alter the lives of thousands of children!

## chapter 1

The Heart of a Gardener:
Vision Born of Passion

Passion is the energy that propels us to action. Jesus' life of sacrifice and death on the cross must drive us to carry on his work. The closer we become to him who died for us, the greater our passion will be. The person who lacks passion may also lack understanding of what actually happened at Calvary!

THE GREAT COMMISSION IN TODAY'S WORLD, CHURCH, AND FAMILY

The work of children's ministry is extreme! It is extremely exhausting, and extremely fulfilling. On any Sunday, you may find yourself sweating, crying, running, hugging, laughing, stooping down, reaching up, wanting to escape, and wanting to savor priceless, eternal moments. I had a perfect example of the extreme world of children's ministry one Sunday morning. Our nursery coordinator had resigned and we had a significant lack of adults to care for the children. I was frantically trying to shuffle volunteers around to cover all the classes while being pleasant and appearing that nothing was wrong. I was so focused on the immediate goal of getting all the rooms ready to receive children that I found myself not even noticing people. My eyes were glazed over with a mixture of sweat and stress. I was standing at a classroom doorway checking on the status of the adult volunteers in the room when I felt my leg being hugged. I looked down to see one of my favorite little worship leaders from our children's church looking up at me with a smile that was right out of Heaven. All my stressed-out circuit breakers were instantly reset.

I knew what God was saying to me in the middle of my busy Sunday morning. God was telling me to remember what I was doing there. He wanted me to remember that the most important thing that could ever happen on a Sunday morning is that one of his most precious children would know him more intimately. My spirit was filled with deep joy as I stooped down and enjoyed the most beautiful hug ever. Little Sandy will never know how God used her that day. I will never forget God's hug and encouragement to focus on the real work of the children's ministry while being distracted by so many challenges.

The Great Commission is Jesus' command to go out and be involved in the world! If it weren't for the Great Commission, I could imagine a large percentage of Christians simply sitting back and enjoying life in the "Saved lane." The Great Commission drives us to be about the Lord's work. In today's busy world, the Great Commission requires more from us. We have to keep up with the pace if we want to have a voice or affect those around us. The increased expectations of this accelerated society force us to examine ourselves often. If we get complacent or lazy, the world will pass us by! Our personal relationship with God must be actively deepening if we expect to minister in today's busy world.

Are you sure of your calling and ability to lead the children's ministry at your church? Do you know the presence and joy of the Lord in your daily walk with him? Is there something about overseeing the children's ministry that makes you thrilled about going to work in spite of the challenges? Do you sense God's favor and blessing as you do what he has laid in front of you to do? If there is any doubt in your mind about these questions, this chapter will lead you to find definite answers regarding these critical foundations of ministry.

After reading this book, I hope you will be able to say that you know what you need to do to prepare yourself to be a gardener in God's ministry field. You should be able to identify areas of spiritual need in yourself and make definite plans to strengthen those areas with God's help.

You may be thinking, "This is too basic, I want to get on to the important things like creating a camp program or making a board presentation." Be patient, we'll get there. I believe this first chapter is the most critical chapter in this whole book. Ministry is not about knowing how to do things, but about knowing Who is really doing them. Your personal, spiritual preparation for ministry will either open the floodgates of blessing into your life and ministry, or it will block God from powerfully moving in your work. Take the time to absorb the information in this chapter, and seek God's wisdom and discernment as you prepare to reap a wonderful harvest for him.

The comparisons of becoming a gardener to becoming a fruitful child of God are significant. Jesus told several stories about farmers and gardeners in order to call attention to the qualities of the heart that God was looking for in his people. We will look at the similarities between the qualities of a gardener and the qualities of a fruitful child of God. Before we do, let me say that these qualities are expectations that God places on all who serve him. The fact that you are reading this book says something significant about you, your calling, and your passion for his Kingdom. You picked up this book because you desire to be a significant influence in children's ministry. You want to somehow direct or lead others. That's good. God needs more people with the desire to lead, but before you are able to lead others, you must first become a follower yourself. Joseph Stowell, president of Moody Bible Institute, says, "Following is the beginning and the end of what it means to be a Christian. Everything in

between is measured by it" (Joseph Stowell, *Following Christ*. Grand Rapids: Zondervan, 1996; p. 12). God requires a clearly defined character of his followers. He has even more to say about the character of a person he chooses to place in a position of leadership.

SPIRITUAL PREPARATION FOR MINISTRY

It is true that today's world is complex and busy, but it is also true that the Gospel message is still the same! God still wants to become real to the children of today's world, just like he did thousands of years ago. The children are growing up sooner, and children's ministry is definitely more complex than ever before. These changes in our world do affect what we do in children's ministry, but nothing will ever change the basic requirements of ministry in general: passionate people sacrificing and building relationships with others.

As a children's minister, you must have passion for what you do! Without passion, you will struggle to have the energy needed to continually give what is required of you. Without passion, you won't be able to survive the challenges that stand before you. Without passion, you may find yourself wanting to quit on a regular basis. How do you get this passion? From where does it come? How can you increase the passion you already have? The answers to all of these questions are connected to your spiritual health and perspectives.

It is interesting, and perhaps no coincidence, that some of the qualities of a gardener are nearly identical to those required by God of his people: willingness to work; vision for the end result; patience; concern for individual plants (or people); concern for the whole garden (or world). As you study these characteristics, ask God to help you examine your own readiness to be a passionate gardener in children's ministry.

God's Word is filled with requirements and blessings. God's love is unconditional in the sense that his love is available to all, but his blessings are clearly

Qualities of a Gardener	Biblical References to Character
1. Willingness to work	"Work...as working for the Lord" *(Colossians 3:23)*
2. Vision for the end result	"We have this hope as an anchor for the soul" *(Hebrews 6:19)*
3. Patience	"Wait for the Lord" *(Psalm 27:14)*
4. Concern for the individual plants	"Mourn with those who mourn" *(Romans 12:15)*
5. Concern for the whole garden	"Go and make disciples of all nations" *(Matthew 28:19)*

connected to conditions. If you want to experience a full basket of ministry fruit, you must be willing to develop godly character through commitment, obedience, devotion, and sacrifice. Think about the work that it must take to raise orchids. I've never done it, but I've been told they require specific conditions and endless attention. Once you make the decision to raise orchids, you must read everything you can find on orchids, interview successful orchid growers, and be willing to learn through your mistakes. Becoming a children's ministry gardener is no different. You can acquire all the right tools, be given a fancy title, and even develop a powerful children's ministry logo, but if you are not prepared spiritually your fruit will be scarce.

CELEBRATE YOUR PASSION FOR CHILDREN

It may seem strange, but I have met people in children's ministry who show no signs of any passion for children! Can you imagine how that affects God? He created, gifted, trained, and called us to children's ministry. If we don't passionately care about children, and if that passion doesn't propel us to lead children to God, then God's efforts are in vain. Let's look at passion for a few moments here. While you read these brief descriptions, ask God to help you examine your own passion for children.

Passion

The Characteristics of Passion:
Passion has a sense of urgency

Passion grows over time and can occupy every thought or plan

Passion causes action, sometimes to the point of exhaustion or death

Passion increases with opposition

Passion reproduces rapidly

Examples of Passion:
Fans at a sports event

Political campaigns

Members of organizations such as MADD (Mothers Against Drunk Drivers)

Patriotic celebrations and parades

How you feel about the people whose pictures you carry in your wallet

How Do You Get Passion?
Experiencing an extreme loss or pain

Research/studying

Convictions of parents

Identification with another's loss or pain

In response to another's sacrifice or gift

Spending time with someone who has passion

JESUS: OUR GREATEST EXAMPLE OF PASSION

The passion that drove Jesus' physical life here on Earth came from having created everything, and desperately wanting all of his creation to enjoy what he, as Creator, offered to them. His passion compelled him to take a stand in the face of the most ominous political and military power in the known world. His passion forced him to speak out and take huge risks. His passion caused him to stop and touch a leprous man, a little child, and a woman caught in adultery. His passion kept him silent as his jealous accusers brutally killed him. Do you have passion like that? Does your passion for the lost children of this world keep you up at night? Does your passion for the confused, frightened children of broken homes drive you to make a difference in at least one of them? No matter how much passion we feel we have, there is always room for more!

Are you a passionate gardener ready and willing to plant the seeds of the Gospel in the soil of children's hearts? Maybe this chapter has challenged you to increase your passion about children. Check out the "Passion Inventory" on page 13; it may help you focus on the areas that need some "passion punch" from the Lord! Keep in mind, as you take this inventory, that the source of your passion must be the Lord! You can give yourself all sorts of pep rallies about children or ministry, but if you don't find yourself feeling the feelings of God, you will soon see your pumped-up passion fizzle down to nothing. Seek the Lord's passion. See life and children through his eyes. Feel his hope and anticipation about what could be. Become his voice, hands, and feet as you passionately care for his children!

Pathway of Passion

Passion will increase as you become more intimately connected with the most passionate person ever: God. It makes sense that the people who are examples of the lowest levels of passion are those who are the farthest away from an intimate relationship with God. Those "heroes" of passion (Mother Theresa, Joan of Arc, Paul the Apostle, Billy Graham, etc.) are those whose relationships with God could easily be classed as intimate. Where are you on this pathway?

1. **Establish a firm foundation.** Remember that God saved you while you were a sinner *(Romans 8)* and that you don't have to work to earn salvation *(Ephesians 2:8, 9)*. Remember that God created you with unique abilities *(Psalm 139:14, 15; 1 Corinthians 12:7, 18)* and that it is he who empowers you *(2 Corinthians 4:5-18)*. While God wants to support you *(2 Chronicles 16:9)*, the only condition is that you seek him and want to serve him *(2 Chronicles 16:9; Psalm 1)*.
2. **Build protective walls.** Don't worry about what may happen. Trust God, but guard your thoughts *(Proverbs 3:5; Philippians 4:6-9)*. Be aware of your weaknesses *(Psalm 119:9-11)*, but focus on your goal, your passion *(Nehemiah 6:9)*.
3. **Grow through challenges.** Don't lose hope *(1 Corinthians 15:58; Hebrews 6:19)*. Learn from your mistakes *(James 1:2-8)*.
4. **Plan for progress.** Pray for God's provision and leading *(Proverbs 3:5, 6)*. Then take action based on what you know *(Matthew 25:21)*, and go in his power *(Acts 1:8)*.

Garden Pest:
Passion-Killing Root Worms

Evidence

Because these worms do their destructive work under the soil at the root level, their existence in your garden may not be known until you begin to see the visible signs in your ministry leaves. Some visible signs of the passion-killing root worm are: an increased unwillingness to sacrifice, feelings of futility, a lack of any strong feelings about children, or a desire to quit the ministry all together.

Sources of Infestation

Selfishness, self-centered thinking, apathy, or fear

Treatment

1. Limit your time with dispassionate people.
2. Spend significant time with passionate people.
3. Keep learning: remain humble, teachable, and hungry for more of God.
4. Try new things: methods, curriculum, and programs.
5. Become more intimate with Jesus: purify your thoughts, devote yourself to worship, prayer and stillness, memorize and meditate on God's word. *(Psalm 19:14; Philippians 4:6-9)*

6. Remember what the Lord has done for, and through, you. *(Joshua 4)*
7. Grieve over the pain and hopelessness of this world; "see" with his eyes. *(Matthew 5:8)*
8. Let your security and identity be his; give him what you have. *(Exodus 4:1-5)*
9. Don't give in to discouragement! *(1 Corinthians 15:58)*
10. Worship God no matter what. *(Psalm 27)*
11. Wait on the Lord for more passion. *(Isaiah 40:27-31; Psalm 46:10, 11)*

Passion Inventory

To help you grow in your passion for the Lord, children, and ministry, take this "passion inventory" based on Jesus' words in *Mark 8:34, 35:* "If anyone would come after me, he must deny himself and take up his cross and follow me. For whoever wants to save his life will lose it, but whoever loses his life for me and for the gospel will save it."

For each of the statements, mark either "Absolutely," "Somewhat," or "Seldom" based on your own personal passion. Be honest, and let the Lord show you where your passion needs some boosting!

PASSION CONDITIONS

"If anyone would come after me"
   He wants us to personally want to come after him.

1. I have a personal, private conviction to follow Jesus.	❏ *Absolutely* ❏ *Somewhat* ❏ *Seldom*
2. My passion can't be stopped by outside influences.	❏ *Absolutely* ❏ *Somewhat* ❏ *Seldom*
3. I follow him, not my own ideas or plans!	❏ *Absolutely* ❏ *Somewhat* ❏ *Seldom*

"He must deny himself"
   He wants us to become selfless and free of pride.

4. My passion for the Lord has made me a new person.	❏ *Absolutely* ❏ *Somewhat* ❏ *Seldom*
5. I am a selfless person.	❏ *Absolutely* ❏ *Somewhat* ❏ *Seldom*

"Take up his cross and follow me"
   He wants us to be willing to live or die for him.

6. My passion for the Lord has no limits.	❏ *Absolutely* ❏ *Somewhat* ❏ *Seldom*
7. My passion for children's ministry has no limits.	❏ *Absolutely* ❏ *Somewhat* ❏ *Seldom*

"Whoever wants to save his life will lose it"
   He wants us to risk our security and comfort.

8. My passion feeds on inconvenience.	❏ *Absolutely* ❏ *Somewhat* ❏ *Seldom*
9. I feel a sense of satisfaction because I am not focused on my own comfort.	❏ *Absolutely* ❏ *Somewhat* ❏ *Seldom*

"But whoever loses his life for me and for the gospel will save it"
   He wants us to be consumed with serving him and spreading the Gospel message.

10. My passion produces a new sense of identity, security, and peace within me.	❏ *Absolutely* ❏ *Somewhat* ❏ *Seldom*
11. What I once valued in life has become "cheap" compared to my new joy and satisfaction.	❏ *Absolutely* ❏ *Somewhat* ❏ *Seldom*
12. Those around me want what I have, and will follow Jesus too!	❏ *Absolutely* ❏ *Somewhat* ❏ *Seldom*

Now, look at your responses to the inventory questions. Those questions to which you responded with a "somewhat" or "seldom" are areas for which you might need to ask God for more passion. For those "absolutely" areas, ask God to increase your passion even more. Ask God to make you even more passionately alive and effective in everything you do for children. Ask God to increase your ability to feel the feelings of children today. Ask God to give you more boldness as you grow in your ability to be a spokesperson for the children!

"An understanding of your soil is perhaps the most important aspect of gardening. With that knowledge you will know how to water and fertilize your plants—in other words, how to care for them" (Sunset New Western Garden Book. Menlo Park, CA: Lane Publishing Co., 1979; p. 33).

A father entered our preschool children's church area at the end of our service one Sunday morning. The children's ministry team members took little notice of the man initially because other parents were entering the building to walk through and pick up their children. Instead of walking through the room, the man just stood still. He was looking around the room and listening. After a few minutes, the coordinator of our preschool program approached him. Thinking that the man was having difficulty finding his child, the coordinator asked, "Can I help you?" The man, shaken out of his observations of the room looked at the coordinator and said, "I just wanted to see what you're doing here that is affecting my home." Not clearly understanding, the coordinator asked for clarification. The father, through tearful eyes, began telling a story that blessed our entire children's ministry team.

The father's marriage was in trouble. His wife was angry and never came to church. She fought him about everything having to do with God or the church. The father took their little five-year-old son to church week after week, alone. The boy regularly attends this preschool children's church program in which the preschoolers worship, pray, and learn about God's intimate love for us all. Last week, during one of the mother's bad days, the little boy said to his mom, "Mommy, you should get to know Jesus. He can help you not be so angry all the time." The father turned to the coordinator,

who was also now crying, and said, "Thank you for having an impact on my marriage." It was then that the little five-year-old minister came running up to the man. They shared a sensitive embrace, and then walked to the check-out door.

THE INCREASING VALUE OF CHILDREN'S MINISTRY

Children's ministry is not about curriculum, budgets, programs, or recruiting techniques. It is about being involved with God in shaping the spiritual destinies of children and teaching them how to live in this confused, busy world. As we begin now to consider the soil of your ministry, the children themselves, I'd like to take a moment to remind you of the tremendous potential of your calling to children's ministry. It is the most powerfully-effective ministry available to anyone!

Of course, I'm prejudiced! I suppose every ministry could communicate the philosophical reasons for their ministry's importance over all others. There is something to be said, though, about the unique potential of children's ministry. We all share the same message of the Gospel, and we all have the same goal: to reach all for Christ and to lead them to a close relationship with him which affects their daily lives. There is a difference with the children's ministry that sets it apart from all others. We don't have to deal with so many walls which the people to whom we minister have built up in defense of their past fears or patterns of living. Our goal is without walls, and within view!

Obviously, today's child is different from the child 10 years ago. Today's second grader is aware of the world on a level that you and I were in junior high. Regardless of that fact, Jesus himself said that children were to be examples for us. I think that means fewer walls, less guilt, less pain, more innocence. Studies have shown that over 80 percent of the Christians today made that commitment prior to age 14! What a great area of ministry!

Ministry to children today is more than just passing on Bible stories. It's about effecting change in the lives of the children who then have a powerful influence in the home. No longer are the majority of our adults "church parents" who bring their children to us to reinforce what they are teaching the children at home. The majority of today's children come to us out of desperation and need. The home is not the place it used to be. Concepts like consistency, commitment, faithfulness, security, and truth are fading from our homes. The church is now the "final frontier" for values that we once thought of as accepted or common-place. The children are becoming the missionaries to their own homes.

We recently offered communion during our Sunday morning elementary children's church program. We told the parents weeks in advance of our plans to teach the children about communion, and then to actually serve them communion. We invited the parents to join their children for this important service, if they so desired. We asked our church elders to join us on that morning to assist in the serving of the communion. The children were ready. They had had two or three lessons beforehand on the significance and value of communion. On the morning of our service, we were deeply impressed with the number, and interest, of the parents who showed up to be with their children for communion. The room was packed with parents sitting with their children. Throughout the service we could sense the presence of the Lord as we watched parents and children praying, crying, and participating in communion. Many

parents told us this was the most significant thing that had happened to them as a family. They were very thankful for our partnership with them in the spiritual development of their children.

This event, and the parents' reactions to it, is an excellent snapshot of the condition of today's child, parent, and family. No matter where you live, you can almost guarantee that your parents are getting less and less confident about raising their children spiritually. They need help. They need specific tools. They feel out of touch with their children. What we do in children's ministry is not just for the children. We have to look at what we do as family ministry.

No longer are the children coming to church with wide-eyed anticipation of how the Sunday morning experiences will further the life lessons they regularly get at home. Your area of the world may be different, but a majority of the families today are too busy for spiritual training, or the parents are simply unprepared to train their children in the things of God. The spiritually-weak condition of today's family has definite effects on what we do in children's ministry today.

Those who serve in the children's ministry must view themselves as perhaps the only voice for God in the children's lives. There may be exceptions to this condition, but if we use this viewpoint as our foundation, we will not neglect those for whom it is true. I believe that those children who do receive Godly education and spiritual nurture at home will benefit from the refresher course they receive on Sundays. We will explore advanced training program options for these children later in this book.

THE VALUE OF CHILDREN

This chapter is full of ideas to help you sample the soil of the children in your community. Before we get to those specific ideas, let's look at some general teachings about children from Jesus himself. Jesus was a passionate, outspoken advocate for children! In his day, children were not valued by the adults. The adults viewed children as unimportant because they were not yet adults. Jesus changed all that! Look

How Did Jesus View Children?

Children are to be respected.

"See that you do not look down on one of these little ones. For I tell you that their angels in heaven always see the face of my Father in heaven" *(Matthew 18:10)*.

Children are examples of innocence, teachability, humility, and trust.

"I tell you the truth, unless you change and become like little children, you will never enter the kingdom of heaven. Therefore, whoever humbles himself like this child is the greatest in the kingdom of heaven" *(Matthew 18:3, 4)*.

Children are representatives of Jesus.

"Whoever welcomes a little child like this in my name welcomes me" *(Matthew 18:5)*.

Children must be encouraged to know Jesus as savior.

"Let the little children come to me, and do not hinder them, for the kingdom of God belongs to such as these…. And he took the children in his arms, put his hands on them and blessed them" *(Mark 10:14, 16)*.

Children must be protected from the evils of the world.

"If anyone causes one of these little ones who believe in me to sin, it would be better for him to have a large millstone hung around his neck and to be drowned in the depths of the sea" *(Matthew 18:6)*.

---

at what he taught about the value of children, and how to care for these spiritually-sensitive examples to us all.

EXPLORE THE WORLD OF CHILDREN

In order to adequately minister to a group of people, you must know their world. Missionaries are known for this. A missionary will live with the people to whom he or she is ministering for several months or years before they actually begin their work. A missionary knows the value of becoming familiar with the people, and letting the people become familiar with them, before trying to influence their lifestyle. It is the same with children. The greatest influence a person can have on another person is from within, not from the outside. Jesus was a master at this. He lived among us for 30 years before he began his ministry. There are many accounts in the gospels about Jesus eating, walking, sitting, praying, and fishing with those to whom he had been called to minister. Knowing the children of your community is a critical part of your ministry to them.

Years ago, a book like this could have included a list of characteristics for each age-group of children. You could have read about the specific abilities of the 4-year-old, or the mental differences between the second grader and the fifth grader. Today's child is changing so quickly that it is not as easy to pinpoint specific age characteristics as before. At the end of this chapter are some basic characteristics for each age group. These are given to you as general ideas, and not as definite facts. Instead of trying to tell you what the third graders in your town are like, I will give you the tools with which to create your own list of characteristics for your own children in your own community.

There are four things that influence children: their family, their friends, their community, their entertainment. I'll take each one of these influencers and help you develop your own ability to keep current with the children of your area, wherever it may be.

Before we begin, I have to establish the importance of God's wisdom. You have to remember that ministry is God's idea. Ministry is what he has been about ever since creation. God created those to whom you minister. God cares for them more than you could imagine. God wants to help you accomplish his plans in their lives. Ministry is not about you or your plans. It is about him and his plans. So, to do anything apart from him is worthless. Jesus said this in *John 15:4, 5*: "Remain in me, and I will remain in you. No branch can bear fruit by itself; it must remain in the vine. Neither can you bear fruit unless you remain in me. I am the vine; you are the branches. If a man remains in me and I in him, he will bear much fruit; apart from me you can do nothing."

As you do your research and start to get to know the soil of the children to whom you minister, you must ask God for his wisdom and leading. He knows the children to whom he has called you to minister. He can teach you about them and what they need. Pray for God's wisdom. Pray for him to lead you to people who can help you get to know the children in your community. Ask him to open your eyes and ears as you walk among them.

Children's ministry is changing as fast as the computer industry it seems. Just as soon as you think you have the right computer, you realize that you actually own an antique! What you thought was just right for your needs a few weeks ago, now is too slow or not able to perform up to your expectations. The ways we ministered to children years ago worked well—then.

The Gospel message is unchanging. We are trying to communicate the same message that Peter, James, and John did just days after Jesus was crucified. The basic needs of children are also unchanging. We are seeing different expressions of those needs, and the complexity of those needs is definitely affected by the changing complexity of today's society, but they are still the same needs as always. The difference between how we minister to children today and how we ministered to children years ago is what I call the language of children's ministry.

We have to understand the environments from which our children come before we can communicate with them. Just because we can talk with them in a recognizable language, doesn't mean we are really communicating. When Jesus looked into the tear-stained, frightful eyes of the woman caught in adultery and said, "Neither do I condemn you, go and sin no more," he was speaking the language she needed to hear. He could have spoken that same language without saying anything. He was touching her. He was down on her level. He was looking at her with graceful, loving eyes. He had protected her from her accusers. He was a male who understood. This was the language of ministry for her.

Get to know the language of the children to whom you minister. The Christian message is best spoken, not with words, but with actions. The Christian language is a silent, soul-piercing one!

On the pages that follow, you will be led through a series of experiences and questions about the four influencers of the world of your children: their entertainment, their families, their friends, and their community. Copy these questions, or transfer this information to a computer so you can update and manipulate the information as you collect it. These questions are not intended to be exhaustive. Add your own questions or comments as you go. Have fun doing this!

HOW CHILDREN LEARN

Just as knowing the culture of the children in your community is vital to your children's ministry, so is knowing the various ways that children learn. This information should effect everything we do in children's ministry, not just our individual lessons. Knowing how children learn and applying that knowledge to our curriculum, programs, and training will produce healthier plants and more fruit from our ministry garden.

Every child is different. The ways they learn are different. It is our challenge to "train a child in the way he should go" *(Proverbs 22:6)*. This challenge has enough meaning hidden within it to fill many books, and you have probably read many of them. Let me simply say that there are words here that imply an individualized approach to teaching a child. The old days of lecturing to a class of quiet children seated neatly in chairs with their hands folded is over. That method was probably ineffective then, and it is definitely not good for the children of today. Today's

World Influences Survey

Here is a list of questions you can use to survey the influences the world has on the kids in your community. Of course, all of these ideas are secondary to your own informal discussions with the children at church and in the community. Take advantage of every opportunity to get to know the children in your community. You may feel a bit strange at first, asking children these kinds of questions, but you will soon notice that most children truly enjoy talking about themselves and their lives. They will also feel complimented by an adult who actually cares about what they believe and feel. You will soon be addicted to getting to know the "soil" of your garden, and find yourself inquiring about the condition of children naturally. This is when you actually know you are becoming a "gardener." A true gardener of children's ministry can't wait to get his or her hands in the "soil" of the real world of the children's lives.

THEIR ENTERTAINMENT
Watch Their TV Shows

1. Ask 10 children (of varying ages) to tell you their favorite television shows and why. Then watch the shows for several weeks. During the shows make notes about the characters, the values portrayed, the music played, etc. Ask God to help you see and hear clearly. Make mental notes about the following:
   a. What do the main characters value?
   b. What fears do the main characters have?
   c. Does the program offer "hope"? If so, what is the "hope" it offers?
   d. Does the program offer solutions to life's problems, or is it just an escape from reality?
   e. How do you feel after watching the program? Why do children like this feeling?
   f. During the program, what are the commercials telling you about the children watching the show?
   g. If you were a regular watcher of this program, what would it cause you to think about "church" or "Sunday school" when you went there? Would you go back?
   h. What does God offer the viewers of this show?
   i. What can you do to make God's offers more attractive to the viewers of this show?

Listen to Their Music

2. Buy two or three teen magazines. Read about the musical stars that are popular today. Anything that is popular with teens will be popular with children. Buy some of the music of those musical stars. As you listen to the music, "listen" to the culture of today's child. Ask God to help you see and hear clearly. Make mental notes about the following:
   a. What are the themes of the songs? What does that say about the child's world?
   b. What are the human needs expressed in the songs?
   c. What do the songs say about morals or ethics today?
   d. Are the songs expressing a balance between anger/peace, love/hate, hope/fear?
   e. What does God offer to those who sing or listen to the music of today?
   f. Do you think the church today presents God in an attractive way to those who listen to this music?

Visit Their Internet Sites

3. Find out what internet sites the children of today are visiting. Two very popular sites are Nickelodeon's site (www.nick.com) and Disney's site (www.disney.com). Visit those sites and become familiar with what is offered there. Ask God to help you see and hear clearly. Make mental notes about the following:
   a. What do you think draws children to this site?
   b. What needs are being satisfied in the children while at this site?
   c. After a significant time at the site, how do you feel? How do you think the children feel?
   d. Does this site simply entertain, or does it make the child a better person?
   e. What does God offer to those children who visit this site? Is that interesting to them?
   f. What does this site say about "church" for children?
   g. How can you use what you've experienced here to attract children to Jesus?

THEIR FAMILY
Do a Neighborhood "Drive By"

1. Walk around the neighborhoods of your community. (You might want to do this with another

person or dress to appear as though you are walking for exercise to reduce any fears of being a "strange person.") As you walk, look at the homes, cars, and landscapes to get a sense of the world that your children call "home." If you can listen to people talking or to children playing without stopping and looking, do so. Ask God to help you see and hear clearly. Make mental notes about the following:

a. Note the time of day. Are the parents home?

b. Do you see children playing outside? If "yes," what does that mean? If "no," what does that mean?

c. What is the economic level of the average family here? (Remember that the appearance of the homes doesn't mean they can afford them. Look, rather, at the cars, the landscape, the upkeep, etc.)

d. Read any bumper stickers you see on cars. What do they say about the beliefs of the family?

e. If you see people outside, either adults or children, make eye contact and say, "Hi." Do they respond? What does this say about the fear level of the families in this area?

f. Do you see any signs of neighbors interacting? What does this say about the families?

g. What does God offer these families?

h. What can you do to make God's offerings more attractive to these families?

Go Shopping at Their Stores

2. Go to the local grocery store and do some "shopping." Since a local store attracts local people, you will be able to get a glimpse of the people in the area. It is best to do this during a time when children are most likely to accompany their parents (Saturdays, Sundays, or late afternoons). Actually go down every aisle with a cart and buy something you need. Listen and watch as the families or parents interact. Try not to stand and stare at people. Keep moving and looking at the items on the shelves as you listen. Ask God to help you see and hear clearly. Make mental notes about the following:

a. Are fathers present? Why or why not?

b. How are the children treated while shopping? What could this indicate about their home?

c. Are the families in a hurry or relaxed?

d. Is what they buy mostly healthy or mostly junk food? What could this say about home?

e. Do you see any affectionate touching? What could this say about home?

f. What does God offer to these families?

g. What can you do to make God's offerings more attractive to these families?

Visit Children at Home

3. Invite yourself over to children's homes (or have them invite you) via a "take a teacher home for lunch" program. Not every child or parent will participate in this program. You will most likely be invited into the homes of happy families only. This is OK; you will still get a glimpse of some "behind the scenes" family life. Those children whose homes you do visit will view you differently after your visit. You will now be "a friend of the family." While in the home, ask them if you can see the child's room. (Make sure the parent is with you!) Ask the child to tell you about everything on the walls, the shelves, etc. Absorb it all! Ask, also, to see the family pet, backyard, or anything else that comes up during the visit. Ask God to help you see and hear clearly. Make mental notes about the following:

a. What are the family's values, and how are they expressed in their home?

b. What are the child's interests as expressed by the things on the walls, shelves, etc.?

c. What outside influences (sports stars, heroes, musicians, etc.) are visible in the child's room?

d. Has the child been raised with "traditional family values" (respect for adults, courtesy, manners)?

e. What is the feeling or tone of the home? Is there a prevailing sense of peace or anger?

f. What does God offer to this family?

g. What can you do to make God's offerings more attractive to them?

Interview Those Who Know Them

4. Make an appointment to interview a local elementary school principal. Identify who you are and explain that you are gathering information about the families in the area when you call to make an appointment. This will make your intentions clear. Ask God to help you listen with "ears of understanding" as you ask the following:

a. What is the percentage of single-parent families in this area?

b. What are some of the major issues that challenge the families or parents in this area?

c. What percentage of the parents assist their children with homework?

d. What percentage of the children arrive "ready" for school (with enough sleep, clean, having a good breakfast, dressed well, homework done, with adequate supplies, with lunch or lunch money, etc.)?

e. What can local churches do to better assist the schools in their job of educating the children?

THEIR FRIENDS
Observe Their Gathering Places

1. Go to where the children in your community congregate on weekends or after school (malls, sports fields, arcades, etc.). Do all you can to absorb their culture. Listen to conversations without looking like you're spying on them (maybe bring a book to appear to read). Watch their interactions, understand their need to be together. Ask God to help you see and hear clearly. Make mental notes about the following:

a. What are the ages at this location?

b. What connection do these children have with a parent (transportation, money, etc.)?

c. What do the clothes say about the need to belong, be accepted, or fit in?

d. What does their conversation tell you about their fears, values, needs, or dreams?

e. What is their definition of fun?

f. If Jesus were to walk into this environment, what would he do or say to capture their attention?

Go with Them on Field Trips

2. If possible, volunteer to be an adult chaperone on a school field trip. You might make an appointment with the principal and explain your "research" project beforehand, if you're not a parent of a child in the school. While on the bus and while at the location, listen to the children's conversations. Ask God to help you see and hear clearly. Make mental notes about the following:

a. What do children talk about when they think adults aren't listening? What does this say about their basic value system today?

b. In what are the children interested today?

c. What makes them laugh?

d. What are their fears?

e. What makes children consider others as friends today?

f. What does God offer to the children today?

g. What can you do to make God's offerings more attractive to them?

THEIR COMMUNITY
Go to School with Them

1. Make an appointment with a local school principal. Explain your interest in getting to know the culture of your community to better assist the parents. Ask if you can do a "walk-along" with a recess-duty teacher one day. Assure the principal that all you want to do is to learn by observing. If you are permitted to do this, ask God to help you see and hear clearly. Make mental notes about the following:

a. What is the economic makeup of the children at this school?

b. How is play different from when you were a child?

c. What makes the children angry?

d. How do the children respond to authority figures?

e. What are some moral voids that you notice in the character of children today?

Stay Connected with the Community

2. Read the local newspaper daily. Look for indicators of the general moral, ethical, or spiritual condition of your community. As you read, ask God to help you discern the following:

a. What are some of the spoken and unspoken "laws" of the community?

b. What beliefs does the city council exhibit?

c. What does the crime rate tell you about the community?

d. Are the churches active in the community, or are they just present somewhere?

e. What does God offer the community?

f. What can you do to make God's offerings more attractive to the community?

Go to Their Games

3. Become a spectator in local sporting events such as soccer, little league baseball, city basketball games, etc. While in the stands, observe the families and community at play. Ask God to help you see and hear clearly. Make mental notes about the following:

a. What are the fathers like? Is there a prevailing sense of competition or family support there?

b. Is there more yelling at the referee or cheering for the players?

c. Is the crowd large or small? What does this say about the pace of life in the community?

d. Is there a police presence? What does that say about the community?

e. Do the children on the team touch, encourage, and cheer for each other?

Learning Styles

The various styles of learning have been known by many different labels. They are all connected to a specific character type. The names I have chosen to use are from an excellent book on the subject by Marlene LeFever entitled *Learning Styles* (Colorado Springs, CO: David C. Cook, 1995).

1. The Imaginative Learner
This child learns through the imagination being stimulated. He asks the question, "Does this interest me?" or, "Is this useful information?" before becoming involved in the learning. This child must be attracted with visuals, object lessons, etc. to the lesson content.

2. The Analytical Learner
This child learns through a logical thought process. He must be involved in the learning. He questions frequently, and wants to know the details of the lesson. He asks, "What does God say about this?" This child likes to read or be read to.

3. The Common Sense Learner
This child needs to get his hands into the lesson by doing some sort of craft or project. Personal involvement is critical. He asks the question, "How does this work?" This child needs activity, movement, personal exploration, and hands-on learning.

4. The Dynamic Learner
This child is highly motivated to learn by the application of the information. He asks the question, "How can I use this in my own life?" This child needs the lesson to be placed into the setting of his own life. Role plays or personal stories help tremendously for him.

---

children require and expect variety, activity, visuals, and plenty of application to their current lives.

"SO WHAT?" ANSWERING THE CRITICAL NECESSITY OF BIBLE APPLICATION

Have you ever had a child raise his hand during a lesson and say, "So what?" If you have, you know the effect that that level of childlike honesty has on you as a teacher. You may think that a child who asks, "So what?" is rude and disrespectful. I believe that most of the children in today's children's ministries are asking, "So what?" They may not raise their hands and actually say it, but they're thinking it! Today's child doesn't care that Zacchaeus was a "wee little man" who climbed up in a Sycamore tree to see Jesus. Today's child has too much on his mind to care about something as unrelated to his life as that! They may not say, "So what?" but they're thinking it!

Our challenge in children's ministry today is to introduce the children to a real God who has real things to say that will really help children in their real world. More than ever before, we need to ask God to help us understand the Scriptures, and their applications to today's children. Zacchaeus was a man who was plagued by guilt, emptiness, and loneliness. His desperation brought him to Jesus, this teacher who healed people of their sicknesses. He was so hungry for meaning and hope that he risked his reputation by climbing a tree just to connect with Jesus. When Jesus saw him, he looked at him, and then gave Zacchaeus what he wanted: significant, healing attention from the One who created him. That is the deeper lesson of Zacchaeus. That is the connection to today's confused, lonely, empty child.

Everything we do in programming and curriculum must be designed and evaluated based on its application to the children's daily lives. "If it doesn't apply, let it die" is a good to motto use. We have to answer the "So what?" question before our children even ask it! Our prayer today must be: "Oh, Lord, help me see beyond the teacher's guide and into the needs of the children you have given to me for this hour. I want to be a conduit for your living water to flow into their hearts. Teach me, so I can teach them."

I recently discovered that I'm old. Have you ever had one of those encounters with your age that goes right to your own identity? I'm not that old, yet, and I still view myself as being able to be real with the children of today, but the following experience in my office at church was a wake-up call for me.

My assistant and I were doing some snooping on the internet to update ourselves on trends in pre-teens' music, interests, etc. We had visited several sites, but ended up staying the longest at Nickelodeon's (nick.com), and Disney's (disney.com). While at both of these sites, we discovered that we were out of touch with what our children were viewing on television, and listening to in music. The final blow to our vision of being current came when my assistant's 13-year-old daughter came into the room and started talking about all the things we were viewing on the web site. She knew all the television shows, and began telling us all about the leading characters. We both felt old when this lesson in humility ended. It doesn't take long for us "older folks" to become out of touch with the fast-moving trends in television and music.

One of the side-effects of this encounter with the web sites was that I discovered the importance of fun to children. I've always known that fun was important, but I think I was impressed with the vital, critical role that fun plays for today's busy children. If you stop and think about it for a moment, you can understand the logic: As life gets busier, more frightening, and less personal, the value of laughing and playing increases. Today's child faces huge challenges and crumbling foundations. The family is too busy to relax on the front porch, or even to share a consistent meal time together. The value system of this world is so filled with inconsistencies that children find little security anywhere. In the middle of all this confusion, one thing grows in value: fun!

Children are no different than adults in their desire to laugh and have fun. At the end of a hard day, there's nothing more enjoyable than to play and laugh. For some children the hard day lasts all week long! I believe every event in children's ministry must have a significant fun factor. Today's children will not beg their parents to come back to church if it is too serious or boring. Fun is the attractant to the "meal" of the Gospel that the children don't know they want. When a parent inquires about their child's experience in church today, they usually ask, "Did you have fun?" When a child talks about a pleasurable experience either at church or elsewhere, the commentary usually includes, "I had fun." "Fun" has become the measuring stick for the value of today's experiences. Let's look, briefly, at what the word "fun" may mean to a child.

DEFINING FUN

Fun (according to children): "Things that make me laugh. Things I like to do. Things I want to do again."

- "Things that make me laugh." We all laugh, but we laugh for different reasons. Each session with children must include something that makes them laugh—slapstick humor, ironic situations, etc. Be careful not to make children the focus of a joke!

- "Things I like to do." The critical word is "like." As we already discussed, each child is different, with different likes and dislikes. Variety is more and more critical in programming. The worst thing we can do is to lecture to the children as they sit and learn. Children like being involved, discovering, playing, moving, experimenting, etc. Each session should have a high "like" factor for every child.

- "Things I want to do again." We all want to repeat meaningful moments: feeling good about helping others, fixing a problem, making a gift for someone special, feeling confident, feeling affirmed, etc. These are the things that we all want to do again. These are fun! Each session with children should include something that makes the children want to do it again.

As you think about including fun things in your ministry, it's important to consider the deeper fun of worship, prayer, and service to others. The challenge in children's ministry is to attract children with something simple and lead them to something significant. We may attract them with funny programs, or jugglers, but our goal is to lead them to desire the deeper fun of intimacy with God.

As we consider the needs of children, and especially the need for fun, this would be a good time to introduce the "5 Steps of Ministry" that we have found to be a valuable tool in designing, conducting, and evaluating our children's ministry. Everything we do fits into one of these steps:

MINISTERING TO A CHILD: A FIVE-STEP PROCESS.

1. *Attraction:* Children must be drawn into the environment or lesson with something that interests them.
2. *Participation:* Once the children are attracted, they must be involved somehow. They can't just observe others' involvement.
3. *Confrontation:* If the children are participating, we must lead them to a confrontation with the lesson challenge. This step makes them think and consider personal growth.
4. *Salvation:* After the children are confronted with God's love and his standards, we must invite them to become Christians if they aren't already. The whole process is pointless without this step.
5. *Discipleship:* Once the children are confronted, and then respond to God's salvation, we need to lead them to deeper levels of character development and intimacy with God through mentors and service to others.

A balance of fun and inspiration must be included in everything we do in children's ministry. An unbalanced ministry will not produce fruit that will last. You can create a ministry that packs them in with high-energy, high-fun programs. You may feel successful because your numbers are growing quickly. That's good; we all want to attract children. The les-

sons of life teach us, though, that too much candy is not good for a body. It is the same caution that applies to sweets, money, relaxation, or selfish pleasures: too much can cause problems. Too much fun, at the expense of participation, confrontation, or discipleship can produce children who are only interested in more for themselves. We have to let the children taste the deep fun of giving to others and growing in their personal relationship with God, The same caution applies to too much inspiration at the expense of fun. If we produce programs that are not fun and yet extremely confrontational, we may produce children who are inspired, but not happy.

We all want to repeat pleasurable experiences. That's just how God made us. Children's ministry is about preparing children for adulthood. As adults, we are forced to redefine fun. Those adults who fail to do this have a lifelong struggle with adulthood. They have difficulty with relationships, responsibilities, and commitments. They bounce from one spouse or job to another looking for more fun. I believe God has called us to produce an environment in which children can have the most fun possible while still learning how to find significant pleasure in sacrificing for God and others.

Today's children are less interested in Bible knowledge than ever before. They don't automatically want to know what God says. We have to connect with their world, be examples of godly people, attract them to God, and let them taste his love. Then, and only then, they may be interested in what he has to say to them. Jesus, our master teacher, modeled this process himself:

1. He lived among his students.

2. He attracted them with thrilling visuals.

3. He became valuable to them by caring for their needs.

4. He connected them with God's love.

5. He taught them new things (confrontation)

6. He reinforced the value of belief and faith (salvation).

7. He empowered them to teach others (discipleship).

The lessons of the Bible are more valuable to today's children than ever before. Today's children are receiving less spiritual instruction from their parents, and the world is becoming more hostile to godly standards or morals. They need help! God's instructions in his word must be clearly taught. Children not only need more of God's Word, they need it earlier than ever before. The temptations and challenges of life are being experienced by younger children each year. We must attract the children to "pure spiritual milk" of God's Word *(1 Peter 2:2, 3)* and teach them those things that we have already taught ourselves *(Romans 2:21)* by correctly handling the Word of truth *(2 Timothy 2:15)*. God's Word must be taught well and often to today's child!

The value of worship and prayer in today's children's ministry cannot be over emphasized! I don't believe children will be attracted to God apart from an emphasis on worship and prayer. This opinion comes from a conviction that was reinforced one Sunday morning. We had created a children's church program with a clear focus on worship and prayer. During the worship time, we taught the children adult worship songs from current live-worship adult music CDs. The children learned the words to the songs as they watched the adult leaders worshiping along with the children. When we started this program, the children knew little of worship, and weren't comfortable singing. Within a few weeks, the children were closing their eyes, lifting their hands, and even leading each other in worship. They were "tasting" the deeper fun of worship.

Along with the worship, we devoted significant time to prayer with the children. We encouraged children to pray out loud, and to touch each other as they prayed (participation). We taught them the basics of prayer, then got out of the way and watched God work. We saw children grow in their faith and trust in God. We saw them bring their prayer journals, filled with answered prayers, to share with the rest of the group. We saw their hearts attracted to the deep fun of trusting in God.

We believed it was now time to offer an invitation to the children to commit their lives to Jesus. We were a bit nervous because we knew the concerns about inviting children to make a public response to Jesus. We prayed much. We informed the parents weeks in advance. Then, we did it. We were overwhelmed by the response. During our four services, we had 108 children accept the Lord. I'll talk more about this process later, but let me say that I have never seen this amount of fruit from a purely knowledge-focused program. I believe the Lord blessed our efforts to connect the children with him through worship and prayer. I believe those children were attracted to God before they learned about him. I believe those children are now more hungry for God's Word than if they had just been taught Bible stories without the presence of worship and prayer. They are now ready for the final step: discipleship!

In conclusion, I'd like to challenge you to be aware of the children of your community, and to do all you can to attract them to God without neglecting the foundational truths of the Bible. We can't be so focused on connecting with the children that we lose sight of the Great Commission. We have been commissioned to go out to teach and to make disciples, not to be "good people" and to teach nice, moral lessons. We must connect with the children and then connect them to God by teaching his Word. Without a strong emphasis on God's Word, we are little more than a nice social agency. God is "the same yesterday and today and forever" *(Hebrews 13:8)*. His word never changes or ceases from being "living and active" *(Hebrews 4:12)*, but it is the children who do change with the seasons and climates of life.

A good gardener leans down and picks up a handful of soil. He holds it, squishes it, and sometimes even lifts it to his nose to become totally aware of all of its properties. May the Lord bless you as you lean down and become aware of the children around you.

General Age Group Characteristics of Children

This is a general list of age group characteristics for children. This is a stereotypical list, and is not intended to describe every child of today's world, or every child in your community. Refer to it as you might use a soil chart from your local agricultural agency that tells you the general characteristics of the soil in your area. While this is valuable information for a gardener, you should always take a soil sample to a local agency for specific testing. In the same way, use this list as a general idea of what your children might be like, but please do some soil testing of your own with the tools I've given you in this chapter.

EARLY CHILDHOOD

NURSERY
(Birth–Walking)
General Characteristics
- Helplessly dependent on adults to meet his needs
- Communicates needs by crying
- Requires individual attention (holding, rocking, etc.)
- Sleeps a great deal
- Learns by the attitudes of those around him
Needs
- Loving physical care (feeding, changing, etc.)
- Clean surroundings
- Security at his level:
  –Familiar surroundings (sights, sounds, smells)
  –Familiar people caring for him
  –Consistent schedule
  –The presence of his parents
Level of Understanding
- Absorbs the attitudes of those who care for him
- Can understand simple words
- Beginning to recognize signs of "love"
- Can connect places, situations with concepts of "good" or "bad"

TODDLER
(Walking–Two Years)
General Characteristics
- Constantly moving
- Learning to talk
- Uses all five senses to learn
- Limited vocabulary (two or three word "sentences")
- Imitates actions
- Short attention span (two minutes maximum)
- Requires individual attention
- Developing social skills
- Fearful
- Susceptible to sicknesses
- Tires easily
Needs
- Loving physical care (snacks, changing, etc.)
- Frequent change of activity (variety)
- Frequent rest times
- Activities for large muscles
- Room to explore
- Orderly environment
- Personal attention from "accepted" adults
- Security at his level:
  –Familiar surroundings (sights, sounds, smells)
  –Familiar people caring for him
  –Consistent schedule
  –The presence of his parents
  –Consistent discipline/reward system
Level of Understanding
- Most learning is still through the senses
- Concepts of God, Jesus, and the Bible can be introduced
- Concepts of good and bad can be further understood
Activities
- Conversations about pictures
- Simple stories
- Simple songs
- Action rhymes
- Simple puzzles
- Ball games
- Hiding/peek-a-boo

2'S AND 3'S
General Characteristics
- Extremely active
- Attention span of three to five minutes
- Responds to guided play
- Rapidly growing vocabulary (although still limited)

- Imitative in actions and speech
- Still learns using all five senses
- Susceptible to sicknesses
- Tires easily
- Achieving physiological stability
- Forming simple concepts of "society"
- Learning to distinguish between right and wrong
- Curious
- Learns by repetition
- Plays alongside others rather than with them
- Understands and fears being "away" from parents

Needs
- Frequent change of activities (every 10 minutes)
- Frequent rest periods
- Exploration using senses (coloring, clay, etc.)
- Consistent discipline/reward system
- Large-muscle activities
- Repetition for learning
- Frequent restroom trips
- Security at his own level:
  - Familiar adult figures (teachers, babysitters, etc.)
  - Familiar surroundings (furniture, toys, etc.)
  - Consistent schedule
  - Knowing that parents will always return
  - Loving, understanding, gentle care

Level of Understanding
- Can understand simple, brief stories (retold often with short sentences)
- Understands the concept of love as it relates to self and others
- Appreciates Jesus as a friend and the Bible as a special book
- Knows right from wrong
- Beginning to understand concept of "being sorry"

Activities
- Guided conversations
- Guided play
- Fingerplays
- Simple songs with hand motions
- Simple stories
- Coloring
- Exploring with clay, dough, etc.
- Building with blocks, etc.

BEGINNERS
(Fours and Fives)

General Characteristics
- Very active
- Enjoys imitating
- Attention span of five to ten minutes

- Enjoys playing with other children
- Forming concepts of social behavior (teamwork, partnership, etc.)
- Inquisitive
- Learning to relate to adults other than parents
- Large imagination
- Further developing sense of right and wrong
- Learning to share (with encouragement)
- Growing vocabulary—able to express self in sentences with feeling
- Curious
- Longer attention span (20 minutes)
- Thinks of God in personal terms
- Responds to Jesus with simple trust

Needs
- Loving, supportive care
- Consistent discipline/reward system
- Interaction with adults who are interested in him
- Frequent change of activities
- Consistent models of Christian behavior
- New or different words defined
- Activities that involve physical movement
- Freedom to explore new things (places, thoughts, etc.)
- Security at his own level:
  - Clear signs of love shown to him
  - Respect from those around him
  - Feeling valuable (significant)
  - Unbroken trust/promises
  - Knowledge that God and significant adults will not abandon him

Level of Understanding
- Can understand that God created the world
- Can reason and deal with "why" questions regarding life
- Can learn through humor
- Can learn through role-playing or role-reversal
- Beginning to read simple words
- Still learns, thinks in concrete terms

Activities
- Drama
- Guided conversation
- Guided play
- Fingerplays
- Simple crafts involving cutting, pasting, coloring, folding
- "Reading" picture books
- Building with blocks

THE ELEMENTARY CHILD

The elementary child is a diverse creation. Just when you think you know him, the smoke from his smoldering birthday candles seems to signal a new era complete with personality changes, advanced discipline needs, and expanding horizons. The tricky part of working with this age child is that we are required to keep up with the changes. If we lag behind, we will lose our potential for being a role-model.

Even though the personalities are changing drastically, the basic needs of every child remain consistent. I believe the basic needs of security, significance, and belonging are never packed away with the other "toys" of our childhood. We, as adults, keep them with us forever. If we can understand our needs, we will better understand the needs of those around us.

PRIMARY
(First and Second Grade)
General Characteristics
- Active
- Talkative
- Imaginative
- Likes group activities
- Inquisitive
- Seeks personal attention from the teacher
- Small muscle coordination developing
- Building attitudes about self
- Learning masculine or feminine roles
- Learning to read confidently
- Learning to write
- Developing conscience and sense of morality
- Still thinks in concrete terms
- Honest (generally)
- Eager to learn
- Emotionally immature
- Attention span of 20 minutes or more
- Fashion conscious
- Peer group pressure beginning
- Life's values rotate around having fun
- Selfish, but capable of caring and giving to others

Needs
- Loving, respectful, patient care
- Variety in activities
- Freedom to express himself orally
- Opportunities to exhibit the things he has learned
- Abstract concepts presented in concrete terms

- Security at his own level:
  - Self-worth among his peers (sense of belonging)
  - Self-worth from his teacher (support and belief in abilities)
  - Self-worth from his parents (sense of belonging, unending love)
  - Self-worth from God (sense of unconditional love and forgiveness)
  - Consistent discipline/reward system
  - Freedom to make, and learn from, mistakes

Level of Understanding
- Genuinely loves God and Jesus as real people
- Appreciates the Bible as a special book
- Prays sincerely
- Beginning to understand what a sin is
- Beginning to apply biblical principles to life

Activities
- Drama
- Storytelling
- Games
- Art and crafts
- Music (especially if it is self-played)
- Puppets
- Reading/being read to
- Field trips

MIDDLER
(Third and Fourth Grade)
General Characteristics
- Energetic
- Still thinks in concrete terms (older middlers may think abstractly)
- Likes group activities
- Asks challenging questions
- Enjoys personal attention
- Continuing to build personal attitudes
- Developing specific interests (hobbies, etc.)
- Strong sense of morality, fairness
- Emotionally immature
- Eager to learn about things that interest him
- Memorizes easily
- Wants to help
- Attention span of 20 minutes or more (depending on subject or activity)
- Fashion conscious
- Interested in being popular or "cool"
- Has visions of being older, or capable of doing anything

Needs
- Supportive, loving care
- Variety of activities

- New experiences (educational and memory-building)
- Freedom to express himself within respectable boundaries
- Security at his own level:
  - Self-worth among his peers (sense of belonging)
  - Self-worth from his teacher (support and belief in abilities)
  - Self-worth from his parents (sense of belonging, unending love)
  - Self-worth from God (sense of unconditional love and forgiveness)
  - Consistent discipline/reward system
  - Freedom to make, and learn from, mistakes
  - To be needed and valued (service to others)

Level of Understanding
- Can understand cause/effect relationships
- Can understand order, chronology
- Able to apply biblical principles to life
- Able to know and accept Jesus
- Understands the need for salvation
- Appreciates the value of giving to others and sacrifice

Activities
- Projects
- Field trips
- Drama
- Role-playing
- Puppets
- Games
- Art and crafts
- Music
- Reading to himself
- Using his own Bible
- Local and distant service projects

JUNIOR OR PRETEEN
(Fifth and Sixth Grade)

General Characteristics
- Energetic
- Healthier
- Loud
- Inquisitive
- Talkative
- Imaginative
- Beginning to understand abstract thought
- Has many interests
- Likes competition
- Hero worshiper

- Dislikes outward display of affection
- Gang spirit
- Performance is affected by self image
- Independent
- Attention span of 20 minutes or more
- Can be rebellious
- Can be disrespectful on purpose
- Can be emotional (especially girls)

Needs
- Firm, loving, supportive care
- Consistent discipline/reward system with clear consequences
- To know the results of choices
- To learn from the consequences of poor choices
- Quality adult-like time with teacher, parents, etc.
- Freedom to begin to make significant choices with guidance
- Freedom to communicate feelings, etc. to parents and teacher
- Security at his own level:
  - Self-worth among his peers (sense of belonging)
  - Self-worth from his teacher (support and belief in abilities)
  - Self-worth from his parents (sense of belonging, unending love)
  - Self-worth from God (sense of unconditional love and forgiveness)
  - Consistent discipline/reward system
  - Freedom to make, and learn from, mistakes
  - To be needed and valued (service to others)

Level of Understanding
- Is interested in and understands Bible history and backgrounds
- Can understand the need for learning
- Is able to teach others
- Appreciates the value of giving to others and sacrifice

Activities
- More adult-type projects, etc.
- Research
- Problem-solving
- Field trips
- Interviews
- Panel discussions
- Debates
- Local and distant service projects (weekend, week-long, summer)

## chapter 3

The Gardener's Dream:
Vision for the Ministry

Knowing what you want to accomplish in your garden is critical. Visualizing your garden even before you turn your first shovel full of soil will keep you focused and make gardening more fruitful and rewarding.

Vision is about seeing and perceiving. A ministry vision is just that: seeing what is around you and perceiving what God wants you to do with it. Our lives are filled with vision. We visualize, or dream, about our careers, our children, our retirement, and even our upcoming social engagements or dates. We visualize, because God, who created us, is a visionary. We can see this throughout the Bible: in the commands of creation *(Genesis 1)*, in the promise to Abraham *(Genesis 15:5)*, in the promise of deliverance from Egypt *(Exodus 3:8)*, and in the commission to the disciples *(Acts 1:8)*.

Vision sees beyond. Vision stirs the emotions. Vision directs action. Your ministry vision must do all of this as well. True ministry vision comes from God. He is the One who called you to ministry. He is the One who placed you where you are. He is the One who has the plans, and he must be the source of your vision.

Your ministry vision comes from God, but it will include your passion and your beliefs about children's ministry in general. God has created, trained, and equipped you. He will use all he has invested into you to craft your ministry vision. Your ministry vision is an extremely spiritual tool that God will use to help you create and evaluate everything you do in ministry. This is a wonderful step in becoming a fruitful gardener for God!

YOUR VISION MAKES YOUR PASSION CONTAGIOUS

Your passion for children accomplishes nothing unless you have a plan to affect others with it. Your ministry vision is that plan. Your ministry vision is a simple statement of the process by which your passion and God's plan come together to lead children to him in your church, and community.

Your ministry vision incorporates all you are and all God wants to accomplish in your particular church location. In order to begin crafting your ministry vision, you must understand what you believe about the needs of children today, the church, and the family. These personal beliefs are basically your philosophy of children's ministry. They are general, and not a specific reference to your local church. Your ministry vision is a very specific plan to deal with your specific children and culture which applies your personal philosophy and passion. If you don't have a clear idea of what you believe, the "Philosophy of Children's Ministry Worksheet" on page 30 may help you.

Of course, there could be more to say about your personal philosophy of ministry. If you can briefly state the above views, you are on your way to seeking God for a ministry vision. God will perfect your views as you grow in him. Your views and passion will change as you get older and as you increase in years of ministry. What you believed when you first entered the ministry grew

Philosophy of Children's Ministry Worksheet

What I believe about children

1. I believe the most critical need of today's child is:
2. I believe the most effective way to attract today's child to God is:
3. I believe the most effective way to inspire today's child to a lifelong, intimate relationship with God is:

What I believe about the family

1. I believe the most critical need of today's family is:
2. I believe today's parents are most afraid of:
3. I believe today's parents are most interested in:
4. I believe God wants to help today's family by:
5. I believe the best way to connect with today's family is through:

What I believe about the Church

1. I believe the most critical need of today's Church (universal body of believers) is:
2. I believe the most critical message that today's Church has to bring to the world is:

---

into what you believe today. Just as God's word is "living and active," so is his inspiration to you.

Your ministry vision statement will be a blend of God's inspiration, your passion (chapter 1), and the information you have about today's child (chapter 2).

Inspiration + Information = Vision

A CHILDREN'S MINISTRY VISION STRENGTHENS CHURCH GROWTH

Those churches whose children's ministries have clear, compelling ministry visions experience significant growth. The work you do on creating (receiving) your ministry vision will affect your entire church.

Logic dictates that a healthy children's ministry will attract young families. When two adults visit your church, chances are very good that three children will visit along with them. These children are very likely to be young children, so what kind of an impression is your children's ministry making? Adults who are spiritually hungry are more likely to select a church where their children's spirits are equally kindled than they are to select a church

where their children are bored, ill-cared for, or complacent. Adults will tolerate a myriad of inconveniences and discomforts as long as their children are happy, but if their kids complain, goodbye visitors.

God is the source of all growth. We are given the joy and responsibility of caring for the ministry garden, but it is God who brings the growth (*1 Corinthians 3:6*). By seeking him for a ministry vision, you are simply doing all you can to make sure your ministry efforts are focused on him and his plans. Once that is true, blessings will come! As *Psalm 1:3* states, those who seek God's will will prosper.

You are about God's work. He wants to bless your thoughts, deeds, and programs to accomplish his efforts to attract children to come to him. The frightfully-beautiful essence of ministry is that God will let you and I personalize our ministry vision and goals. All he wants is for us to be yoked to him (*Matthew 11:29*) and to acknowledge him in all our ways (*Proverbs 3:5-7*). He receives pleasure and praise from our worship and our delight in him (*Psalm 37*), and he will establish our ministry.

Before you actually seek God for a ministry vision, let's review the process so far. First, it is important to know what you believe and feel about ministry (your ministry philosophy); then you need to recognize and stir up your passion about children's ministry; then you need to understand the needs of today's children, the church he's called you to, and the community around you; and, finally you now need to ask God to give you a clear ministry vision that will satisfy his will, your passion, and the needs of the people around you. This is basically what Nehemiah did as he set out to rebuild the wall around Jerusalem. In Nehemiah 1 you read about his passion as he wept over hearing about the condition of the wall. Then, he mourned, fasted, and prayed for some days to receive God's blessing and vision for the work. In chapter 2 of Nehemiah, you can read about God's gift of vision to Nehemiah evidenced by his plan. This is the same process you and I need to follow as we seek to rebuild the broken walls in our children, families, and community.

CREATING A MINISTRY VISION

Every ministry vision should focus on the Great Commission. It is our common purpose, and it is what we are all called to fulfill in our lifetimes: "Go and make disciples of all nations, baptizing them in the name of the Father and of the Son and of the Holy Spirit, and teaching them to obey everything I have commanded you. And surely I am with you always, to the very end of the age" *(Matthew 28:19, 20)*.

So, your ministry vision should simply be a picture of how you will fulfill the Great Commission in your children's ministry. A ministry vision, then, has 4 parts to it:

"Go": How will you become aware and involved in today's child's world? How will you go to them? What is God's plan for evangelism?

"Make disciples": How will you attract the children and interest them in Jesus?

"Baptizing them": How will you lead children to make a personal commitment to Jesus?

"Teaching them": How will you teach today's children in a way that interests and motivates them to learn more on their own?

Examples of Children's Ministry Vision Statements

"Crossroads Children's Ministry is committed to changing the faces of children through nurturing their spirit, preparing them to discover and develop a personal relationship with Jesus, and enabling them to face the future in Christ with the heart of a servant" (Crossroads Christian Church, 2331 Kellogg Avenue, Corona, CA 92881; 909-737-4664; www.crossroadschurch.com).

"In Promiseland, we believe that learning should be fun, so we create our own dramas, songs and activities. This results in Bible lessons that are age appropriate, interactive and relevant to today's children. You and your children are invited to visit Promiseland during any weekend service, where you will experience our commitment to working with every family in laying a spiritual foundation children can build their lives on" (excerpt from web site information; Willow Creek Community Church, 67 E. Algonquin Rd., S. Barrington, IL 60010; 847-765-5000; www.willowcreek.org).

"Saddleback's All Stars Children's Ministry exists to SHARE Christ with the children of our community, TEAM them with other Christians, ADVANCE them in their spiritual maturity, help them RECOGNIZE their spiritual gifts and to SURRENDER their lives to God" (excerpt from web site information; Saddleback Community Church, 1 Saddleback Pkwy., Lake Forest, CA 92630; 949-609-8000; www.saddleback.org).

"To Obey": How will you disciple the children and lead them to obedience and service? How will they be inspired to teach others?

Your ministry vision should be visual and stir the emotions in those who hear or read it. It should contain words like, "We believe," or "We see." It should transport the reader or hearer into a visual tour of your ministry.

Your ministry vision should include answers to the questions:

1. What will you accomplish in the lives of the children?

2. How are you going to accomplish it?

3. What will you see when your goals are accomplished?

Your ministry statement can be a condensed version of a longer document that fully explains your vision. This longer document can include your beliefs and what you see.

A GREAT COMMISSION VISION
"Go"

1. We will Go into the world of today's children with trained, passionate, godly adults who carry the message of the Gospel.

2. We will Go into the church, community, and the schools with a children's ministry image that attracts children.

3. We will provide a safe, nurturing environment so that parents can rest assured that our children's ministry is a positive place to which their children can Go.

"Make Disciples"

4. We will Make Disciples by drawing children into the presence of God through dynamic worship.

5. We will Make Disciples by teaching children how to pray and providing opportunities for them to experience God's presence and provision.

6. We will Make Disciples by teaching children the truths contained in the Word of God, and by providing opportunities for them to explore these truths for themselves.

"Baptizing Them"

7. We will develop a process of child evangelism which leads children into a relationship with Jesus Christ.

8. We will train our team members in the child evangelism process.

"Teaching Them"

9. We will train our team members in effective Teaching methods based on the interests and needs of today's children.

10. We will Teach Them with relevant curriculum which emphasizes both biblical content and fun!

11. We will establish a variety of child-targeted programs that Teach Them how to apply the truths of God's Word in their daily lives.

12. We will inspire and challenge adult team members to Teach Them by becoming role models and by developing significant relationships with the children.

13. We will support the parents in Teaching their own children through printed materials, seminars, and conferences.

"To Obey"

14. We will teach children To Obey the commands of God by participating in supervised service projects.

15. We will teach children To Obey Jesus' command to be "salt" and "light" to others through their words, actions, and choices.

16. We will expect the children To Obey Jesus' Great Commission by volunteering to help in the children's ministry.

YOUR MINISTRY VISION AFFECTS ALL YOU DO IN MINISTRY

Once you have created your ministry vision, you will use it to define and refine all you do. Every program option will be tested before, during, and after using your ministry vision. Your curriculum, training process, and facility should all reflect your ministry vision. We will look at the budget later, but your budget is your ministry vision expressed in numbers. Everything is driven by your vision!

The Ministry Vision Wheel

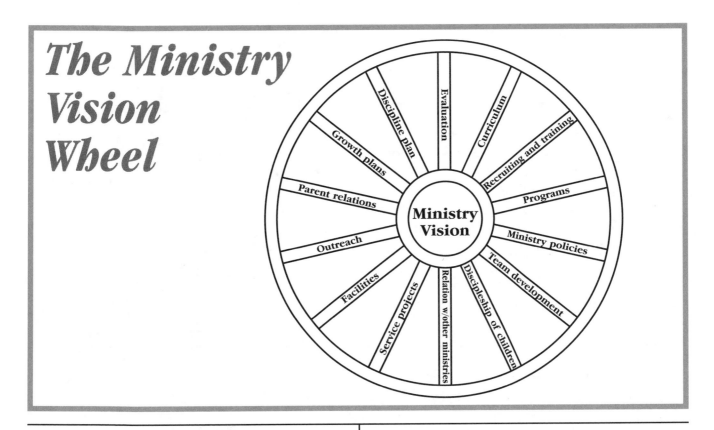

Wheel segments (clockwise from top): Evaluation, Curriculum, Recruiting and training, Programs, Ministry policies, Team development, Discipleship of children, Relation w/other ministries, Service projects, Facilities, Outreach, Parent relations, Growth plans, Discipline plan. Center: **Ministry Vision**

VISION & THE CHILDREN'S MINISTRY JOB DESCRIPTION

In a perfect world, your job description would perfectly reflect your ministry vision. Everything you are expected to do, and the basis for evaluating your success, would be related directly to your vision. That would be nice, but you don't serve God in a perfect world. Your job description may be as broad as, "Do everything related to children," or as complex as a multiple-page government document. Even your area of ministry may not truly reflect your passion. Your church may define children as being anyone under the age of 21. The challenge of receiving, clarifying, and writing your ministry vision is just the beginning. The next challenge is to make your ministry vision fit into your job description.

If you've been given a job description, that's good. If you serve at a church that doesn't use job descriptions, you may need to craft one for yourself. There is a clear division of opinions about job descriptions among those in ministry. Some believe job descriptions limit the work of the Lord. Some believe job descriptions protect the work of the Lord. I believe they can do both. I believe a job description needs to be loose enough to permit the Lord to move and adjust things according to his will; but I also believe

that a job description needs to be tight enough to protect the vision from being diluted into areas that don't relate to your calling or vision.

A job description is a strange thing. It sounds so legal and binding, and yet when reality strikes, it becomes one of the most flexible pieces of paper you'll come across administratively. A job description becomes prey to personnel differences, corporate policies, unspoken standards of behavior, and a fine collection of other legitimate reasons for adjustment. In spite of all this apparent inconsistency it is vital that there be some attempt at clarifying just what it is you do with all your time and talent.

It may be easier to first describe what the job of children's minister isn't before we talk about what it is. Doesn't that seem to be the way things go anyway? You find yourself in a new position, and the most important things you try to learn are what not to do rather than what to do.

Basically, the children's minister gathers and communicates the information the senior pastor needs to oversee the total congregation. The senior pastor is the one who is ultimately responsible for the spiritual health of his congregation; it is the children's minister who supports the pastor by being in touch with the needs and condition of the children. When discussing

Garden Pest:
Visionblight Fungus

Evidence

Beginning slowly, unnoticed by the gardener, a powdery mildew forms on the leaves. Soon, if not treated, the mildew forms a thick layer of bacteria that totally blocks out the light from above. The gardener's ability to see the vision lessens as the focus shifts to the problems or fears of the ministry. A slow death to the vision is certain if this fungus is not stopped.

Sources of Infestation

Traditions, fear, complacency, fatigue, or short-term thinking

Treatment

1. Value traditions only as foundations for the future. Don't throw out traditions or be controlled by them; build upon them! Move beyond the past and focus on the future.

2. Don't focus on your fears; focus on God's power and vision. Growth requires risk. Moving forward requires change. Move forward cautiously, sensitive to people's needs, and with much prayer; but move! "Vision replaces fear with energy and hope" (Aubrey Malphurs, *Developing a Vision for Ministry in the 21st Century*, Baker Book House: 1992; pages 122-129).

3. Remember, restore and protect your passion! Read books and magazines about children's ministry and passion. Network with others in children's ministry. Pray for more passion! Complacency can kill passion.

4. Fight fatigue, both physically and spiritually, with plenty of sleep, protected days off, and a "sabbath" which includes worship. As a ministry leader who deals with matters of eternal significance, you must be rested before beginning the work.

5. Ask God for the ability to focus on the future, not on today. The "fires" of today are demanding. They can easily produce short-term thinking in you and your team. Remember that God's vision for a ministry may well outlive the person who first had the vision. You are a part of a bigger picture! Look beyond!

---

the job description of a minister, whether he ministers to adults or children, there are two lessons that share the spotlight as "Best Supporting Lessons": how to be a servant, and how to disciple others.

BE A SERVANT

The greatest thing you, as a minister, can do, whether you work with children or adults, is to prove yourself to be a servant first. This can easily be done in a matter of months as you do the menial tasks that could be assigned to an underling. This is not done to call attention to your great humility, but, rather, with the attitude of service to the Lord. It is also done in order to experience what each phase of the ministry requires. Those who you later direct in those areas will respect you, knowing that you understand. Jesus did this when he took on the menial task of life on this earth, doing such things as washing the disciples' feet.

What Is a Children's Minister?

A CHILDREN'S MINISTER IS

The person called and equipped by the Lord to serve as an overseer, under the authority of the senior pastor, of all the functions and responsibilities pertaining to the children of the local congregation, and to all who disciple those children.

A CHILDREN'S MINISTER ISN'T

- The sole person responsible for the spiritual growth of the children.
- The person who "keeps the teachers in line."
- The person who does it all in order for it to be done right.
- The person who gets the glory for the things that are done.
- The person who tells the senior pastor what should be done for the children.

DISCIPLE OTHERS

The second greatest lesson that you should learn is how to disciple others. It would not be healthy for you to continue doing the menial tasks for a prolonged period of time. The Lord has called you to carry the Gospel to children, and you should seek the Lord for workers who could be trained to do the menial tasks. This would then free you to devote your total attention to creating and shepherding. This is the same dilemma the early apostles faced in *Acts 6*. Your ego must be laid aside in order that others might be used to enhance and multiply the ministry.

To give you some idea of just what it is that most churches expect from a children's minister, take a look at the list of typical functions performed by those who are in full-time children's ministry positions. Keep in mind that it would be impossible for any one person to care for all of these areas, but you should be prepared to do them just in case.

As you can see, the children's minister may be expected to have his thumb in many church pies. This is very healthy! You will be a feeder ministry to the rest of the church. Children will be trained and equipped for service under your guidance; then, they will be channeled back into the church body to serve and hopefully disciple others themselves.

The Typical Functions of the Children's Minister

- Attend Church Board Meetings
- Attend Conventions
- Be Involved in Church Calling
- Counsel With Workers and Families
- Develop and Maintain the Budget
- Develop and Run Summer Programs
- Develop the Camping Program
- Direct Seasonal Programs
- Disciple Coordinators
- Discipline Children
- Evaluate and Revise Curriculum
- Lead a Mid-Week Bible Study
- Oversee the Christian School
- Oversee the Daycare Program
- Recruit and Train Workers
- Teach a Sunday School Class

Being confident in whom you are (vision), and what is expected of you is critical to your success in the ministry. Although I can't give you a ready-to-copy-and-implement ministry job description, I can give you some principles. (A sample job description is included on pages 37 and 38.)

Principles of Developing a Healthy Job Description

1. Clearly connect the position to the ministry vision
2. Clearly define the general area of service (age-group, etc.)
3. Clearly define the "chain of command" administratively
4. Clearly define the specific responsibilities and expectations
5. Clearly define the criteria for evaluating success
6. Clearly state the salary
7. Clearly state the hours of service
8. Clearly define the process for updating or enlarging the responsibilities

YOUR PASSION "GILGAL"

These first three chapters are the foundations of growing a healthy ministry garden.

As we move into the rest of the book, I urge you to remember the principles established here.

When the people of Israel finally ended their 40 years of wandering in the wilderness, they crossed through the Jordan river at a place called Gilgal. After God parted the river and all the people had crossed through, God told Joshua to do something very significant. He told Joshua to have one man from each of the 12 tribes go back into the river and pick up a large boulder. They were told to make a pile of the boulders on the banks of the river. This would be a place of remembrance for them and their children. In *Joshua 4:19-24*, Joshua tells the people to remember what God did "so that all the peoples of the earth might know that the hand of the Lord is powerful and so that you might always fear the Lord your God." For years later, you can read about the people of God "returning to Gilgal" either before, or after significant battles or decisions. They came back, as God had commanded them, to restore their focus and remember whom they served.

Remembering is very important to God. Forgetting is a tool of the enemy. If you forget who God has called you to be, or what he has told you to do, you will lose heart and eventually lose your ministry strength.

Let these first three chapters be a Gilgal to you. I encourage you to return to them periodically throughout this book, and even after you've finished the book. As you deal with politics, budgets, personnel, or problems, you must remember! You must return to your Gilgal, and restore your focus and passion.

Children's Minister Job Description

The Children's Ministry Vision
(Write the children's ministry vision for your church here.)

The Children's Minister and the Ministry Vision
The children's minister oversees the creation, fulfillment, and revision of the children's ministry vision. This involves the "casting" of that vision to the total team, and overseeing the development of that vision in all areas of the ministry. The children's minister also oversees the recruiting and developing of the children's ministry team members. Team members will be recruited and developed according to the ministry vision.

The Church "Chain of Command"
(The specific "chain of command"—who reports to whom—for the church is described here.)

Job Responsibilities
The Age Group
The children's ministry is defined as dealing with children twelve years old and younger.

General Job Responsibilities
The most basic responsibility of the children's minister is to continue to grow in his or her own relationship with Jesus through personal devotions, Bible study, fellowship, and service. The children's minister will oversee all activities, programs, supplies, curriculum, budgets, and personnel associated with children.

Specific Responsibilities
The children's minister will oversee, or delegate limited supervision to others, the following responsibilities. Even though others may be recruited or "trained" to perform aspects of these responsibilities, it is the children's minister who will be ultimately responsible.
1. Stay "current" with the needs and "culture" of children nationwide and in the community.
2. Stay "current" with the trends in children's ministry nationwide.
3. Stay connected with other children's ministry directors in the community.
4. Communicate the needs and current trends to the senior pastor or other administrative pastors as often as possible.
5. Oversee the spiritual development of the children with whom we come in contact through children's ministry programs, events, and classes.
6. Develop the children's ministry team through recruiting, orientation, training, organizing, encouragement, and socials.
7. Develop, oversee, and evaluate all programs, events, and classes
8. Develop, oversee, and evaluate the curriculum used for all programs, events, and classes.
9. Develop, oversee, and evaluate the children's ministry budget and all expenditures.
10. Develop the children's ministry "image" based on the ministry vision.
11. Oversee the safety of all children during all events, programs, and classes both on and off-campus.
12. Develop, oversee, and evaluate the parent support programs, curriculum, and efforts.
13. Develop, oversee, and evaluate all outreaches and service projects to the community.
14. Develop, oversee, and evaluate "cross ministry" support and partnerships with other ministries within the church.

Criteria for Evaluating "Success"

Success will not be based purely on the number of children attending children's ministry programs, events, or classes; but, the attendance figures will be used as an indicator for probable success in the following areas:

1. Satisfying the needs of the parents (who bring the children to us).
2. Satisfying the needs (physical, emotional, mental, spiritual) of the children.
3. Leading children closer to God (inspiring them to deeper intimacy and trust in God).

Other more tangible signs of success in the children's ministry will be:

4. A growing number of children who accept the Lord yearly.
5. A growing number of people serving on the children's ministry team.
6. A growing number of team members being "cultivated" for leadership.
7. A growing number of team members taking leadership (paid and volunteer) positions.
8. A growing number of youth (junior, senior high school age) returning to serve in the children's ministry.
9. New programs of outreach and service being designed and successfully (goals met) executed.
10. A growing budget that is monitored, evaluated, and expanded to service new ministry growth.
11. A majority of parents who are pleased and supportive with the efforts of the children's ministry.
12. A majority of church board members who are pleased and supportive with the efforts of the children's ministry.

Salary

(Write the salary figures—including benefits—for the specific job here.)

Hours of Service

The children's minister will be expected to serve at least forty hours per week. It is understood that there will be weeks in which more hours are required for either unforeseen situations or planned events. The children's minister will be given "executive trust" for "executive performance." Flexibility will be granted for office hours to compensate for late night programs or work. Days off must be personally protected by the children's minister. The children's minister is expected to discuss situations affecting hours of service with an administrative pastor.

Job Territory Enlarging Process

The children's minister is hired to perform the responsibilities stated in this job description. It is understood that the senior pastor is the executive director over all church personnel. If, at any time, the senior pastor desires to "add" to the children's minister's job description, it is his right to do so. The children's minister has the ultimate responsibility to serve the senior pastor. If, by enlarging the children's minister's "territory," other critical responsibilities are negatively impacted, the children's minister has the right to let the senior pastor know of these impacts. If, after discussing the impacts with the senior pastor, it is decided to continue with the responsibility additions, the children's minister should do all he or she can to "make it work." The children's minister may ask the senior pastor for wisdom in dealing with the impacts of the changes on the children's ministry.

Term of Service

This job description is applicable for the duration of the contract. If the contract is a probationary contract, this job description may be revised at the end of the probationary period. The term of service for this job description is linked to the contract's term of service.

_____

Employee Signature   Date

_____

Employer Signature   Date

"*A garden can be a place to provoke thought and seek inspiration, a refuge to rest in, an area to play in, or a place simply to look at. It can take on many forms, provide varying sensory experiences, and accommodate many types of activities. It can be as simple or as complex as you wish to make it*" (Landscape Plans, San Ramon, CA: Ortho Books, 1989; page 5).

In my earlier years as a children's minister, I served at a large church in Riverside, California. The church was growing, but was still in its first facility. We had purchased a building that another church had built. It was a one-room sanctuary with three small classrooms upstairs. We also had, on the same property, an old house on a granite hill and four modular trailers. The "house on the hill" and the modular trailers became our children's ministry home. I can remember story after story of memorable moments in the house and trailers.

We had children everywhere in that old house! We had one swamp cooler for the whole house. When I arrived on Sunday mornings, I would go first to the house and turn on the swamp cooler. It was not very efficient, but those who served during the first service appreciated a cooler environment. By the middle of second service, the "little swamp cooler that could" began to say, "I don't think I can!" The house began to be too warm with all the windows closed, so we would turn off the swamp cooler and open the windows. To this day, I still don't understand why none of the windows in that dear little house had screens, but there must have been a good reason. When we opened the windows to permit some flow of air through the house, we all shifted into "window patrol" mode. The windows were all low, wide, and easy to crawl through. We had to watch the windows to make sure none of our little angels escaped.

One Sunday morning was particularly memorable. We had a child escape through a window and fall to the ground. Fortunately, our "house on the hill" angels were there to cushion the fall, but he still got a good bruise on his head. We put some ice on the bump and waited for the parents. When the service was out, we watched as the nicely-dressed women climbed the railroad tie stairs to the house on the hill. One woman was wearing spiked high heels. This was a well-known safety hazard! Before any of us could say, "Be careful," it happened. One of those finely-sharpened stiletto heels sunk into a hole in the railroad tie and down she went! Rushing out to her aid was our professional crew of "house on the hill" EMTs. We extracted her, rescued her stiletto, apologized, and walked her up to the house. When she arrived, shaken and "out of sorts," she said the words we never dreamed of hearing, "I'm Joshua's mother, I'm here to pick him up." I'm sure she didn't understand why we all stood and stared at her with mouth-open disbelief. She had no idea what was about to be told her.

It was her son, little Joshua, who had fallen out of the window that morning. I'm not sure, but I think our overall church attendance dropped by two after that day. *It is sad, but true, that your facility can either attract people to or repel people from your children's ministry.*

First Time Visit Survey

1. Park your car and get out. Look around for where to take your children. Are there any signs? How do you know where the children's ministry is located?

2. If you have to ask someone where to find the children's ministry, was it easy to find someone to ask, and were they helpful?

3. Once you arrive at the children's ministry facility, what is your first impression? What catches your eye first? Do you see trash, peeling paint, dirt, or signs of disorganization? What does the facility "say" about the quality of care your children will receive?

4. Now that you have found the children's ministry area, do you know where to take your child? Are there signs for the various age group ministries?

5. If you have to ask someone where to take your children, was it easy to find someone to ask, and were they helpful?

6. What do you hear, smell, and see as you walk to your child's area?

7. Once you arrive at your child's area, what is your first impression? What catches your eye first? What does the room or area say about the quality of care your children will receive here?

8. Are you greeted by a member of the children's ministry team? (Obviously, this will happen because of who you are. If you can, observe the arrival of real visitors to get a sense of the welcome they receive.)

9. If you can look into the room, do so. What is your first impression? What catches your eye first? What does the room say about the quality of care your children will receive? Can you get an idea of what the topic of study for the morning will be based on the decorations of the room?

10. Walk away, as if you were going to the adult service, and think as a first-time visitor. Do you feel free to worship in peace? Would you consider returning next week? (Obviously, the answer to that question is based on more complex factors than just a first impression, but your first impression is valuable.)

If you do this little experiment, you will gather some significant data that could affect improvements in both your facility and in your overall ministry. I hope you do this homework assignment. It's fun and informative!

In a perfect, Christian world parents and children would overlook the facility problems and only see the joys and fruit of your ministry that happens inside the facility; but, we don't serve in a perfect world. The only time I have seen the majority of church folks overlook the facility flaws was when our church moved into a tent while our new facility was being built. While we were in a tent, the whole church had a pioneer spirit. We were all flexible and understanding because "we were in the tent." That pioneer spirit quickly reverted back to the normal insensitivity and grumbling soon after we folded up the tent and moved into our new facility. I've learned that there is no such thing as a perfect facility. No matter what we do, there will always be those who complain about our facility. The only thing we can do is to do all we can to dress up our facility to make it as clean, efficient, and friendly as possible.

That is the goal of this chapter: to give you the tools you need to evaluate your current facility and to make sure it is a place where children, parents, and team members feel welcome and happy. I will also give you some considerations for designing a new facility if you should ever get to do that.

SURVEY YOUR FACILITY: THE FIRST IMPRESSION

I'll give you a homework assignment. Yes, I said, "Homework." Don't complain, or I'll keep you in during recess. This won't be too hard; in fact, I think you'll enjoy it. Here's what I want you to do: This Sunday, walk around your facility as if you were a first-time visitor. Pretend that you have never been to your children's facilities before. The survey above lists some things to do on your first-time visit to your facility.

SURVEY YOUR FACILITY: EVALUATE ITS USE

One of the greatest threats to your ministry could be your facility. This seems silly, but it's true. Let me briefly explain how this could be true. We minister to children who are dependent on their parents. The parents are the ones who bring the children to our ministry. If the parents are offended or bothered by the facility (too cramped, dirty, needing repair, disorganized, etc.), they may decide not to bring their children to you. It is possible that a smelly nursery could stop you from being able to minister to a child's sixth grade sibling! We need to take our facility's impact on our ministry seriously!

Most people in children's ministry are stuck with their current facility for à very long time. Some people get to be a part of designing a new facility, but that doesn't happen too often. We are all challenged to be good stewards of the facility the Lord has given us. What we have may be all we'll get! We need to be like my wife's mom. She and her husband survived the Nazi occupation of Holland during World War II, and she learned the priceless ability to make something from nothing. There have been many times that they invited us over for dinner with, what I would consider, an empty refrigerator. I peek into the refrigerator and think, "There's no possible way to create a meal with the food that is in here." I've learned to ignore my lack of faith in her resourcefulness. Time after time, she calls us to the table which is filled with an amazing meal that, according to her, she simply "threw together." Using what you have wisely is a lesson "from the old country" that directly applies to our children's ministry facilities.

Do you know your facility? You can get very comfortable with the status quo of your facility. You can get used to the crowded hallways, underused rooms, or piles of storage, and not even notice them anymore. When you did your first-time visit homework assignment, did you notice things that you had either not seen before, or things that you had grown used to? On pages 42 and 43, there is a facilities evaluation that will help you evaluate your facility and its use. For each item, check the appropriate "Always, Sometimes, or Never" columns on the right. Once you have evaluated your facility and considered the results of that evaluation, set some goals. It's great to dream big, and set goals after evaluating; besides, God knows what you need: "Your Father knows what you need before you ask him" *(Matthew 6:8).*

FACILITY GOALS: COMMUNICATING YOUR VISION

Ideally, your facilities should be statements of your ministry vision expressed in concrete or wood. When

---

14 Ways to Communicate Your Vision With Your Facility

1. Professionally-created posters or banners
2. Vision statements painted on exterior walls
3. Vision statements painted on sidewalks
4. Clean, well-landscaped grounds
5. Freshly painted facilities
6. Vision messages playing on video monitors
7. Music played in hallways
8. Vision messages heard in hallway speakers
9. Testimonials (children, parents, team members) displayed on walls
10. Vision statement summarized in framed displays on walls
11. Vision messages displayed in classrooms
12. Tables and chairs that are clean and not needing repair
13. Clean carpet in all areas
14. Deodorizers in rest rooms and nursery

Children's Ministry Facility Evaluation

Condition   **Rating**

FIRST IMPRESSIONS

1. Is your facility free of trash outside the buildings? ❏ *Always* ❏ *Sometimes* ❏ *Never*
2. Is your facility free of trash inside the buildings? ❏ *Always* ❏ *Sometimes* ❏ *Never*
3. Are your floors clean? ❏ *Always* ❏ *Sometimes* ❏ *Never*
4. Are your building exteriors freshly painted? ❏ *Always* ❏ *Sometimes* ❏ *Never*
5. Have visible repair needs been fixed immediately? ❏ *Always* ❏ *Sometimes* ❏ *Never*
6. Have "storage piles" been eliminated in rooms? ❏ *Always* ❏ *Sometimes* ❏ *Never*
7. Is your ministry vision obvious in the exterior of the facilities? ❏ *Always* ❏ *Sometimes* ❏ *Never*
8. Are there clear direction signs for parents and children? ❏ *Always* ❏ *Sometimes* ❏ *Never*
9. Does your landscape reflect your professionalism? ❏ *Always* ❏ *Sometimes* ❏ *Never*
10. Does a first time visitor hear crying children? ❏ *Always* ❏ *Sometimes* ❏ *Never*
11. Does a first time visitor hear children's music? ❏ *Always* ❏ *Sometimes* ❏ *Never*
12. Does your nursery area smell clean? ❏ *Always* ❏ *Sometimes* ❏ *Never*
13. Do the non-nursery areas smell clean? ❏ *Always* ❏ *Sometimes* ❏ *Never*

ROOM USE

14. Are your children's rooms assigned to avoid crowding? ❏ *Always* ❏ *Sometimes* ❏ *Never*
15. Are there rooms that aren't crowded? ❏ *Always* ❏ *Sometimes* ❏ *Never*
16. Is there a possibility to rearrange room usage to adjust to room population? ❏ *Always* ❏ *Sometimes* ❏ *Never*
17. Are there rooms that are being used for storage? ❏ *Always* ❏ *Sometimes* ❏ *Never*
18. Is the equipment (tables, chairs, etc.) in the rooms age-appropriate? ❏ *Always* ❏ *Sometimes* ❏ *Never*

FLOW OF PEOPLE

19. Does the check-in flow prevent crowds in hallways? ❏ *Always* ❏ *Sometimes* ❏ *Never*
20. Does the check-out flow prevent crowds in hallways? ❏ *Always* ❏ *Sometimes* ❏ *Never*
21. Is there a free-flowing, "in and out" direction for each classroom or area? ❏ *Always* ❏ *Sometimes* ❏ *Never*
22. Are there centralized check-in points for certain age-groups? ❏ *Always* ❏ *Sometimes* ❏ *Never*

SAFETY/SECURITY

23. Are the doorways of your facilities monitored to prevent intruders? ❏ *Always* ❏ *Sometimes* ❏ *Never*
24. Is there a check-in/check-out process that protects children? ❏ *Always* ❏ *Sometimes* ❏ *Never*
25. Is your playground fenced with latched gates? ❏ *Always* ❏ *Sometimes* ❏ *Never*
26. Are there fire extinguishers in each room? ❏ *Always* ❏ *Sometimes* ❏ *Never*
27. Are there fire extinguishers in the hallways? ❏ *Always* ❏ *Sometimes* ❏ *Never*
28. Are there evacuation procedures posted in the rooms? ❏ *Always* ❏ *Sometimes* ❏ *Never*
29. At night, is the lighting bright and adequate? ❏ *Always* ❏ *Sometimes* ❏ *Never*

TEAM MEMBER FRIENDLY

30. Are there adequate cabinets in each room?	❏ *Always*	❏ *Sometimes*	❏ *Never*
31. Is there a supply room?	❏ *Always*	❏ *Sometimes*	❏ *Never*
32. Is there a supply requisition process available to each team member?	❏ *Always*	❏ *Sometimes*	❏ *Never*
33. Are there air conditioners and heaters in every room?	❏ *Always*	❏ *Sometimes*	❏ *Never*
34. Do the air conditioners work?	❏ *Always*	❏ *Sometimes*	❏ *Never*
35. Do the heaters work?	❏ *Always*	❏ *Sometimes*	❏ *Never*
36. Do the windows open?	❏ *Always*	❏ *Sometimes*	❏ *Never*
37. Is there an AV requisition process?	❏ *Always*	❏ *Sometimes*	❏ *Never*
38. Is the lighting bright enough in each room?	❏ *Always*	❏ *Sometimes*	❏ *Never*

CHILD FRIENDLY

39. Are the restrooms child-sized?	❏ *Always*	❏ *Sometimes*	❏ *Never*
40. Are there several drinking fountains, within view?	❏ *Always*	❏ *Sometimes*	❏ *Never*
41. Do the drinking fountains work?	❏ *Always*	❏ *Sometimes*	❏ *Never*
42. Are the drinking fountains child-sized?	❏ *Always*	❏ *Sometimes*	❏ *Never*
43. Are the walls of the rooms colorful, and bright?	❏ *Always*	❏ *Sometimes*	❏ *Never*
44. Are there adequate tables and chairs in each room?	❏ *Always*	❏ *Sometimes*	❏ *Never*
45. Are the tables and chairs age-appropriate?	❏ *Always*	❏ *Sometimes*	❏ *Never*
46. Are there adequate supplies for each child?	❏ *Always*	❏ *Sometimes*	❏ *Never*

INTERPRETING THE RESULTS OF FACILITY EVALUATION

Go back to the items for which you marked "sometimes" or "never," and highlight them with a felt tip marker. On a separate piece of paper, make notes as you think through the following questions for each item you've highlighted.

1. ***What is the reason for the item's "low" score?***
   a. Financial reasons
      • Have you requested funds to "fix" the situation? (Connection to vision!)
      • Have you advertised the need for donations?
   b. Personnel reasons
      • Have you asked people for specific help in this area?
      • Have you organized a "work day" to solve the problem?
      • Have you approached existing team members for help in this area?
      • Can you use youth or children to solve the problem?
      • Can you make this a "family project"?
   c. "Tradition" reasons
      • Have you advertised your ministry vision well enough?
      • Have you "sold" people on the values of the change?
      • What are you waiting for? Set a date, advertise, and move!
   d. Facility limitations
      • Can you rearrange other facility uses to provide for this need?
      • Can you combine other facility uses to provide for this need
      • Can you advertise the vision, and solicit volunteers to remodel the facility?
2. ***If you can't "fix" the situation, how can you "work with what you have"?***
   a. Change the schedule?
   b. Change the facility use?
   c. Change the perceptions—entertain, laugh, smile during the situation?

you visited your facility for the first time, did you see your ministry vision? If you were truly a first-time visitor, would you know anything about the ministry vision as a result of walking around your facility? These are the challenges of making our facilities work for us, not against us.

Letting your facilities express your vision can be as simple as putting up professionally created, full color posters or banners with your ministry logo or slogan on them, or as complex as giving your entire facility a face lift to reflect your vision.

FACILITY GOALS: CREATING CREATIVE LEARNING ENVIRONMENTS

Your buildings should be pleasant to look at and express your ministry vision, but don't forget that your rooms are the "greenhouses" of learning and spiritual inspiration. What happens inside the rooms and how that affects the children is the real focus of your facilities. Your facilities, just like greenhouses, are carefully-designed environments in which plants can flourish.

Making your learning environments creative is critical. Your classrooms or large assembly areas may be the first attraction your children experience. Children should be attracted by what they see and experience in your facilities. If your environments attract them, they may mentally stick around for deeper things. If your environments are cold and sterile, the children may mentally leave before you even begin your lesson.

One of my most memorable experiences with a creative learning environment was when I turned a room into the belly of the whale for a study of Jonah during an evening family program. I wanted the children to experience (taste, feel, smell, hear) the feelings of Jonah as he tried to run away from God. I began by preheating the room during the afternoon. When I turned on the heater, I also spread 4 cans of tuna on aluminum foil squares in each corner of the room. To add that final touch, I set a couple of humidifiers to work all afternoon as well. By 6:00

p.m., the room was ripe. About a half an hour before the program began, I entered the room to tie some wet pantyhose to the T bar ceiling so they hung down to the level of the children's faces. I also began playing a taped recording of the ocean waves gurgling in and out of the rocks that I had made days before (if you don't live near an ocean, you can record water sloshing in a bath tub as well). When it was time to begin, I turned out the lights and kept the families outside the room. Before I let them in, I stood outside the closed door and told them that they were going to experience the inside of a whale. When the families entered the dark, hot, humid, smelly room, the children all said "Ew, yuk" as they walked in. After a few minutes of reactions, I began to read the story of Jonah in that dark room with only the light of a penlight flashlight. We then went into another room to let the families discuss and interact.

Years later, I had children and parents tell me how much they enjoyed that experience, and that they would never forget it. That was a fruitful use of a facility! The planning and work that went into transforming that environment from a cold, sterile room to the belly of the whale was well worth it. Although that was an extremely successful experience, I couldn't do that sort of thing each week. Totally transforming a room environment is something you might plan on doing once a quarter. To do it more than that would be unrealistic unless you have a set construction crew at your disposal.

Other than totally transforming a room, there are other things you can do to make your rooms creative, fun, and full of attraction for the children.

Creative Walls

When the parents or children first see the room, they should be attracted to your lesson topic. A good teacher makes the walls a part of the lesson. Fight the temptation to just stick a picture from your curriculum on the wall! That doesn't interest anyone! You don't have to produce a piece of art each week, just ask God to help you create a word, a statement, or something that intrigues the children or makes them ask, "What's that for?" as they walk in. For instance, if your lesson topic is about controlling your anger, you might write the question "Is it ever right to fight?" on the board. As the parents or children see that question, they will begin to think about the answer, or even talk about the question among themselves. You've attracted them to the lesson topic without even saying a thing! You can also put up a picture or series of pictures that pertain to the topic without any explanation. Then ask the children to figure out what your lesson topic is for the day. Consider the use of the bulletin boards, white (chalk) boards, windows, upper wall cabinets, or plain wall space.

Creative Ceilings

A creative classroom includes things that are unusual, or that don't normally show up at church or in the room. Hanging things from the ceiling is a good technique to capture the children's attention and attract them to the lesson. Writing things on paper that is taped to the ceiling is also a good use of the ceiling. Make sure that what you hang from the ceiling isn't heavy and won't fall down on the children. Don't leave the items on the ceiling after the class session. If a creative item is left up for more than one session, it is no longer creative.

Creative Lighting and Sounds

Changing the lighting of a room definitely attracts attention! The average classroom has florescent lighting. Florescent lights are efficient, but very unattractive. The use of floor or table lamps from home, spot or flood lights, black lights, Christmas lights, a color wheel, colored gels on lights, flashlights, or glow sticks will all send the attraction factor through the roof!

Sounds can also be very powerful tools in making your classroom a creative environment. Adding sound effects, background music, recorded songs, audio stories, or children's television theme songs adds to the attraction factor of your room or lesson. Make sure the sounds connect with the lesson topic somehow, or you could actually be training your children not to listen to the sounds for any connection with the lesson.

Creative Doorways

If you think about it, the doorway is the first thing the parents or children actually see as they approach your room (unless you are standing outside greeting them). There are things you can do to the doorway that make it a tool of your lesson as well. You can decorate it with some lesson-related decoration. You can build a puppet stage in the doorway and perform a short introductory show either before the children enter the room, or right after they come in. You can hang things from the doorway so the children have to walk in through something that introduces the lesson topic. You can also make a doorway cut-out that the children walk through. Think of your doorway as the entrance to the learning environment!

Creative Scenery and Sets

This is a next step up from the simple use of your walls. You can build a set in your room that is a scene that relates to your lesson topic. This can be a biblical scene, but it would be more interesting if it wasn't. You can also build a puppet stage in your room. The goal is to transform the room into something else (like the belly of Jonah's whale).

Creative Floors

Floors are perhaps the most under-appreciated surface in your room. Floors can be fun. You can draw on them with masking tape, tape messages on them, or transform them into a game board. You can also place unusual, lesson-related objects on the floor. You can create a "lesson treasure trail" that the children follow and experience lesson centers along the way. You can also rearrange, or remove, the furniture to suit your lesson topic.

The bottom line of transforming your room into a creative learning environment is to think outside the box of your own habits or preconceptions. If you get

Garden Pest:
Tradition Termites

Evidence

These termites hang onto the past with pinchers attached to whatever they can grab. The most obvious signs that you have Tradition Termites in your ministry is the lack of new use of your facilities. The rooms are always the same, with the same use. New uses of the rooms or the removal of walls sends these people into a swarm! Thinking outside the box is foreign or offensive to them.

Sources of Infestation

Fear of change, or lack of awareness of the needs and interests of today's children are the greatest source of these termites. Most of the termites spring from years of membership in the church.

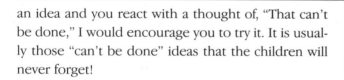

Treatment

1. Spray on liberal amounts of children's ministry vision.
2. Advertise the fruit of the new facility use before the changes are made.
3. When the changes are made, make sure to highlight the positive comments.
4. If the person continues to grumble or eat away at your team, remove the person from the team.

---

an idea and you react with a thought of, "That can't be done," I would encourage you to try it. It is usually those "can't be done" ideas that the children will never forget!

FACILITY GOALS: CREATING A SUPPLY ROOM

It's hard enough to increase the ranks of your teaching staff without telling them to "make bricks without straw" or teach children without the appropriate supplies and resources. If you want your teachers to be creative and add to the curriculum, you can't expect them to supply all those extras out of their own pockets. There are many supplies that will be needed by all on a regular enough basis to warrant them being purchased in bulk and stocked in a supply room. Other supplies may have to be provided on an as needed basis.

Every children's ministry should have a supply room. There's no excuse not to. If you are a small church with little or no budget resources from which to purchase supplies, there are still some great ways to gather those needed supplies.

Inventory Current Supplies

You can't adequately order supplies unless you have inventoried those supplies you already have stored away in some forgotten shelf under the old magazines. If this is the first time you are doing this, it will be a large task. If you have done this in past years you will simply do it again. There are two purposes of the inventory:

1. To discover items that aren't used.
2. To determine what quantities are used and needed.

Another side effect of the inventory is to drive your

teachers or yourself to doing some spring cleaning. You'll be amazed at what you find. You will come across useable items that you didn't know you had, and some other items that you can store in the big green storage bin out behind the church (you know the one with the flies).

The inventory can be done by the teachers or coordinators themselves, but it might be best for you to do it yourself. Regardless of who does the task, here are some suggestions for carrying it out:

1. Formulate a list of supplies you will provide. Ask for specific needs from each department.

2. Print an inventory sheet listing the supplies you are interested in inventorying.

3. Ask for the supplies to be counted and the totals put on the sheet which is returned to you, or:

4. Ask for all the supplies listed to be returned to the office

The purpose of doing this is to clean out any catch-all areas and to determine which supplies are, or are not used. I suggest bringing all the craft, audio visual, or other supplies to a central area (your office?) for this inventory.

Formulate a Supply List

If you use key teachers from the various departments, you should be able to build a list of supplies. Keep in mind that the curriculum-related craft needs change from quarter to quarter; so if you can peek ahead to see what will be needed, that would help you be prepared. Specific supply needs will exist from the nursery and toddler departments. There will be special needs at special times (V.B.S., camps, etc.). If you do a year's calendar, you should be able to plan to purchase the needed items ahead of time.

Formulate a List of High-Frequency Supplies

You need to determine what supplies are needed on a frequent enough basis to warrant their purchase in bulk and storage in the supply room. The means by which you can formulate this list are:

1. Ask teachers, or their coordinators, from each department to provide a list.

Basic Supply List

brass paper fasteners	masking tape
construction paper	name tags
crayons	paper towels
drawing paper	paste
dry erase markers	pencils
erasers	pens
facial tissues	scissors
first aid supplies	scotch tape
glitter	staplers
glue	staples
handi-wipes	tempera paint
markers	tissue paper

Basic Nursery Supplies

3 oz. cups
apple juice
baby wipes
bubbles
crackers
diapers
disinfectant spray
facial tissues
latex gloves
paper towels

2. Review past curriculum-related supply requirements (crafts, lessons, etc.).

3. Interview children's ministry directors from other churches.

Designate a Room as the Supply Room

This room may be a closet, cabinet, or even the trunk of your car. It would be great to have a room available, but you may not have that luxury. Use whatever space you can creatively organize. There

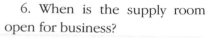

are only two places that should be considered out of bounds for this use: the pastor's office, and his pulpit.

When considering a room, make sure you check it all out with the pastor before you do any changing. Remember, he can be your best supporter only if he knows the same things you do, and agrees with your plans. Here are some hints:

1. The room should be big enough to support adequate shelf space.

2. The room should be centrally located near the classrooms.

Prepare the Room

There are some things the supply room needs to make it smooth-running. Some of these items can be done later, some should be done before the room is opened.

1. Build the shelves.

2. Build or buy the cabinets. Make sure they're locked.

3. Label the shelves.

4. Make a check-out counter (half door?).

5. Make a Supply Room sign for the door or wall.

Prepare Yourself

The worst thing you could ever do is to advertise the opening of the supply room before you are sure of the policies and procedures involved. You will find that it is the gray areas that will give you the most problems. Do all you can to think everything through. The following questions will help you develop some basic policies and procedures:

1. Who are the supplies for? Teachers only? What about other ministries?

2. How are the re-useable supplies checked out or returned?

3. What quantities of the supplies do you give out?

4. Should any supplies be kept in the classrooms? How are those supplies inventoried or replenished? How are those supplies secured? Will you use supply tubs (see note below)?

5. Who is allowed in the supply room? Who gets keys to the door, or cabinets?

6. When is the supply room open for business?

7. Who is in charge of the supply room?

8. When are the supply orders, and inventories done? Who does the orders?

Prepare the People

You won't have any problem getting the people excited about having the supply room. This will be water to a thirsty land! The difficulty will come in your organization of the actual working of the room. If you've done the necessary work suggested in the previous step, you should be fine. Remember to keep your ears open for adjustments or additional policies during the first few months of operation. Here are some ideas for preparing the people:

1. Prepare and print a Supply Room Handbook stating all of the policies and procedures you designed in the previous step.

2. Teach the children's ministry workers about the supply room during an all-teachers meeting. Review the Supply Room Handbook.

3. Post posters and signs around the children's ministry area announcing the date of the supply room's opening, etc.

4. Print flyers and distribute them to children's ministry workers.

5. Communicate your policies (via the Handbook) to the ministries, other than the children's ministry, that will be able to use the supply room (if any).

Order Supplies

A teacher who has been provided with all he needs to do his job is a sight to behold. His or her creativity is supported by a supply room filled with paste, glitter, crayons, construction paper, and other materials that have been organized and distributed in a professional manner.

The ordering of supplies can either be a somewhat tedious task, or that last fling that sends you over the deep end. It all depends on how the supplies are inventoried and ordered.

Your supply order will take some significant time to

Supply Request Form

Team Member Requesting Supplies: _____ Date of Request: _____

Room #: _____ Service Day: _____ Service Hour: _____

Supplies Needed:

Quantity: _____ Item: _____

Quantity: _____ Item: _____

Quantity: _____ Item: _____

Please leave this form with the supply room coordinator. The supplies will be delivered to your room.

---

develop and receive so do this as early in the process as possible. Remember to pray for the Lord of the supply harvest to provide what you need! Don't budget God out of your ministry by failing to ask and trust him for your needs! Also, give the body of Christ a chance to work by advertising your needs in the church bulletin, and letting the people donate what you need. If you have to purchase supplies, do so.

Recruit and Organize the Supply Room Personnel

Don't kid yourself, you aren't super-human! You need to delegate the huge responsibility of overseeing and running the supply room to someone you trust and who can take charge and see that the job is done correctly. It would be great if you could have a coordinator who oversees the whole room and workers who would be in charge during the various services.

Once the Lord has supplied the people to run the room, you need to formally introduce them to the teachers and other staff people who will be using the supply room.

Maintain the Supply Room

Once the supply room is opened, you may be tempted to just let it run itself. Don't! This is one of those ministries that requires consistent care and

Supply Tubs Suggestion

Even though you do your best to collect the right supplies and cage them all nicely inside your supply room, they still have ways of escaping. To protect your budget and your teachers' emotional well-being, here is an idea that has worked for me! Buy plastic tubs (one for each classroom), and label them each with their classroom number. Decide what each tub should have in it. If you can come up with a standard list of supplies that every classroom tub includes, this is easier. Each age group may have different supplies. Make a list of the tubs' standard supplies and post that list on the inside of the supply room as well as in the classroom. The supply tubs are kept in locked cabinets in the classrooms. If supplies are needed, the teacher fills out a "Supply Request Form" and leaves it with the supply room coordinator. The supply room coordinator fills the supply needs and then delivers the supplies to the classroom as early as possible.

loving support from you. It is a non-glory ministry with a high level of pressure and potential for problems. Here are some hints:

1. Physically support, by your presence and compliments, the supply room staff.

2. Oversee the inventories and orders—support a job well-done.

3. Have public (teachers' meetings?) "we appreciate you" times for workers.

FACILITY GOALS: CREATING OR REBUILDING A PLAYGROUND

Playgrounds can be a great part of a fruitful, vision-driven facility, but they can also be risky, unusable, eye-sores as well! The difference is in the design. Children need to play. Play is a critical part of children's ministry. To design a playground that attracts children while, at the same time, doesn't put them at risk, is a huge challenge. That is why there are people who are experts in playground design. That is why there are companies who charge a life's savings for a store-brought playground. That is why I now have all their catalogs in my file drawer! (An excellent source for playground development is the company called KaBoom! They can be contacted at their web site at www.kaboom.org or written to at 333 S. Wabash, Suite 16 South, Chicago, IL 60604-4107 or called at 312-360-9520.)

The goal of building a playground is to attract the children while satisfying the safety-conscious parents and children's ministry team members. You can build a playground that is filled with challenges for the children, but if it is not safe the adults in charge won't let the children use it. The most critical challenge in building a playground is designing a playground that is age-appropriate, safe, challenging, and right for the space available. Here is a list of components of a good playground.

Components of a Fruitful Playground

1. A useful location (near the classrooms)

2. A safe location (fenced, away from cars, free of debris)

3. Accessible to all children (visit www.access-board.gov/play/summary.htm for details)

4. Age-appropriate (specific ages, or blend of all)

5. Variety of activity (active, creative, cooperative, sensory)

6. Durability (withstand weather and children)

7. Low maintenance (not requiring constant sanding, painting, repairing)

8. Visibility (no areas hidden from supervision)

9. Fun (provides physical challenges, stimulates imaginations)

Playground design must not be done by a novice. I encourage you to invest whatever time or money is needed to assure yourself, your parents, and your church that you have done your best in the design phase. Consulting with your city planning department, the parks and recreation department, local elementary schools, other churches, or organizations such as KaBoom! could save you years' worth of problems!

When either building or rebuilding a playground, it would be wise for your to consult those agencies which regulate public playgrounds. Even though your playground may not be considered public, you would be wise to make every effort to conform to these standards should the laws change. In the event of a lawsuit, your efforts to make your playground conform to accepted standards will be to your church's benefit. See page 51 for a list of the agencies to consult.

Whatever you do in the area of children's playgrounds, do it well! If all you have is a cement strip for hopscotch, make it the most beautifully painted, well-organized hopscotch area the world has ever seen! Remember that parents will take one short look at your play area and judge your entire ministry's value based on what they see. Let your playground be an excellent "spokesperson" for your vision.

Sometimes "Free" Is Too Good to Be True

Building a playground for free, with donated materials and volunteer labor, sounds so good to most of us who love children and have a tight budget. I've been there, though. I can tell you that the dream of a free playground may sound good at first, but it may end up being a nightmare.

I built a "free" playground below "the house on the hill" that I mentioned earlier in this chapter. I had no money with which to build a playground, but I knew the children needed to play. My get-it-for-free nature kicked into high gear. I scrounged around town looking for storage yards of building materials, cement pipes, and old tires. After just a few days, I had connected with some wonderful companies who were willing to donate everything I needed. I was thrilled! I had a tractor tire company who was willing to donate two huge tractor tires. A demolition company gave us a very large cement pipe and all the used lumber I needed. I was set! What I didn't understand, though, was that the term "free" sometimes means "a huge amount of work." We had to move all of these "free" materials to our playground site! That meant renting trucks and recruiting men. I learned that moving free tractor tires was very expensive. To move a tractor tire requires a huge truck with a specially-made crane. We got two free tires, but they cost us $300 to move them. The free lumber all had to be sanded and prepared. The free cement pipes also cost us $200 to move. By the time I had finished building our free playground, I had paid, just in material costs alone, nearly $800! Now, when I am tempted to use the word "free," I turn around and run!

Playground Regulatory Agencies

- U.S. Consumer Product Safety Commission (CPSC), Washington, DC 20207 (800) 638-2772 www.cpsc.gov
- American Society for Testing and Materials (ASTM), 100 Bar Harbor Dr., West Conshohocken, PA 19428-2959 (610) 832-9585 www.astm.org
- International Play Equipment Manufacturers Assoc. (IPEMA), 8300 Colesville Rd., Suite 250, Silver Spring, MD 20910 (800) 395-5550 www.ipema.org

THE IDEAL CHILDREN'S MINISTRY FACILITY

You may never be able to be involved in building a new facility from the ground up, but if you do, it is a fun experience! The children's ministry facility is much like the Christian life in the sense that we have a perfect example (Jesus) to which we aspire, but none of us will actually accomplish perfection this side of Heaven (even though God views us as complete and perfect in Jesus). We all may dream about the perfect facility, but we will probably never experience it. That doesn't mean that we shouldn't work toward it, though. We may not have a totally perfect facility, but we may be able to have bits and pieces of that dream facility.

Even if you don't have the perfect facility, there are some things that should be included in each room or area. See page 54 for a list of those items.

The Perfect Children's Ministry Facility

GENERAL EXTERIOR IDEAS

1. A nicely-equipped, safe, enclosed children's playground. A well-designed, secure environment that challenges the children physically while stirring their imaginations. This can either be "store-bought" or self-made. The goal is safety, longevity, and low maintenance.

2. Clearly marked room numbers and age assignments outside classrooms. These should correspond with some "Parent Directory" or other way for the parents to find the rooms.

3. Nice, efficient drinking fountains set at child-level. A weak drinking fountain, or one set too high, can give the wrong message to thirsty visitors.

4. External speakers. These speakers can be valuable in "setting the mood" for the children's ministry area, as they play worship music or children's songs during the service.

5. Some sort of "information center." This could be a gazebo-type free-standing building, or simply a room with an exterior window or door. The information center needs to be right on the traffic path for parents as they come into your children's area. It should be marked by clear, large, friendly signs.

6. Vision-related banners. The external walls must communicate your vision. This will attract both the parents and children to your ministry. This will also assist in times of recruiting.

GENERAL INTERIOR IDEAS

1. Large classrooms. Small classrooms may seem to "save money" by getting more rooms into the overall facility, but almost without exception, churches later end up tearing out walls or building on. Rooms should be no smaller than 20 feet by 20 feet; they should be at least 25 x 25!

2. An intercom system into every room. This adds a tremendous level of communication support for the teachers. This could be used for messages from "the office" to the teaching team, or requests for assistance from the teachers.

3. Speakers in every room. These are both for ambiance (worship or children's music) and for announcements from the children's ministry office.

4. Extra wide interior or exterior hallways. In your planning, when you think you've designed them "wide enough," widen them by another 2 feet. As you grow, the comfortable flow of parents and children at drop-off and pick-up periods is vital to safety and public relations. Interior halls are affected by classroom doorways opening into the hallways and drinking fountains on the walls. If you don't have a centralized check-in area (see #12, #13), the check-in lines at each classroom will always flow into the hallways! Interior hallways of 12-15 feet are great!

5. Child-sized restrooms. This design feature says, "We care about children!" Small, low toilets and sinks are better than steps up to adult-sized facilities. A mixture of adult-sized and child-sized toilets is OK. Mirrors and towel dispensers should also be within reach for the little ones.

6. Teachers' supply room. This is one of the greatest supports to your loyal, servant volunteers! The room should be centrally located to the classrooms. The door should be a "Dutch door" that can be used as a check-in and out counter. The room should be as large as possible; don't go any smaller than 15 x 20 feet. You will always use every inch! If possible, this room should have a sink and counter in it for cleaning the supplies.

7. Plenty of storage. Another mistake we tend to make in facility design is the lack of storage. Consider who needs to store stuff, and plan for it! You cannot keep "stuff" away by not building storage; it will find places to live, and it will always occupy space that should be used for ministry!

8. Classroom cabinets. Together with storage for "stuff" outside the rooms, each room should have lockable cabinets inside as well. Even though you may have a centralized supply room, you will still have ministry-related stuff to store in each room. *CAUTION:* these cabinets can quickly become junk storage if they aren't regularly cleaned out!

9. A children's ministry office with reception area. This is a welcoming area that says, "We care, and we're professional about it!"

10. Plenty of restrooms. The restrooms are usually at the end of the hallways. This can cause problems for the younger children and their teachers who have to walk a long way during emergencies. You might consider building your classrooms in "pods" with restrooms in each pod. This is especially valuable in the toddler area where children are being potty trained! There could be four classrooms around a central restroom facility. These classrooms would all have access to the restrooms, and the restrooms would be sized according to the age of the children in the pod. Make sure your restrooms are well ventilated! There is nothing worse than stale restroom air! When you calculate the size of exhaust fan needed for the restroom, order one size larger!

11. Sinks in every classroom. This is a luxury. It's a nice addition to a supportive facility. Sinks in the middle and upper grade classrooms aren't as necessary. If you are adding sinks, remember to include drinking fountains in the sinks! Make sure they are set at child level so you don't have to include steps!

12. Check-in and check-out doors. Children under 7th grade should be checked-in and out by parents or guardians. In multiple worship service situations, two doors increases the efficiency of the parent flow. If parents have to stand too long, they may not want to return next week! A centralized check-in center (see below) will reduce the stress at the doorways for both the parents and the team members!

13. Centralized Check-in/Information Center. This is a great support to the classroom team members! Children are checked-in at a centralized location. At this center, parents are greeted, security measures are monitored, and ministry information is given. Once checked in, the parents take their children to the rooms for quick drop off. This center should be within view of the parking lot. If this can't be, make sure its location is well-advertised with signs.

14. Elevated classroom windows. Distractions can be reduced by placing the classroom windows above the "view line" of the children. As parents or others pass by, the children will not be able to see them. The classroom doors should still have lower windows for viewing into the classroom.

15. Large, assembly room. Your facility should have a large room where most of your children can assemble at one time. This room should have a stage and sound system. There could be a kitchen adjoining this room for potlucks, etc.

16. Medium, large room. You might want to build "double wide" classrooms with sliding partitions in a couple of areas in your facilities. These are valuable for versatility!

17. Thermostats in every room. A good temperature is vital for a good learning environment. If you can't afford thermostats in every room, one thermostat for two rooms is OK. Make sure these two rooms have a door linking them so the teacher can stick his or her head in and make suggestions for temperature adjustments without leaving the room. (Accessible timer switches that control the thermostats will prevent the air conditioners from staying on for days.)

18. A communication link to the sanctuary area. If you aren't sure if you need this, lay a large conduit (5-6 inches) with a pull cord for later. This may be used for transmitting the service or sermon into the children's area, paging parents, or for other communications. It is one of those "plan for the future" things.

NURSERY/TODDLER FACILITIES

1. Excellent air circulation. If the air is slow-moving, the smells will build. Build larger vents and capacity than is really needed in these rooms. (Accessible timer switches that control the thermostats will prevent the air conditioners from staying on for days.)

2. Washer/dryer. This is a great support to the wonderful servant who will volunteer to do the laundry for this ministry.

3. One-way windows. Parents like to see in, and your volunteers benefit from knowing they're looking. You can post a sign "Watch us love your children!" over the window on the outside. The inside is covered with a mirror film so the children cannot see their parents and begin to cry.

4. Noise and smell barriers. The nursery/toddler area may be the most critical area for attracting new church attendees. If this area is smelly or filled with the sounds of crying children, first time visitors may get the wrong impression of your care for the children. Build a second door and buffer area for both sound and smell. (See the illustration on page 55.)

Ideal Room Equipment

NURSERY

CD player
Changing tables
Check-in counter
Crib area
Cubbies for diaper bags
Fire extinguisher
Lighting control to dim lights
One-way viewing windows for parents
Refrigerator
Rocking area
Shelves
Sink
Supplies storage
Swing area
Toilet
Toy storage
Walled play area
Washer/dryer
Workers' coat rack

TODDLER

Changing table
Check-in counter
Crib area
Cubbies (for diaper bags and other belongings)
Fire extinguisher
Large toy play area
One-way viewing windows for parents
Refrigerator
Shelves
Sink

Supplies storage
Toilet
Toy storage
Toys on walls
Various "experience areas"
Walled play area
Washer/dryer
Workers' coat rack

2's–5's

Appropriate number/size of chairs
Appropriate number/size of tables
Black/whiteboard
Bulletin board
Carpet/linoleum space
Check-in counter
Coat racks
Counter/cabinet space
Fire extinguisher
Play area
Sink/drinking fountain
Toy storage

1st–6th GRADERS

Appropriate number/size of chairs
Appropriate number/size of tables
Black/whiteboard
Bulletin board
Coat racks
Counter/cabinet space
Fire extinguisher
Sink/drinking fountain

THE POLITICS OF A WELL-USED FACILITY

When the Lord blesses your church and your children's ministry (notice I said "when" because I believe that he will if you are following him), you will experience the thrills and challenges of a well-used facility. You will experience limited room availability, shared cabinets, and messes you didn't create.

When a healthy garden grows, it creates its own problems. The watermelon vines creep into your tomatoes. The corn overshadows the broccoli. Your squash just went wild this year! Healthy growth thrills the gardener, but it demands thoughtful trimming, pruning, or dividing.

When ministries grow, they need more room. They will take or be given the room they need based on their direct relation to the overall church vision. The interpretation of their connection to the overall church vision is the right of the senior pastor. You may believe that the singles' use of room 15 is not as

A Check-in Friendly Nursery Design

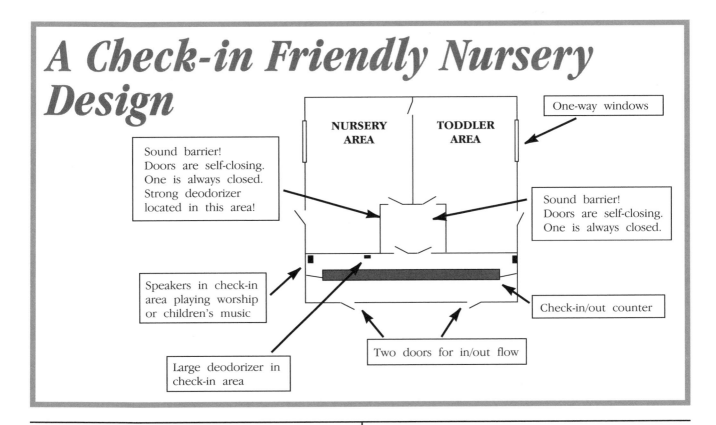

NURSERY AREA

TODDLER AREA

One-way windows

Sound barrier! Doors are self-closing. One is always closed. Strong deodorizer located in this area!

Sound barrier! Doors are self-closing. One is always closed.

Speakers in check-in area playing worship or children's music

Check-in/out counter

Large deodorizer in check-in area

Two doors for in/out flow

---

valid or important as your fourth grade's service center. You may believe that the singles can walk a little further to room 22 which is not being used during that hour. What you believe may or may not matter! If the senior pastor believes that the singles' ministry, in this case, is more significantly connected to the overall church vision, the fourth graders will walk to room 22, and you will be thankful and gracious to have room 22!

Be flexible with room use. If you can make room for other ministries without compromising your vision, do so. Be patient with changes in the room set up. Plan for surprises! Arrive in your ministry area before the program's start with enough time to completely set up the room. Even though you may have clearly defined your room needs to other ministries or to your maintenance staff, don't be upset when things fall apart. In a busy church, there are probably programs happening every night of the week. In a perfect world, those who use the facility should be sensitive to the needs of the program that uses the room next. They should either leave the room as they found it, or assist in setting up the room for the next program. That would be nice, wouldn't it? Wake up! You're dreaming! This is not a perfect world. We, you and I, are perhaps the only perfect people here.

The rest of the people will probably leave the room in a mess and let you be surprised when you arrive in the morning. The only way I have found to keep myself from permanently checking into "Happy Acres Rehabilitation Center" is to plan on surprises. Then, when I arrive to find the room messed up, I'm not surprised. If I arrive to find the room set-up as I had requested, I'm thrilled, and I treat myself to a little more peace for the morning.

Don't misunderstand me. I'm not saying that you shouldn't make your requests known to the other ministries who will use the facilities. I am just cautioning you to ask God to help you do so with grace, honor, and humility. You can, and should, be upset with others' lack of the same grace and honor; but you should only express that frustration to the Lord, and to your spouse. Everyone else should only hear your calm expressions of your desire for a team mindset about the facility, and your humble suggestions for improvements.

We, in children's ministry, must always campaign for what we believe to be important. We must not be too soft or weak when it comes to the rights and needs of the children; but when forced to comply with the needs of other ministries, we must be positive, supportive, and gracious. This is not hypocritical.

Thirty Goals for Your Facility

GENERAL EXTERIOR GOALS

1. Create a safe, attractive, clean, enclosed play area for children. This can be inside or outside.
2. Clearly mark rooms with large numbers or signs to assist the parents.
3. Create a directory or map to the rooms. This can be either a brochure, wall display, or both.
4. Provide clean, efficient drinking fountains at child-level.
5. Install external speakers for ambient music.
6. Create a children's ministry information center within view of the parking lot.
7. Display ministry vision-related banners around the church campus.

GENERAL INTERIOR GOALS

8. Design creative learning environments in which to attract children to God: large rooms, creative use of walls, floors, doorways, ceilings, and windows; creative use of lighting and sounds.
9. Install an intercom system in every room.
10. Install speakers (for music and announcements) in every room.
11. Create the largest hallway space possible. Remove any obstructions. Control the flow of people.
12. Build or refurbish the restrooms to be more child-friendly.
13. Guarantee the maximum efficiency of the restroom exhaust fans.
14. Create a teachers' supply room.
15. Clean out and maximize the storage areas.
16. Provide lockable classroom cabinets for the teachers' use.
17. Create or refurbish the children's ministry office/reception area.
18. Provide sinks in every classroom.
19. Provide two doors in every room for efficient flow of people during check-in and check-out.
20. Create a central check-in area for the entire children's ministry or for each age group department.
21. Provide windows in every classroom. Restrict the children's view of parents with one-way film.
22. Create a large assembly room for worship and fellowship.
23. Plan for versatility in classroom use by replacing some solid walls with moveable walls.
24. Provide efficient, easily accessible temperature control for as many rooms as possible.

NURSERY/TODDLER FACILITY GOALS

25. Provide excellent air circulation.
26. Provide a washer/dryer in the facility.
27. Provide one-way windows for parents.
28. Create noise and smell barriers.
29. Create experience areas for the toddler children.
30. Provide an internal restroom for potty-trained children.

This is professional. Submission is the determined act of placing your power or ability under the authority of another. Submission is not a weak move; it is a powerful act. We are called to submit to the authorities placed over us (see *Romans 13:1, 2*).

Campaign boldly and with a smile, but if you lose, support the decision as if it was your idea in the first place! Believe me, God will bless this characteristic and he will create favor for you, your team, and your ministry.

"*Conditions in your garden or neighborhood can create microclimates that will be somewhat different from the general climate of your area*" *(Sunset New Western Garden Book, Menlo Park, CA: Lane Publishing Co., 1979; page 9).*

If only I had known sooner that I should never have tried to discuss finances with Bill Smith or tried to move Kathryn's Wednesday morning Bible study out of the Fireside Room! Things seemed so clear to me; I had taken the required courses in psychology; I was together! I think they saw me coming.

It wasn't just that I had to get acquainted with some key people, but I also had to learn (by trial and a sufficient amount of error) what those people meant in terms of the power structure of the church. After a few months, I felt like I was ready to run for the Presidency. I had developed a circle of advisors who could whisper in my ear before those gala events, and I had finally uncovered the complex, underground communication network between the pulpit and the elders. This may sound a bit blown out of proportion, and well, OK, it may be. Nevertheless the political structures that exist in the church should be part of every children's minister's training. This section is designed to help you become aware of these unspoken structures with a minimal amount of "Oh, I didn't know" time in the boss's office.

Every gardener knows that the soil in a garden needs to be "turned" before it is planted. Turning the soil accomplishes many things:

1. The crusty top surface of the soil is broken and softened.

2. The leaves, sticks, or dead plant materials on the surface are rotated under the soil to decay and enrich the soil.

3. Oxygen is infused into the soil.

All of these are very valuable, and they must be done. But the gardener turns the soil for another reason that somehow transcends all the other reasons. He turns the soil to see what's going on below the surface. As he turns the soil, he looks, smells, and even leans down and feels the soil. He looks for bugs, worms, peat, roots, fungus, clay, or any other condition that could benefit or impede his plants. This first turning of the soil is a critical step toward his enjoying a juicy watermelon on a hot Sunday afternoon.

Turning the soil of your ministry site is just as important. In chapters 2 and 4 you observed children and your facility. To some extent, that was a surface observation of your garden site. Now, it's time to get out the shovel and dig deeper into the belief systems and political structure of your church. What you will find as you turn the soil in your ministry garden will either thrill you or concern you. Either way, you need to look deeper to discover what goes on below the surface. You will be looking for political structures, power people, belief boundaries, traditions, or anything that might hinder or further your ministry to children.

I have always told my co-workers and students, "If you can learn how to work with people, you can work with anyone!" Children's ministry is about working with people. Our focus is, of course, on the young people, but we can't hide from or offend the older people in the process. A children's minister soon realizes that his or her typical day at the church is spent dealing with adult situations more than with the children. It is our job to minister to the adults who are ministering to the children. I have also been surprised to hear so many people say that politics shouldn't exist in the church. In my early years of ministry, I used to try to ignore political situations. I thought I was above all that bickering over such petty issues. I soon realized that I could not run from the politics. I had to learn how to work with the power structures and use them to further my goals.

Since ministry is about people, we must ask God to make us better at dealing with their differences, opinions, and their power struggles. Can you imagine how difficult it must have been for the God of perfection, power, and all creation to come to the political world of the Roman Empire and deal with human politics? He could have just spoken his way though the process; instead, he showed us how to work with and within politics to accomplish the purpose of the Gospel.

JESUS, A MASTER "PEOPLE PERSON"

Jesus was a masterful example of walking among the politics and using powerful people to influence other powerful people. Jesus was a master at getting to know people. Even though he knew them from the beginning of time, he still showed us how to step off of our busy path to connect with the face in the crowd. He knew he had to do this in order to win their respect along with feeling their feelings. Jesus didn't spend much of his time in the temple. We find him going there to fulfill the law or to earn the respect of those around him. He was much happier out in the streets with the real people. His love for people stems from the fact that he made every one of us! He knows us—all of us! He disliked the religious people who set themselves apart from the common folk of the day. To refresh your focus on the value of the common folk to Jesus, look at his encounters with an outcast Samaritan woman *(John 4)*, a sinful woman *(Luke 7:36-50)*, and a hated little man *(Luke 19:1-10)*.

Jesus' face-to-face dealing with real people is an example to us all, especially those of us in ministry. We are commanded to be with the people. We cannot run away from those who bother us. We have been called to love them even more! I have often said, humorously, that church work would be a lot easier if we didn't have to deal with people! There are times that we all struggle with our calling to minister to people, but it is important to remember that we are part of God's efforts to restore his people back to him. This is not about us! It's about him.

"PR" STANDS FOR "PERSONAL RESPECT"

You'll find many pages dealing with people and their needs in this book. If you can learn to understand the needs of people, you will do well in being able to work with, and eventually like, even the most offensive church members. That is ministry.

Many years ago, the Lord blessed me with a successful, fruitful ministry in a mega-church. For eight years I enjoyed designing, planting, and growing a children's ministry and Christian school. God had given me insights about people and administration that produced, in his power, a strong team of volunteers. The Lord moved me to a new ministry just recently, only a few miles away from my previous fruitful garden of years ago. I felt fairly confident in my abilities based on the experiences at the other church. In many ways, I said to myself and to God, "No problem, I'll just do what worked before." I didn't consider the climate differences between the two garden sites. Just about everything that had worked at the previous children's ministry location failed at the new site. I discovered I was dealing with different people, a different culture of volunteerism, and a significant difference in our overall church vision. I had to lay all of my ministry plans aside while I became familiar with the new environment and sought the Lord for a fresh design for this new garden.

Whether you are new to a church or you have a gold pin for your years of attendance, you must get to know the people who are in the know. Don't deny their existence or try to work around them; they have always been there and will still be there when you move on. Division-causing arguments are typical with people, Christians included. Anytime you have a group of people together, you will find a hierarchy developing. It is comforting to know that even the early disciples had disputes and struggles amongst themselves. For an earful, read the first chapter of *1 Corinthians*. You might as well get with the system, or as Paul said it so beautifully: "I have become all things to all men so that by all possible means I might save some. I do all this for the sake of the gospel, that I may share in its blessings" *(1 Corinthians 9:22, 23)*.

If you are entering a new ministry, don't be too excited to come in "with your guns blazing." You should work with the ministries and people already functioning whenever possible. This is a good way to show that you respect what has been done and those who designed it. If the people involved ask you for help or suggestions, then is the time to suggest some changes, but not before. After a few months of involvement in these ministries, you will eventually earn the right to be heard with the people and slowly make some adjustments.

Remember that authority is earned; power is taken. Authority supports people; power seeks to control them. The fruit of power is rebellion, distrust, and administrative loneliness devoid of any followers. The fruit of authority is respect, trust, and a growing list of followers. The effectiveness of your data-gathering time rests solely on your heart's attitude. All the information you could possibly collect wouldn't benefit you at all if your purpose was to increase your power over these people. The reason you are gathering this information is to be better able to serve those with whom you work. Remain a servant who is always ready to deem others more important than yourself.

Remember, your motive is to become aware of any conditions that might affect your ministry now, or in the future. Your motive is not to change any condition that you may find. This is the site to which the Lord has called you. He will help you deal with the conditions of the site. Remember, it is the Lord who is growing your garden, not you!

OBSERVING THE CONDITIONS OF YOUR SOIL

Every church is unique. We all share a beautiful connection with a common commission, but how we carry out that commission can be significantly different. As you get ready to turn some soil at your church, remember, you are looking for things that might influence the growth of your tender, young plants. There can be quite a few things that can influence your children's ministry garden.

The list of "Ten Soil Conditions to Consider" tells you what to look for as you "turn the soil" in your church. Let me warn you that what you're about to do may be risky. Some people may question your motives. Remind yourself and others about your reason for asking the questions: You want to do all you can to make sure the children's ministry garden has the best chance to produce as much fruit as God can give you.

Ten Soil Conditions to Consider

1. Denominational influences
2. Tradition/history of the congregation
3. Past experiences of the congregation (successes, traumas, legal battles, etc.)
4. The average age of the members
5. The vision of the church
6. Financial influencers in the community
7. The senior pastor's views on ministry
8. The church board's influence
9. Location of the church (rural, inner city, etc.)
10. The number of children attending your church

General Misconceptions About Politics in Ministry

1. "Politics are bad." The existence of politics is not an indicator of the presence of evil. Whenever you have people working together, you'll find politics. It is how we deal with politics and what our motives are that determine whether they are good or bad.

2. "There shouldn't be politics in the Church." The Church is made up of people. All people are sinful and need a savior. The only difference between the Church and other large corporations is that the Church has a commission to follow which dictates that we "think of others as more important than ourselves." The Church should have less political powerplays in which people are hurt or ministries destroyed, but we cannot delude ourselves into believing the Church will be devoid of all politics because all politics are not necessarily evil.

3. "Even though there are politics in the Church, I'm not going to 'play'"! It would be nice if we could be successful in ministry without dealing with people. After years in ministry, you will begin to dream of the "perfect" church: one in which no one complains, there are no power-plays, every one gets along with each other, and you are always respected for your work. That church would have to keep 85% of all people out of its "holy grounds." The Christian life is about people! The Great Commission is about dealing with those people! Your call to ministry is about your learning how to deal with people! You must learn about politics in order to survive and thrive within the structure of the local church!

4. "I'm going to get to the 'top' so I can make sure politics don't run my church." In politics, the final word is "power." We all have that bit of God in us that says, "There will be no other gods before me." The quest for "the top" is not a bad thing if your desire is to serve God more effectively or further his Kingdom through that level of leadership. If, however, you want to be at "the top" to permit you to always be right or free yourself from the hassles of working with people, be careful! Those motives may not be listed in the "To Be Blessed" category on God's chart.

THE PROCESS OF TURNING THE SOIL

Remember, a healthy awareness of the rocks, climate, and soil conditions affecting your garden can only benefit your overall ministry; however, there are some cautions I need to give you before you put on your boots and gloves, and begin turning the soil.

Rules for Turning the Soil

1. Meet with your senior pastor before you do anything to tell him of your intentions. Make sure he gives you permission to do your observations. Tell him what you want to do in detail, and do only what he permits you to do. Offer to report to him at the conclusion of your observations to show him your discoveries.

2. Never observe financial records without permission of the keeper of the records.

3. If you are not given permission to do your observations, don't! "No" means no! Respect for authority and boundaries is more valuable than a ton of information gathered wrongly.

4. Respect the office of a board member. Disclose your purpose clearly and ask for permission to speak to the board member before proceeding. If the board member is not willing, stop. Thank him or her for their understanding and reinforce your respect for the decision to not participate.

5. Never attend a board meeting unless invited to do so. Board meetings are serious meetings during which sensitive information is shared. Respect the significant role of the board.

6. Deal with political connections within the church very carefully. Knowing these connections is like holding a lit match. Handled correctly, the fire can warm or cook food, but a lit match handled wrongly can cause much destruction and pain.

Turning the Soil With the Senior Pastor

Ask the senior pastor for an appointment. Once in a meeting with him, tell him of your plans to become familiar with some of the conditions of the church that might affect the children's ministry. Assure him that your motive is to better produce, with the Lord's help, a growing children's ministry. Tell him all that you plan to do in your observations. While there, ask him if he would answer a couple of questions. If he agrees, ask him:

1. "What is your vision for the overall church, and how does that relate to the children's ministry?"

2. "What can the children's ministry do to better support your ministry here?"

3. "What are some of the 'untapped potentials' for the children's ministry?"

4. "In your opinion, what are some obstacles to growth that face the children's ministry?"

5. "Are there any denominational beliefs or doctrines that directly affect the children's ministry?"

6. "What are your views about volunteers in the ministry?"

7. "What are your views about paid staff in the ministry?"

Turning the Soil With Administrative Assistants

Visit with the church's Administrative Assistant for an informal interview (if he or she agrees). Affirm his or her value in the strength of the church. Ask the following:

1. "In your opinion, what are some areas that need to be improved in the children's ministry?"

2. "What is the general reputation of the children's ministry among the congregation?"

3. "What are some suggestions you might give for making the children's ministry more fruitful?"

Turning the Soil With the Financial Manager

Ask the financial manager if he or she would be willing to answer some questions about the children's ministry budget. If the answer is "yes," ask:

1. "In your opinion, what are the financial limitations facing the children's ministry?"

2. "What are some suggestions you might give for making the children's ministry more financially stable?"

3. "May I review the past children's ministry budgets?" (If applicable)

Turning the Soil With a Church Board Member

With permission of, or referral from, the senior pastor, make an appointment with a member of the church board. Thank him or her for the opportunity to meet. Review your goals for this interview, then ask the following: (Remember, if he or she is not comfortable answering the question, respectfully move on to the next question.)

1. "What role does the children's ministry serve in the overall church mission?"

2. "What is the relationship between the church board and the children's ministry?"

3. "In your opinion, what are some successes of the children's ministry in the past?"

4. "In your opinion, what are some mistakes the children's ministry has made in the past?"

5. "What would you like to see the children's ministry accomplish in the near future?"

Turning the Soil by Observing Social Connections

Your church has a social structure. Observe these political lines that are stretched throughout the church by keenly observing the social connections. Knowing who not to offend or with whom to clearly communicate your vision are critical bits of knowledge. Don't be bothered by politics in the church. As

I said earlier, politics exist whenever two people are in the same room. To ignore the existence of politics is to travel an obstacle course with your eyes shut.

Let's take another look at the social maneuverings of Jesus. He was a master at recognizing and using political connections. His meetings with Nicodemus *(John 3)*, Zacchaeus *(Luke 19)*, and Matthew *(Matthew 9)*, prove Jesus' recognition of the political structures in place. He used these relationships to his advantage. Ask God for discernment as you quietly observe the following:

1. With whom does the senior pastor visit at church during the week?

2. With whom does the senior pastor socialize during off-work hours (golf, etc.)?

3. With whom does the chairman of the board socialize both at church and outside church?

4. Who attends the longest-functioning adult Sunday school class?

5. Who attends the newest adult Sunday school class?

6. Who has been on the church board the longest, or for the most terms?

7. Which group or ministry gets the most "press" in the church newsletter or bulletin?

8. With which ministry of the church is the senior pastor's wife most involved? Does the age of their children have anything to do with that?

Using the Information You Have "Turned Up"

As with any survey, the information gathered is only as valuable as its use. If you simply log all the information the Lord has let you learn as a result of your "snooping," and then put it in a file drawer, you have wasted your effort. You've turned the soil of human relationships and looked at it from all angles. Now you have to do something with the information.

The wise gardener will re-arranges his plans, or make new ones that will better use the natural setting or the type of soil he has inherited. It is much easier to adjust your plans to suit the existing terrain of your site rather than try to change the site to suit your plans. There are instances when your plans are

important enough to warrant the effort it takes to adjust the site, but that decision comes with much thought, consultation, and time.

The information you've learned from your observations will most likely affect all you do in children's ministry. You've learned about your senior pastor's vision for the church and the children's ministry. You've discovered some valuable information about the past experiences of both the church and the children's ministry. You've spent time with some significant people, and observed the inner workings of the political structure of the church. Now, you should take all that information and carefully document it in some format that will help you reference it easily in the future.

I believe that one of the greatest things we can do administratively is to reduce the potential for negative situations that drain so much time and energy away from any advancement of our ministry vision. Knowing some of the potential problem areas in advance might protect you from getting distracted from the joy of leading children to the Lord.

THE SENIOR PASTOR: YOUR MOST POWERFUL ALLY

Without a doubt, the most critical influence of the health of your children's ministry garden, apart from the presence, power, and leading of the Holy Spirit, is your senior pastor. The second most critical influence is your relationship with the senior pastor. Who your senior pastor is, what he believes, his administrative style, and how he treats his staff all have a monumental effect on your children's ministry. You have been called to this ministry; therefore, in the power of the Lord, work alongside him with loyalty and integrity.

In this next section, I will share some insights about developing a working relationship with the senior pastor. I realize that, as I do this, I am venturing into dangerous soil. I think about those signs that you may have seen which read, "STOP, underground

The Church "Soil Conditions"

Go back to the "Ten Soil Conditions to Consider" and plug the information into the appropriate areas. Give some thought to what effect that information has on your children's ministry. Here is a sample to guide your thoughts.

1. Denominational influences

I discovered.... (Insert your information; for example, "Our denomination has concerns about children accepting the Lord before 10 years old.")

This affects our children's ministry by.... (Weigh the effects of this discovery against your children's ministry vision. How will this information effect your progress toward your goals?)

2. Tradition/history of the congregation

I discovered.... (Insert your information.)

This affects our children's ministry by.... (Weigh the effects of this discovery.)

3. Past experiences of the congregation (successes, traumas, legal battles, etc.)

I discovered.... (Insert your information.)

This affects our children's ministry by.... (Weigh the effects of this discovery.)

4. The average age of the members

I discovered.... (Insert your information.)

This affects our children's ministry by.... (Weigh the effects of this discovery.)

5. The vision of the church

I discovered.... (Insert your information.)

This affects our children's ministry by.... (Weigh the effects of this discovery.)

6. Financial influencers in the community

I discovered.... (Insert your information.)

This affects our children's ministry by.... (Weigh the effects of this discovery.)

7. The senior pastor's views on ministry

I discovered.... (Insert your information.)

This affects our children's ministry by.... (Weigh the effects of this discovery.)

8. The church board's influence

I discovered.... (Insert your information.)

This affects our children's ministry by.... (Weigh the effects of this discovery.)

9. Location of the church (rural, inner city, etc.)

I discovered.... (Insert your information.)

This affects our children's ministry by.... (Weigh the effects of this discovery.)

10. The number of children attending your church

I discovered.... (Insert your information.)

This affects our children's ministry by.... (Weigh the effects of this discovery.)

power cable buried here! Before digging, call...." You must be aware that there is a power cable present before you start up your rototiller and begin turning your soil. The power cable is a good thing! Not knowing about the power cable would definitely be a bad thing.

At the very beginning of this section, I'm going to say something that may bother you. I need to say it now so I can go on and explain what I mean. Are you sitting down? Take a deep breath. You may feel a little pressure.... I believe we, in church ministry, are called to do two things: (1) to further the Gospel by carrying out the Great Commission in the area to which God has called us and (2) to serve our senior pastor

Developing a Working Relationship With Senior Pastor "A"

The fine art of supporting, communicating, and understanding

PASTOR'S PERSONALITY	SUGGESTED CARE

Relationship With Children

1. Very popular with entire families. Speaks with children with eye-to-eye smiles.
2. Openly shows affection and respect to his own children, who return the gesture.

1. Praise God for such a great example and compliment him both publicly and privately.
2. Make sure to invite and include him, whenever possible, in children's ministry events.

Relationship With the Support Staff

1. Hires support staff to assure those areas get the best ministry possible.
2. Meets with his support staff regularly, and displays interest and ideas for those areas.

3. Permits the support staff "freedom in bounds" to develop and maintain efforts.

1. Respect the trust and faith he has in you. Ask him for his opinion and suggestions regularly.
2. Never break an appointment; thank him for meeting with you; listen to and apply his suggestions when possible; report back to him regarding the results of his ideas. Thank him!
3. Never overstep your bounds! If unsure, ask! Do nothing to damage the trust. Thank him for his trust and style. Do more than is expected of you.

Budget Concerns

1. Realizes that ministry takes money, and is willing to support strong budget bases for ministry ventures within means.
2. Remains focused on the Lord's provision while being a wise steward of the finances.

1. Be a conservative, wise steward of the money entrusted to you.
2. Keep excellent records; report to him regularly regarding the use of the funds. Thank him for his support.

Views of the Church Service

1. Enjoys children in the service, may even have a "children's time" in the program.
2. Provides time during the service periodically to announce children's activities.
3. Provides time during the service periodically to recognize quality teachers.

4. Provides time during the service periodically to announce areas of need in the children's ministry and reinforces the value of the ministry himself.

1. Praise God for this! Thank him publicly and privately.
2. Be cautious to take less than the time given. Be positive and ask for his "critique" periodically.
3. If possible, let him decide when this is to be done (with your input). If he desires, let him do the recognition. Thank him for his support as pastor.
4. Thank him privately for his support. Reinforce to him the impact his support has on the church's response.

Personal Time

1. Makes an effort to attend teacher meetings or appreciation banquets whenever possible.

2. Periodically visits the teachers or other volunteers before, during, or after the service whenever possible.

1. Recognize his effort and presence openly. Let him feel a part of the program whenever possible without making him feel obligated to attend. Make sure he is aware of the dates of the meetings well in advance. Thank him privately. Appreciate him formally, periodically.
2. Encourage the teachers to write him notes thanking him for this "extra-mile gesture." Thank him privately.

Developing a Working Relationship With Senior Pastor "B"

The fine art of supporting, communicating, and understanding

PASTOR'S PERSONALITY	**SUGGESTED CARE**
### Relationship With Children	
1. Focuses attention on adults, ignores children, children ignore him.	1. Pray for him to become more sensitive to children. Wait and watch for an opportunity to support his attention to a child.
2. Very rarely is he seen with his own children.	2. Invite him and his children to a banquet or outing periodically. Reinforce the healthy value of seeing them together to him afterwards.
### Relationship With the Support Staff	
1. Hires support staff to free himself from having to be "bothered" by the busywork of that area.	1. Regularly relay "praise reports" from your ministry to him. Regularly ask for his counsel regarding the ministry.
2. Has an "open door policy" with his support staff. They may make an appointment with him whenever they feel the need to talk.	2. Reinforce the value you place on his support. Ask to meet with him every other week at first, then weekly. The purpose of the meetings is to help you know how to better support him.
3. Dictates the functions of each support staff member through the job descriptions he has designed.	3. Do your best within these boundaries. If you do suggest changes, do so only after reaffirming your respect, etc.
### Budget Concerns	
1. The main church budget takes priority over all other areas. If "offering is up," there may be money for the other areas such as the children's ministry.	1. Be frugal! Try to strike a balance between wanting more money and yet designing a program with little or no church money required.
2. Very seldom does he talk of faith or trust in the provision of the Lord for the church.	2. "Season" your financial comments with references to the Lord's provision, trust in Him, etc. without being obnoxious.
### Views of the Church Service	
1. Would rather not have children in the service due to the distraction.	1. Pray! If there are no changes, do your best with what you have. Don't whine!
2. Views announcements as a waste of time: "That's why we spend the money to print a bulletin."	2. Reduce the announcements to a bare minimum. Thank him for letting you do the announcements. Use less time than allotted.
3. Will not recognize one area of the support staff because, "Then they will all expect it, and there's not enough time for that. They have to be content with God's recognition."	3. Pray! Do the best you can at the teacher appreciation banquets instead.
### Personal Time	
1. Is really too busy to attend meetings or banquets: "That's why he hired you."	1. Personally invite him as your guest. Support, compliment, tell him how valuable he is to you and the entire staff of teachers. If he does come, make a "big thing" out of his coming (have everyone stand, clap, etc.).
2. Is rarely seen in the children's area, and never talks with any of the volunteers.	2. Invite him to speak as a guest or answer questions, in a children's class periodically. This will have to be scheduled around his service duties. Have the children and teachers write him "thank-you" cards even if he doesn't come to see them.

to the best of our ability. If we are called to serve at a local church, we can't do one without the other.

There, are you OK? I have been a college professor for many years. I tell my students that our job is to please the senior pastor. You should see the reactions in the students! Those who have had good experiences with senior pastors smile and nod agreeably. Those who have had less-than-positive experiences with senior pastors gasp in shock! Let me spend a few moments explaining my theory before I go on to talk about what this means to us in children's ministry.

At the very foundation, we must realize that we, in ministry, are called to work with humans. Humans are difficult and complex creatures. God has had a lot of trouble with humans ever since he made them. He even got so frustrated that he cancelled the whole project and started over with a control group whom he could trust. God's family is not made of perfect people. We are all sinners and basically messed up by the sin tendency inherited through Adam and Eve, and greatly influenced by the world around us. The Church is nothing more than a group of sinners who have been given mercy and forgiveness, and who are

Five Goals for Supporting Your Church Leadership

1. Understand each person's dreams, fears, and motivators.

2. Build a professional relationship with those in leadership based on #1 above.

3. Do all you can to serve in such a way so as to make the jobs of those in leadership easier.

4. Give regular (weekly?) children's ministry updates to those in leadership (either written or verbal).

5. Protect the integrity of your ministry vision while submitting to those in leadership positions.

on the way to restoration. We know the way. We aren't totally there yet. The senior pastor is a human who has a high calling on his life to be a leader of a local church. He is not much different from you or me except for the fact that he carries a very large responsibility of shepherding a group of humans. We are told to respect that calling on his life. There are many Scriptures that clearly tell us to respect him as we would respect the Lord, who gave him his authority and position (Romans 13:1, 2; Colossians 1:16; Titus 3:1, 2; 1 Peter 2:13, 17). (See pages 64, 65.)

THE SURVEY:
TURNING THE SOIL OF OPINIONS

No one knows the condition of the children's ministry better than the precious men and women who work the current system. Become familiar with these people and the ministries they operate. Get a feel for these ministries' successes, failures, goals, etc. Prayerfully ask the Lord to help you be a "fruit inspector." Are these ministries producing the kind of fruit they should? Does the fruit justify the effort? Is there a better way of doing the same thing? Could the ministry be reorganized? Could the workers be re-trained for a greater crop?

As you begin to turn the soil of opinions, remember to ask God to give you wisdom and discernment. Don't base your ministry on opinions or feelings. God can use the counsel of many to give you wisdom (Proverbs 15:22), but always seek him directly for discernment.

You may find that people are more than willing to share their views with you. You may hear things you don't really want to hear. There are two reasons for doing this turning of the soil: to learn and to earn. You will learn much about the people and the ministry, and you will earn their respect as you listen to their opinions. The greatest way to show respect is to ask someone for their opinions. Let the loyal team members talk. As you listen, ask God to help you weed out the opinions and views that don't apply, but keep those with value.

A great way to turn the soil of opinions is to create a survey. I have found that a survey will give you priceless information upon which you can base your projected changes. You can discover the answers to important questions by following the suggestions on this page for designing and conducting a survey of your current ministry team.

Using the Information

The results of the survey should be semi-confidential. You may not want all of the data to be publicized, but some of the data should be made public property within the children's ministry team. Ask the Lord for wisdom as you pour over this freshly-harvested crop of information. You would be wise to have a team of respected friends or co-workers help you total, or sort the answers.

The survey's purpose should be foremost in your mind as you attempt to assimilate the responses. Your goal is to diagnose the needs in the ministry and to assist you in prescribing changes. In discerning the actual needs versus those which may just be good ideas, consider the following criteria:

1. Does this stated need align with both the church's philosophy of children's ministry, and my own?

2. Is this need practical, considering the finances, personnel, and facilities of the children's ministry?

3. Would this need, if satisfied, deepen the children's relationship with Jesus?

4. Would this need, if satisfied, increase the children's ministry's effectiveness in handling, and ministering to, the parents as well?

5. Is there a better way of doing this?

6. Is the timing right?

Once you have whittled your list of needs for possible changes down to a realistic size and filed the others in a "maybe later" file, you are ready to take the next step in this complex process of becoming

Designing a Survey

1. Scope:
  a. Sample a broad cross-section of people, if not all the people.
  b. Take into consideration people's age, character, and ministry differences.

2. Design:
  a. Each question or section must provide you with some valuable information.
  b. Each question's responses should fit into a particular category.
  c. The survey should not be any longer than is absolutely necessary.

Conducting a Survey

1. Pastor's Support:
  a. Give the pastor as much time with the rough copy of the survey as he needs in order to feel confident with it.
  b. Remember that he has the ultimate authority over the children's ministry, not you.
  c. He should be as excited about the outcome as you are as a result of your time devoted to getting him involved in the survey.

2. Prepare the People:
  a. Let the people know ahead of time that a survey is coming so they won't be surprised when they are handed this ominous set of papers with all these serious questions.
  b. Make sure they know how the information will benefit the children's ministry.

3. Set a Time and Place for This Survey:
  a. It is not good to give a survey as a take-home. Doing it all together, at the same time, would mean that they would all turn the surveys in together, instead of having them trickle in through the mail or under your door.
  b. Conduct the survey during a regular team meeting. Make sure there is food and fun at the same time.

Children's Ministry Survey

In order to better serve you and to strengthen our overall ministry to children, we have designed this survey. Please take a few moments and prayerfully respond to the following inquiries. Your responses will be kept in confidence. The results of this survey will be used to assist us in developing curriculum, organizing facilities, training teachers, and setting goals.

Take as much time as you need to adequately respond to each question. If you need more room, feel free to write on the back. You may also write any additional comments or suggestions on the back. We will read each comment, but do not expect all of your suggestions to be utilized. Pray for us as we seek the Lord's guidance.

THE CHILDREN'S TEAM MEMBER

1. What is the area of your service? Please check the appropriate spaces below:
   - ❏ Sunday morning aide
   - ❏ Sunday morning teacher
   - ❏ Sunday evening teacher
   - ❏ Sunday evening aide
   - ❏ Mid-week teacher
   - ❏ Mid-week aide
   - ❏ Other: _____

2. Are you satisfied serving the Lord in your capacity? Why or why not?

3. What, in your opinion, could be done to make your ministry more satisfying?

Training

4. Do you feel you received adequate training? If not, what did your training lack?

5. What suggestions would you give to improve the training process?

Curriculum

6. Are you comfortable with the curriculum you are currently using? Why or why not?

7. What, in your opinion, should a "good" curriculum include?

8. Do you use all of the curricular components every week? Describe your usual methods of deciding what to use, when.

9. Do you feel "locked in" by the curriculum? Should there be any steps taken to enhance your creativity?

Supplies

10. Are you satisfied with the craft supplies available to you? What, if any, additional supplies would you like to see provided?

11. Is the current method of distributing the supplies effective or in need of improvement?

Facilities (Your room #_____)

12. Is your room size adequate for the number of children you teach?

13. Are the cabinets adequate for the supplies, curriculum, and miscellaneous storage space needed? What additions would you suggest?

14. Are you satisfied with the chairs and tables in your room? Are they the right size? Do they need repair or replacing? Do you have enough of them?

15. Is the room's location easily found and conducive to efficient traffic flow?

16. Is the temperature in your room adequate? If not, why not?

17. Is the lighting in your room adequate?

18. Are you pleased with the condition of the flooring in your room? Would you like to see improvements made? If so, what?

19. Are the restroom facilities adequate? What improvements would you suggest?

Miscellaneous

20. Are you happy with the time schedule for your service or area of ministry? Would it be better to do it differently? Please give suggestions.

21. What could be done to increase the effectiveness of your ministry?

22. Do you get the kind of support you desire from the children's parents? Why or why not?

23. Apart from this survey, do you feel that the communication between you and the leadership of the children's ministry is good? What would you do to improve it?

24. What can be done to encourage the people in the church to become involved in the children's ministry?

COMMENTS OR SUGGESTIONS:

Thank you for your time in responding to these questions. The responses will all be treated with much care and attention. Remember, if you feel an area hasn't been dealt with, please use the back of these pages to share your thoughts with us. Pray for us as we now ask the Lord to give us wisdom in assimilating all this information.

the kind of ministry that attracts children and introduces them to the Lord. Actually, getting this far was the easiest part! The next few miles of pathway are known for their pits and thistles. Remember that the Lord must direct your path; don't do anything without him going first.

Once you have collected your information, you can begin to set goals to implement improvements in your existing team members. This chapter deals with the existing soil conditions of your church. We will look at recruiting, training, and developing relationships with new team members in chapters 13-15.

SETTING GOALS FOR THE EXISTING TEAM

Your existing team members are, perhaps, your most loyal, consistent servants in your church! Treat them with respect. Tell them and show them your appreciation! Here are some ideas for making your appreciation of your existing team members obvious.

Ten Ways to Appreciate Existing Team Members

1. Hold an awards banquet for the children's ministry team members. Everyone should be recognized and presented with an award (certificate, trophy, etc.) for their specific service.

2. Invite small groups (10 or less) out for pie (you buy). Being invited, by you, to a local restaurant just for pie can be a thrill for many people. While eating, thank and encourage them. This gesture will effect greater fruit than you can imagine!

3. Personal notes sent in the mail. These are notes of thanks and appreciation for their commitment and service. The more specific the praise, the greater the impact.

4. Ministry "after-glows." After the service is over, while they are cleaning up the room, spend some time with team members talking about the encounters of the past hour. Verbally thank them and support their work.

5. Invite small groups (10 or less) to your house for dinner. During the evening, listen to ministry stories and thank them for their service.

Twenty Goals for Supporting Existing Team Members

1. Become acquainted with every person's position and related responsibilities.

2. Pray for each team member's needs, fears, dreams, and potential.

3. Provide training in the areas needed.

4. Provide curriculum.

5. Provide the necessary supplies.

6. Create or clarify the leadership positions within the team.

7. Build or refurbish clear communication lines between supervisors and team members.

8. Create, or increase the children's ministry budget.

9. Plan regular fellowship gatherings.

10. Create regular team meetings (large/small group).

11. Change the focus of the team from "me" to "we."

12. Cast the new or revised vision to every team member (individually, small group, or large group).

13. Hold regular appreciation banquets.

14. Guarantee that every team member at every service is personally touched and encouraged.

15. Invite small groups (less than ten) of team members to your home for dessert or dinner.

16. Write personal letter or emails to team members whose service is above and beyond.

17. Pay for and send team members with leadership potential to ministry conferences.

18. Utilize leaders (or potential leaders) from within the team in training. (Especially after #17.)

19. Begin new ministries or programs to kick start vision and passion.

20. Utilize the senior pastor in as many of the above goals as possible.

HOW TO MAKE A PRESENTATION TO THE CHURCH BOARD

Since we've talked about setting some significant goals, we now need to discuss how to present those goals and related changes or improvements to those

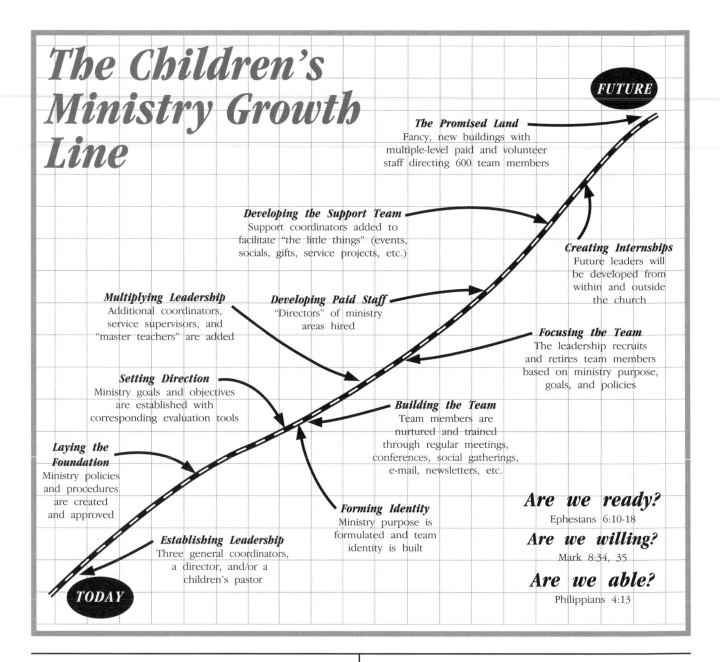

The Children's Ministry Growth Line

FUTURE

The Promised Land
Fancy, new buildings with multiple-level paid and volunteer staff directing 600 team members

Developing the Support Team
Support coordinators added to facilitate "the little things" (events, socials, gifts, service projects, etc.)

Creating Internships
Future leaders will be developed from within and outside the church

Multiplying Leadership
Additional coordinators, service supervisors, and "master teachers" are added

Developing Paid Staff
"Directors" of ministry areas hired

Focusing the Team
The leadership recruits and retires team members based on ministry purpose, goals, and policies

Setting Direction
Ministry goals and objectives are established with corresponding evaluation tools

Building the Team
Team members are nurtured and trained through regular meetings, conferences, social gatherings, e-mail, newsletters, etc.

Laying the Foundation
Ministry policies and procedures are created and approved

Forming Identity
Ministry purpose is formulated and team identity is built

Establishing Leadership
Three general coordinators, a director, and/or a children's pastor

TODAY

Are we ready?
Ephesians 6:10-18

Are we willing?
Mark 8:34, 35

Are we able?
Philippians 4:13

---

who oversee the church: the church board. There are different views on the role and position of the church board. Some churches place the church board over the senior pastor; some church boards are under the senior pastor; and still others are placed as advisory boards only. There are also some churches who do not believe in church boards, and who function without any formal advisory groups. In your turning the soil, did you discover how your church views the role of the church board? Did you discover what the relationship is between the children's ministry and the church board?

If your church does not have a church board, or if the church board has no authority over the direction of individual ministries, this next section will only be mildly interesting to you. I do believe, though, that there are some principles of working with powerful people that are hidden within this next section. These principles can apply to your work with the senior pastor or other administrative supervisors even if you don't have a formal church board

As the director, or pastor, of the children's ministry, you are charged with the responsibility of overseeing every function of the ministry. You are only a shepherd. You are not the Provider! Before we jump into how to make a board presentation, I need to remind you that you are simply a voice and tool of the Lord. You also need to remember that the board is also only a tool of the Lord. Ultimately, it is the Lord's favor, leading, and blessing that you should seek, not the board's. We have been told to honor and respect the authorities over us, so you make this presentation out of honor for the Lord and in response to his command to honor those in authority over you. Regardless of the answer of the board, you must seek God's answer and leading. If the board denies your proposal, God must have another plan for you. Pray before, during, and after the presentation! Trust him, and move forward with what you know!

Now, with that as a foundation, let me encourage you to become a positive, strong, thrilling advocate for what you are about to present to the board! A board presentation demands convincing enthusiasm for the vision the Lord has given you! You need to call down fire from Heaven, read all the manuals on influential speech, spare no expense in producing a full-color brochure, an inspiring video, or a polished power point presentation, all the while remaining humble and respectful. Basically, this is a job for Super Communicator!

The greatest garden tool you could polish and oil before your presentation is your confidence. There are many ways to prepare this priceless quality within you. Most of the tricks you will stumble across will have little success uncovering this personality jewel that seems to be buried under the soot of past failures. The greatest source of true confidence can only be found at the foot of the cross! That is the headwaters of all that is good and worthy of praise. Your confidence cannot originate solely from your own efforts or glossy portfolio entries.

The apostle Paul is a man who had his priorities straight. In *Philippians 3:1-8*, Paul teaches us that compared to his relationship with Jesus, and what that can give him, all of his past accomplishments are worthless. That is the principal upon which Paul based his later years. He knew where he gained his strength, and who gave him his breath, but that doesn't mean that Paul forgot what he had learned! Didn't he use his gifts and abilities he had learned as a Pharisee to influence the Pharisees? Didn't he use his background as a Hebrew zealot to exhort the legalistic Jews of his day? There is a balance in Paul's life that you and I must long for in our own. He set Jesus, and all his knowledge and wisdom, as the foundation, and then he let his past experiences build upon that base as a brick wall. Together, this sure foundation produced a man who would not be tossed about by every wind of doctrine. He had a confidence designed in Heaven and respected on Earth!

If you know Jesus loves you and that you have been placed in this ministry for a purpose, you will have the basis for a confidence that is unbreakable. You must do everything within your power to make your presentations appealing and successful, but don't ever leave Jesus in your dust. He never takes a back seat to our goals or plans! He tends to "get out and walk" instead. Take some of the following steps prior to and during your presentations so that you can be prepared and confident.

Preparing the Presentation

1. Attend board meetings prior to making your presentation. (You must be invited to attend before attending!) The process and protocol of the meeting is something you must be aware of. You should visit at least two meetings before you present your ideas. Ask the Lord to help you see and hear everything you need to help you be an acceptable part of the process.

2. Gather the data to support your presentation. This can be done through the use of a survey, interviews, photographs, past history, attendance statistics, or simply your vision for the ministry.

3. Acquaint the pastor, or associate pastor, with the need that your presentation's idea will address. Remember that the pastor may only know what you tell him. Make sure he has the same data that you have upon which he can base his understanding of your idea's value. Invite him to come and see the situation for himself, if you feel that's important.

4. Investigate other churches' handling of the

problem. If you can visit other churches who have done what you are proposing, this information tends to lend a certain credibility to your ideas. Even if there have been mistakes made by those churches, show how you can learn from their mistakes and do it more successfully.

No board likes to take chances. The reason the board members are on the board is to protect the church from needless mistakes and haphazard decisions. By showing them that other churches have found success by applying similar steps your presentation brings no threat to the safety they all desire.

5. Prepare a printed presentation of your proposal. The basic introduction should be in the form of a notebook for each member of the board. The notebook can supplement any other media (video, PowerPoint presentation, etc., but it should be the flagship of your presentation. The notebook, and other parts of the presentation, should be artistically near-perfect! You should use multiple colors, expensive paper, and professional-looking graphics (no clip art!). Your printed presentation should include:

   a. An attractive cover page
   b. A summary of the data gathered (survey results, figures, etc.)
   c. A projected budget, or financial impact of this proposal
   d. Impact on the facilities (rooms used, hours, changes, etc.)
   e. Impact on personnel (recruitment, training, flow-chart, etc.)
   f. Impact on other ministries within the church
   g. An implementation calendar (beginning, evaluations, end, etc.)

Be sure to give these printed components of your presentation to the pastor in advance of the board meeting. Never surprise the pastor with new material at a board meeting. He should see the rough drafts prior to the meeting so that he has the freedom to request changes.

Making the Presentation

1. Pray for wisdom and a fine blend of humble confidence. Don't walk into the board meeting feeling so secure in your preparation that you slam the door on the One who helped you get prepared! You are his associate, he is not yours!

2. Dress professionally. Even if you are the only one who does so, you should dress up for the meeting. Ladies should wear a conservative, yet attractive dress; men should wear a suit and tie.

3. Be on time. Arriving late to the board meeting is the worst thing you could do short of arriving in your pajamas! Being on time, or even ten minutes early, shows respect and your ability to handle responsibilities in a professional manner.

4. Be friendly! Even though you may be terrified out of your socks, don't let that fear drive you to that safe chair in the back of the room. You need to greet as many people as you can, introducing yourself if necessary, letting them know how glad you are to be there. Don't be too friendly; you'll make them instantly uncomfortable with you. Ask the Lord for a balance. His confidence will help!

5. Have your printed materials prepared. Have your papers or folders ready for speedy hand-out when it is your time to speak. All pages must be typed and free of errors.

6. Be friendly and professional in your speech. Greet the audience with an affirmation of how pleased and honored you are to be at the meeting. Place yourself "at their feet" by respectfully recognizing their authority in the church. Never tell a joke or kid around at the meeting; this is unprofessional and immature.

7. Briefly review the parts of the notebook. Establish the need for your proposal or idea. Give them a brief overview of the data upon which you based your evaluation of the need. They must feel the same feelings you do regarding this issue! Don't be afraid to loiter at this stage until you are convinced the majority of the board members understand the need.

8. Compliment and support questions and opposing viewpoints. When a board member asks you a challenging question that seems to be loaded with potential explosiveness and opinions, how you respond to that question is often more critical than what you say. Always thank the person for the question and his thoughtful involvement in the issue. Don't do this by way of the same words used each time; this can become an insulting practice. Solomon learned that "A gentle answer turns away wrath, but a harsh word stirs up anger" *(Proverbs 15:1)*. Some of the ways you can respond are:

    a. "Thank you for asking that."

    b. "That's a good question."

    c. "I appreciate your concern for this issue."

    d. "I hope I can respond adequately to such a challenging question."

    e. "You obviously care a great deal about this (church, issue, etc.), thank you."

    f. "You're correct in your concern about...."

    g. "I'll do my best to respond to your question; feel free to ask a follow-up question."

9. Stay within the time limit. Before you begin, find out how long the chairman wishes you to spend on your presentation. Keep an eye on your watch or clock! To go over without the expressed permission of the chairman is disrespectful. Pace yourself based on how much time you think each section of your talk should take. If you see yourself getting behind, mention that fact, then move on. During your last question/answer time, note the fact that your time is out, but leave the chairman with the option of granting you more time. This is the only justified reason for going over your allotted time period. There are two catchy sayings that will help you stay on track with the time: "Keep it simple, servant!" (KISS), and "Stand up, speak up, and shut up."

10. Accept their decision, if one is rendered instantly, and respectfully submit to it. If the board decides to accept your proposal, rejoice. If they reject it, or suggest some re-working, respectfully submit and agree to do your best in preparation for the next meeting. Remember that you have prayed for the Lord to have his way with you, the church, and the children. That means that you have to respect the authority of those in charge. If God wanted your proposal to be passed the way it was, don't you think he could have done so? Go back to the beginning, ask the Lord for wisdom, and make some changes.

To better assist you in understanding and serving those on your church board, I have put together a sample listing of some typical church board members on page 74. This is an unusual section. I almost feel like you should tuck it under your pillow or some other hiding place. It isn't that there is anything wrong with its subject, but unless someone reads it with the right attitude, there could be a grand misunderstanding of its purpose. At the very beginning I want to say that the purpose for this section is to do all I can to improve communication between you, the children's minister, and the leadership of the church. Getting to know the people with whom you are going to be working is vital to your success.

Keep in mind that these are fictitious, general characteristics. The names have been changed to protect the innocent. You may never come across some of these personality types, but I guarantee that you will meet many of them. You may already know some of them.

A person's character is fashioned much like the sandstone sculptures found in many of our country's deserts. It takes years of rubbing shoulders with the good and bad forces of life to carve out those subtle or obvious qualities that people come to know as that person. Some of those qualities are products of the environment, and some are gifts from the Creator. Good or bad, created or developed, you can't change them. If there are changes that need to be made, the Holy Spirit is the one to do it, not you. Your only job is to love each person and be the kind of Christ-like example that would make those around you thirst for that same lifestyle and attitude.

The purpose in knowing the types of people you may share the board room with is to give you some insight into their fears, desires, and dreams for the church. If you can become sensitive to their feelings,

Board Members I Have Known

Here are some of the types of people you may find serving on a local church board:

"This-is-the-greatest-church!" Charley

This person is totally excited about the church and its potential. He will usually support anything that is "good for the church." The church can do no wrong in his eyes.

"I-like-this-church-the-way-it-is!" Sam

This person doesn't like change. He feels that things are running well the way they are, and if they aren't he hasn't noticed! You must spend an extreme amount of time and effort justifying the need for the change, and guarantee him that the change will work. Ask him for his opinions, involve him in the process as much as possible. He must experience the excitement you feel.

"What-about-our-adults?" Allen

This person has trouble seeing the need for as much effort and money that you are proposing for the children. He would much rather see that same effort put forth in the name of adults. He is possessive of the adult Bible school classes, and their associated ministries. You should do all you can to show this person all the benefits the adults will derive from the changes you propose. The adults' involvement in the children's ministry is healthy!

"I-like-him/her" Harold

This person likes you because you're young and "fresh out of college." he will support you and be your friend simply on those qualities. This person may be the board contact you've been praying for!

"Nobody-ever-listens-to-me!" Mel

This person has a chip on his shoulder that comes from the Ark! His self-concept has been trampled over the years until now it is downright negative. He desperately wants to be significant. He wants his ideas to be listened to and even used to benefit someone else. He generally has a good heart. The best thing to do with Mel is to listen to him! Ask for more of his ideas, go out to lunch with him, etc. Don't ever promise to use all his ideas, but show him respect by listening. You may find a solid supporter in this person after a while.

"How-much-will-it-cost?" Carl

This person is very concerned about the Lord's money. He has taken the challenge of being the "watcher of the bucks" upon himself. He feels that no one else is as concerned about this area as he is. Give this person plenty of support. Ask him for counsel (whether you use it or not). Make sure you have your figures together before he has a chance to see them. Don't ever give him a reason to doubt your stewardship. Remember this somewhat fleshly equation: Happy children = regularly-attending adults = larger offerings.

"I've-been-here-for-20-years!" Eugene

This "historian" of the church has seen many programs come and go. He has become cautious over the years. He is not necessarily resistant to change; he just isn't excited about getting excited anymore. Use his knowledge. Ask him for counsel. Use him as a contact to the older folks in the church.

"The-children-deserve-the-best!" Bill

This person will sell his boat for the children's ministry. He's all for the children, and he will be your vocal support in the meetings.

"I-don't-like-anything!" Andrew

There's not much you can do with Andrew. Respond to him with gentle answers. Pray for patience, and plenty of room between the two of you. This is perhaps the hardest person you will come across. He seems to put down everything. Find out what his hobbies are and become interested in them as well! If you can become his friend, you may see some improvement. The Lord will use this person to sharpen your character.

"Let's-have-another-meeting" Mike

No matter what you have decided, Mike will want to have another meeting before a decision is made. A good review of the progress that has been made in the present meeting will slow him down. Make sure you highlight the fact that your goals have been met and that you are ready to make a decision. You may have to emphasize the time factor with him. If he has legitimate questions, answer them.

"Let's-find-out-what-the-Lord-says" Scott

Scott will be a great person to have around. In the midst of the debates, discussions, or arguments he will speak out with "I think we need to pray about this." He will be a good source of counsel and wisdom.

Garden Pest:
Team-eating Slugs

Evidence

You may begin to see holes in your ministry plants. These holes could be in the form of negative attitudes or a loss of team members.

Sources of Infestation

Grumpy people who want "the good old days" and who are unwilling to accept the new vision.

Treatment

Team-eating slugs cannot be ignored! They won't go away on their own. They reproduce rapidly and their offspring inherit all their destructive abilities. You must be aware of their presence and deal with them swiftly, directly, and with focused attention. If you hear of someone complaining or spreading negative comments, you must go directly to that person and report what you've heard. After listening to the person's side of the story, challenge the person with the value of team unity. Restate the ministry vision or goals related to the negative complaints, and ask him or her to consider his or her continued position on the team. If the person is unable to be a positive, vision-focused team member, he or she will be asked to consider serving in some other area of the church.

If the person chooses to remain on the team, do all you can to support his or her positive behavior and commitment. If he or she reverts back to being a slug, restate your challenge and warning.

---

you can work together with them in the Body of Christ toward the same goal. If you can't understand them, you will have to part company and work separately. I think we can all agree on the only choice that would please our Lord.

HOW TO HANDLE THE "REAL WORLD" OF CHURCH WORK

One of the most frustrating things about my very first ministry position was that I soon felt very unprepared for the frustrations of the job. I wasn't trained in conflict management or in compromise. I thought everyone would like me and come running to my little ministry party. Ha!

Since my first "boy, I'll never do it that way again"

ministry, I have been determined to better prepare those who are entering the ministry for the first time. So I pass this on to you in case you have never considered this process before. There isn't anything holy about this process, but it has helped me from overreacting. I have to tell myself that the ministry is about people, and people are about feelings and opinions, and opinions are about disagreements. I have learned that God is less interested in the actual frustration as he is in my reactions to it.

Establish Your Vision

- Prayerful development of your hopes and dreams for your ministry. Dream big! Pray faithfully!
- Visualize the unfathomable joy of positively

influencing moldable lives for God! Hang onto that vision! Prayerfully brand it into your spirit.

Make Plans
- With the leading of the Holy Spirit, "toy with" some plans by which you can see your vision come to life. (Leave room for God's way of doing things.)
- Consider some "what-if" variations of your plans.
- REMEMBER YOUR VISION!

Expect Frustrations
- Plan for the worst, then be pleasantly surprised.
- Seek the Lord's wisdom regarding flexibility, patience, sensitivity to others' needs.
- Be prepared to put off the accomplishment of you goals while you do some "investing in the future."
- REMEMBER YOUR VISION! Remember that your vision involves people, not programs.

React Carefully
- Ask God for insight into the people who frustrate you. There is usually a good reason for a person being the way they are, and God can show you how to be sensitive to that reason.
- Ask God for insight into the "system" that frustrates you. It has been years in the making; you cannot change it without first proving that you can be a productive part of it. Earn the right to suggest changes. TIME!
- REMEMBER YOUR VISION! Your vision is for relationships with people. You can have your vision in any environment! Find joy and hope even in the face of frustration!

Adjust Your Plan
- Prayerfully consider your plan to accomplish your vision. Based on the "hurdle" you just encountered, do you need to make any changes?
- You may need to become better educated in some aspect of your work. Be teachable! Seek wisdom from other ministers.
- REMEMBER YOUR VISION!

Adjust Yourself
- Prayerfully consider your role in this "hurdle." Is there something about you that caused this frustration to occur? (Psalm139)
- Seek "the counsel of many" regarding the possible log in your eye.
- REMEMBER YOUR VISION!

Staff Relations
If you have ever visited different churches, or children's ministries, you know there is something that you can almost taste about those ministries that are successful and growing. You can see it in the eyes and smiles of all who serve in the ministry! If you haven't visited other churches, you really need to. You'll see what I mean.

What we can sense, as outsiders looking in, is the healthy, fulfilling relationship amongst the ministry staff. This is true for the entire church ministry staff, or simply the children's ministry staff. When people are happy with each other, they can't help but show it! When the staff works together toward a common goal, the goal is reached and the Gospel is advanced!

On page 77 I have tried to graphically portray the sensitive relationship between the various staff members, and the importance of each member. There is nothing more destructive than a staff that is only concerned for their own areas. Each member of the ministry staff needs the other members! If the children's ministry staff thinks that they are the only ones who truly minister to the children, that perspective will soon cause serious problems in the health of the entire church staff.

As you build your ministry staff, or as you exist as part of the church staff, ask the Lord to help you serve as a strong wall to hold up the roof. Build your staff on a common foundation. Talk about that common foundation often! When you plan events or programs, invite the other "walls" to help. Look for ways to support other staff members' programs and

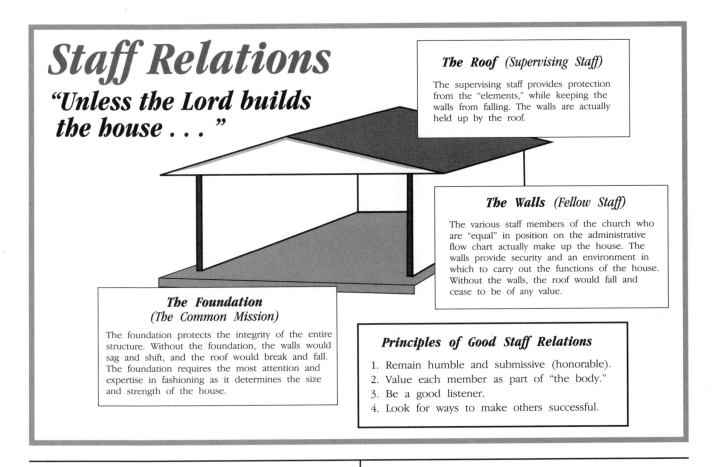

Staff Relations

"Unless the Lord builds the house . . . "

The Roof (Supervising Staff)

The supervising staff provides protection from the "elements," while keeping the walls from falling. The walls are actually held up by the roof.

The Walls (Fellow Staff)

The various staff members of the church who are "equal" in position on the administrative flow chart actually make up the house. The walls provide security and an environment in which to carry out the functions of the house. Without the walls, the roof would fall and cease to be of any value.

The Foundation
(The Common Mission)

The foundation protects the integrity of the entire structure. Without the foundation, the walls would sag and shift, and the roof would break and fall. The foundation requires the most attention and expertise in fashioning as it determines the size and strength of the house.

Principles of Good Staff Relations

1. Remain humble and submissive (honorable).
2. Value each member as part of "the body."
3. Be a good listener.
4. Look for ways to make others successful.

---

successes! Use plenty of strong nails and glue as you build a ministry staff that will protect the children of your ministry for years to come!

How to Understand People

Since we have a common Creator, we have many common behaviors and reactions to life! If you are quick to hear and slow to speak, you will be able to see some similarities in the people with whom you work. Don't dream, or even pray, that all the difficult people would go away; they won't! I believe that God lets difficult people stay around us to keep us growing, learning, and on our knees before him. Instead of wishing some of these people an early retirement, learn to understand them and work with their uniqueness! Notice the universal remedy at the bottom of page 78.

God taught me a huge lesson in people perspective one cold Sunday evening. I had endured a long Sunday morning, and I arrived back at the church with a car-full of bad attitude! I'm not sure what came first, the bad attitude, or the bad evening, but the moment my throbbing feet arrived in the children's area there was trouble. I had several team members decide that they had "something better to do" that night; oh and by the way, they forgot to get replacements for themselves, or notify me that they weren't coming! I was faced with a cold night and a colder reality: I was going to have to deal with a couple of rooms full of unsupervised children, all alone! As the exodus of parents and children continued to flow into our facilities, I quickly shuffled team members around and begged them to fill in briefly as I tried to get some help. I went outside and begged God for mercy. I didn't see anyone glowing with the presence of the Lord right away, so I began my trek to the "promised land": the worship service. I told God I would walk around inside the building and see if I could find anyone who might be willing to volunteer. So I and my stinky attitude began searching. The service began, and I had to stop my search. I felt like those fishermen who came in from a whole night of fishing with no fish! I walked out of the building with a dangerous mixture of frustration, fear, and hopelessness. Yes, my eyes were definitely on me! I began walking up to the children's ministry area ready to do whatever I had to do to take care of the children.

How to Understand People
And How to Help Them Understand You

Premise: There is a reason or explanation for every person's attitude or action. To understand the reason is to understand the person.

STEP 1 - IDENTIFY THE SYMPTOM

After observing the attitude, action, or behavior, identify the general category into which it could fit. The major categories are:

Defensiveness: Characterized by swift, rash reactions; forceful opinions even when they are obviously wrong; seeming to always be ready for a fight; few friends.

Offensiveness: Characterized by a pushy, powerful character; must get his or her way; hungry for power; few friends.

Anger: Characterized by a "chip" on the shoulder; hot temper; high emotions, or low depression; quiet personality most of the time especially prior to an angry outburst; little things set him or her off; few, if any, friends.

Introvert: Characterized by a withdrawn nature; infrequent eye contact; hesitance to share feelings or opinions; few friends.

Jealousy: Characterized by inability to support others' successes; fits of anger; putting others down; comparing him or herself with others; talking about his or her own accomplishments.

STEP 2 - UNDERSTAND THE BACKGROUND

Once you have identified and categorized the behavior or attitude, you can now try to understand the reason behind it. You may never truly know the reason unless you get close enough to know the person. Let the behavior "go by you" as you become an understanding friend. Here are some possible backgrounds:

Defensiveness: This person feels threatened because he or she has the impression that others don't pay attention to him or her. Possible family/childhood roots; he or she may have never gotten enough attention or love. Possible poor self-concept.

Offensiveness: Same as above with the addition of the desire to control as a result of his or her lack of nurture.

Anger: This person may have the impression that everyone is out to get him or her. Possible family/childhood roots; may have been abused or mistreated by a domineering parent. Possible poor self-concept.

Introvert: This person may be living under the impression that he or she "is no good." His ideas and feelings are of no value or incorrect. Possible family/childhood roots. Definite poor self-concept.

Jealousy: Same as above.

UNIVERSAL REMEDY FOR ALL ABOVE SYMPTOMS

Love, as expressed by an interest in opinions, friendliness, compassion for past, compliments on ideas, and support of successes.

Existing Ministry Team Evaluation

CONDITION	EVALUATION
	Yes! Unsure No
1. I have personally visited/observed each team member in action.	❏ ❏ ❏
2. I understand the functions and responsibilities for every position.	❏ ❏ ❏
3. I have personally encouraged those who go beyond in their service.	❏ ❏ ❏
4. Most (75%) of those currently on our team serve the Lord with gladness.	❏ ❏ ❏
5. I have personally encouraged those who aren't serving with gladness.	❏ ❏ ❏
6. Those who currently serve have the curriculum they need to teach.	❏ ❏ ❏
7. Those who currently serve have the supplies they need to teach.	❏ ❏ ❏
8. We have monthly opportunities for team fellowship, appreciation, and/or training.	❏ ❏ ❏
9. Team members with leadership potential have been personally approached.	❏ ❏ ❏
10. Most (75%) of those currently on our team can summarize our ministry vision.	❏ ❏ ❏

I need to take a break from this story to give you some background information. There was a lady who became a "special friend" to me over the course of several months. Have you ever had an obnoxious person who always wanted to talk with you? This was that special friend. She wasn't a regular team member, but she volunteered from time to time. Whenever I would see her, I have to admit, I would make some selfish effort to avoid her because she always had some pointless story to tell me that would take much too much of my time. She was my "little blessing from God." There, now, I'll continue with my Sunday night story.

As I walked up the hill to the children's ministry, I felt very alone. I was sure that God had left me "out in the desert to die." I was well into my own, private pity-party when I heard this voice that sent a chill up my spine. "Oh, Steve...." It was her. "Steeeeve...." I pretended to not hear her. This wasn't the time! I couldn't take her tonight! "Steve, Steve!" There was no use; she saw me. I stopped and turned to greet her with the best fake smile I could muster. "Hi," I said, "Did you need something?" Then, God did it. He pushed the "conviction knife" into my hard heart and slowly twisted it. This lady, who had been a "problem" to me for so long, now became an angel from Heaven with her next words. "Steve, I was just sitting down in the church, and, well, I was praying and singing, and then God told me to come up here because you needed me tonight."

Standing outside, with the cold wind swirling around us, God the Father was holding class. I was his only student, and the lady was his master teacher. How many times had he tried to teach me to look at the heart, and I wouldn't learn? How many times had I taught others to see beyond the outer appearance of people and look for the presence of the Lord inside? That night, I finally got it.

God sees what makes people the way they are. He sees what makes us the way we are. Pray for God's eyes as you look past the obnoxious exteriors and into the heart of his "angels in disguise." God bless you as you learn to love the unlovely.

## chapter 6

Gathering Your Tools:
Financial Goals

"*Whether garden maintenance is pleasant exercise or just hard work depends, in part, on having the right tools to accomplish the tasks at hand. This doesn't mean that you have to buy a multitude of tools for your outdoor work; it suggests that you should own precisely the tools needed to accomplish the routine work in your garden*" (*Sunset New Western Garden Book, Menlo Park, CA: Lane Publishing Co., 1979; page 89*).

It would be wonderful if we didn't have to deal with money, but there seems to be no way around it. Just when you think you have your financial life in control, some bus load of surprises parks in your driveway! The best way to survive financially is to learn from the past and try to plan for these drop-in visitors.

Budgeting is not fun. It is a challenge, and it can be rewarding to see it all work out, but it's not fun! The scariest part of the budgeting process is that you must try to predict the future. That's impossible. Sometimes it is like trying to guess how much food you will need to feed the elephant that may come and stay with you in the spring. But there are some tools you can use to clear away the fog from your view into next year.

THE BUDGET: YOUR VISION IN DOLLARS!

The budget is your ministry vision expressed in dollars! A person should be able to look at your children's ministry budget and see your vision. If you are spending a huge amount on curriculum, and nothing on training, that says much about the values placed on team development. What do you believe to be your ministry's core values? What has God called you to accomplish at this church? How are you going to accomplish it? What do you

need in order to accomplish the vision the Lord has given you? These are the critical questions that will lead to the creation of your ministry budget.

Seven Steps to Creating a Budget

Without restating what was covered in chapters 1-3, here are some thoughts to get your "budget wheels" moving in the areas of vision and core values. Think about what your ministry vision requires financially (advertising, recruiting, training, guests, curriculum, supplies, service projects, outreach, trips, brochures/handbooks, etc.). What are your ministry's core values, and what do they require financially? (Bible teaching that is real and applicable, parent support, inspiration of children, meeting children's needs in the church and community, getting children involved in service at an young age, recycling leadership through discipleship of children, etc.) Can you accomplish your ministry vision goals without money? Sometimes it is good to consider how you might accomplish your goals without money. This forces you to rely on God, and not your budget! If you have money, that is an added blessing!

Step #1: Consider the Needs

Think of all the needs that were identified in the previous chapter's survey. Add the needs of the children in your community, and their parents, to the needs mentioned in your survey. You might review your discoveries in chapter 2. Don't limit yourself at this point. For right now, pretend you have all the money you need. We will whittle these dreams down closer to reality later. Here are some thoughts to help you identify the needs in your community and in your church:

1. What do the children in your community need? (Clothes, food, stability, security, safe places to play, healthy peer groups, positive role models, help with school, spiritual challenges, wholesome activities, etc.)

2. What do the parents of your community need? (Help in raising their children spiritually/sexually/emotionally, networks for support from other parents, ideas for family fun, etc.)

3. What do those who serve in your children's ministry need? (Curriculum, supplies, training, social interactions, facilities, team identity, etc.)

4. What do all these needs mean financially? (Printing, advertising, books, bus rentals, gifts, supplies, team wear, equipment, personnel, postage, meals, audio/visual equipment, etc.)

Step #2: Identify Your Categories

The needs you have, and the related expenditures' categories will become the budget's account categories unless you already have church-wide accounts that you must work within. Check with your pastor or the church accountant for this information. The categories should include:

- Audio Visual
- Capital Expenses
- Craft Supplies
- Curriculum
- Equipment
- Food
- Furniture/Fixtures
- Maintenance
- Nursery Supplies
- Office Supplies
- Postage
- Printing
- Publicity
- Special Events
- Teacher Training/ Staff Development
- Miscellaneous

Step #3: Survey Past Budgets

Next to the time devoted to the survey and its results, this phase should use the greatest amount of your midnight oil. If you have an already-established budget with a respectable expense record for the previous years, your job is half done. If you don't have a reliable record from which to draw, you will have to gather up your detective equipment and go to work.

A good place to find records of past expenditures of the children's ministry is, of course, the church's financial records. These may, or may not, be open files to you. If they are not available to you, compile a list of categories (such as the one above) that you would like to have data on and ask someone who can access those files to supply you with that informa-

Budget Areas
that should NOT be under-budgeted

1. Team development will be just like a tree in your front yard: The more you fertilize it, the bigger it will grow! If you only allocate $100 to your entire ministry team's development, you will probably only get $100 worth of growth!

2. Curriculum is an area that should be fairly easy to predict. If you choose the curriculum you want, the components you will order, and the number of children you will order for you should be able to put your finger on the correct price.

3. Operational Supplies (craft supplies, nursery supplies, snacks, etc.) is another area that shouldn't be under-budgeted. Without the proper supplies, the ministry will struggle.

tion. Make sure you have the pastor's backing before you approach anyone for these records.

When looking at past figures, consider the size of the children's ministry at that time, the number of classes, and any extra programs that were in operation (V.B.S., etc.). Also, try to discover the scope of the expenditures. Did every teacher use curriculum? Were all of the rooms used? Did every teacher get craft supplies?

Step #4: Project Growth Cycles

Have there been any consistent attendance records kept for the past 3 years? If so, these will tell you, if you do some simple graphing of the figures, what the growth cycles have been. Have you grown more, or less, in the summer? Does attendance drop in the fall? Has the overall children's ministry population consistently increased in a way that you can predict for next year?

Remember, that a growing church in a growing community is the most challenging environment in which to project next year's budget. If your church has "big plans" for growth, you have to have bigger plans reflected in the children's ministry budget! Keep in mind that for every new parent or married couple added to your church, your children's ministry may grow by two or three children! In a growing church, you must plan big!

Now, go back to your list of budget categories and put a check by the ones that are affected by attendance figures. The categories from the list above that are affected are: Craft Supplies, Curriculum, Maintenance, Nursery Supplies, Teacher Training, Postage, Furniture/Fixtures, Printing, Food, and Miscellaneous.

Step #5: Set Your Figures

Remember that the first time a new budget is attempted, it is simply that: an attempt. If you have done your homework in the steps prior to this point, your figures will be justifiable, and relatively close to reality. You should involve others (senior pastor, elder, other children's pastors, etc.) in this process as you scratch out some figures for the first time. This will give you an umbrella of protection of sorts as you discuss the figures with the pastor.

One big question will go whirring through your mind, blowing your notes and data off of their neat little stacks: "Should I add a bit more to each figure for safety?" The point is a valid one, and should be considered, but the opposing side needs equal time. If you pad too much, you may end up not needing it and then the following year's figures will be affected by that slush. Any increase in the budget must be justifiable, either by way of a percentage increase in growth, or an increase in the scope of the ministry. For the first year, I would suggest aiming a bit low, establishing the need for the figures, and then, if needed, proposing an increase next year based on your black and white figures. If this is not the first year for your budget, aim a bit high to give yourself some room to march toward your vision with confidence.

I had a Director of Operations challenge my assistant and me with a new way of designing our budget. He asked us to present our budget based on the "Top Five Children's Ministry Efforts/Areas" for the coming year. This forced us to prioritize our ministry efforts, and then to determine the costs involved in accomplishing those efforts. Use the template on page 85 to help you define your costs and set your budget figures based on this process.

If you use the "Top Five" process, you have to consider the other ideas that don't fit into the "Top Five" areas as "optional." If you choose to become involved in something that isn't one of the "Top Five" areas, you can do so only if you have a surplus of money or if you receive support from outside your budget.

Step #6: Itemize and Justify Your Figures

Some of your figures may require some justification or itemizing, especially if your budget is new. This may seem like a large amount of work for something that is obvious to you. That's just it. The reasons for the figures may be obvious to you, but if they aren't clear to the ones who approve the budget you may not get the support for which you hope.

If a figure on your budget is the sum of smaller purchases, you should itemize those smaller figures, for example:

Craft Supplies

Glue:	$45.00
Construction Paper:	$150.00
Scissors:	$75.00
Total Craft Supplies:	$270.00

Remember, your job is not to tell the pastor what to do, but rather to give him the same information that led you to your decision. Hopefully, this will let him see things the way you do. If he disagrees, your only option is to trust him and the Lord, while knowing that you've done your best.

A figure that is new or very large needs justification. As a pastor or chairman of the finance committee could tell you, it's better to be safe than sorry when it comes to money. The running of a church's finance is not an easy job. The pastor must walk a thin line between being a good steward of the Lord's money, and also a visionary who invests in new directions in order to further the cause of Christ. Before you complain about justifying a figure, spend a day "in his pulpit" I think you'll find yourself wanting to do all you can to help the pastor in any way possible.

A sample justification for a new CD player for the children's ministry office would be:

Capital Expenses

CD player (for office): $200.00

Notes: We propose the purchase of a new CD player.

1. Because of the need to play music to the children as they enter the fellowship hall for Children's Church.

2. Because of the need to play a repeated announcement greeting the parents and children on Sunday morning.

3. Because of the need to have a dependable player on which to play music background CD's during Bible studies.

Now, those who will review your capital expense proposals will know what they need to know to understand the requests.

#7: Trim the Fat

Perhaps the budget was returned to you with the recommendation to reduce the bottom line. Now you start to live in the real world. Put each category and figure through a rigorous examination. For every figure, ask these questions.

Bottom-line Budget Questions

1. Can we get along this year without this purchase?
2. Can we accomplish the same goal less expensively?
3. Is this purchase vital to our ministry vision?
4. Is the timing right for this purchase or expense?
5. Have we done all we can to justify this expense?
6. Does past experience support such a purchase?
7. Are we willing to bend on this purchase?

Since your budget is your ministry vision expressed in dollars, you have to carefully respect your overseers' recommendations without compromising your vision, whenever possible. There will be times when financing your vision may need to be slowed in order that you and the children's ministry fit into the total church picture. There is nothing that carries more potential for future bread-drawer mold than to be labeled a maverick. The hardest part of the entire budgeting process is to realize that, no matter how well you do your homework, there will still be those who don't see the vision through the same eyes as you do.

Whenever faced with the decision between standing up for your rights or submitting to your pastor's will, recall the basic rule for the ministry: be a servant! This doesn't mean that you never state your feelings or differ with a decision, but it does mean that you respectfully commit to support the decision for the sake of unity. There's so much more involved in the children's ministry budget than making sure

The Budgeting Process

The budget is your philosophy of ministry expressed in dollars!

Things to Consider When Budgeting

- Goals
- Philosophy
- Last Year
- Present Conditions
- Prayer

Determine Your Needs

1. Consider your goals.
2. How much was spent last year?
3. What worked or didn't last year?
4. Consider the present financial conditions of the entire church.
5. Can you afford "new ideas"?
6. When possible, set figures high.
7. New areas are a "shot in the dark."
8. "Funnel" everything through prayer.

Be Confident

1. If you are sure of your goals, you can be sure of your budget.
2. Financial people respect confidence, but despise "cover-ups."

3. Have a "Plan B" ready, but don't give up on "Plan A" too quickly.
4. "Team players" always get more than "Lone Rangers," eventually.

Monitor and Record

1. Remember that a penny misspent or unrecorded = dollar's worth of trouble!
2. This year's budget will enhance or impede next year's ministry!
3. It is better to have too many receipts.
4. Be ready to recognize better or cheaper ways of doing things.
5. Responsibility cannot be delegated!
6. Don't budget the Lord out of your ministry! Remain dependent on him.
7. It is better to have money unspent than to overspend. Overspending is never a good reason to increase the budget next year. New ideas are!
8. Unspent funds may be interpreted as unneeded, and may be cut next year.

---

the end of the year statement has more black ink than red. Here are some perspective-building thoughts that need to be courted:

1. If you were told that you had no money available to you next year, would you quit, or go on? Could you be effective?

2. If you had spent literally hundreds of hours developing the budget, and then most of it gets cut, would you be objective or subjective about it? Would you take it personally?

3. Which is more important to you, unity with the church and submission to authority, or seeing your vision supported?

To create a budget from scratch (which many of you have had to do during your first ministry) takes much prayer and thoughtful counsel. Your ministry vision, your ministry goals, your geographical area,

and the church's condition financially affect your first budget as well as all budgets thereafter. When people look at your budget, they see what you believe. Be careful not to drastically over budget or under budget. There are problems associated with both. If you do either one, your detailed records will help you in explaining your errors.

To some, your budget is more important than your records of which children accepted the Lord during the year. I am not saying this is good; it's just a fact. You have to treat the budget, and your record-keeping, like it was an infant after a big feeding. You don't throw him around, or drop him! Have a personal goal of being so detailed in your record-keeping that you are told to calm down by your superiors. It is better to be told that than to be asked, "Where did all the money go?" and not have an answer.

Budget for the "Top Five" Priorities in Children's Ministry

Children's Ministry Vision: (Briefly state your vision)
The "Top Five" ways we will accomplish our ministry vision this year will be:

	Monthly	Yearly

Priority #1:
_____

	Monthly	Yearly
1. Curriculum costs	$____	$____
2. Craft supply costs	$____	$____
3. Non-craft supply costs	$____	$____
4. Printing costs	$____	$____
5. Advertising costs	$____	$____
6. Audio/visual costs	$____	$____
7. Postage costs	$____	$____
8. Food costs	$____	$____
9. Equipment costs	$____	$____
10. Team development costs	$____	$____

SUB- TOTALS: _____

Priority #2:
_____

	Monthly	Yearly
1. Curriculum costs	$____	$____
2. Craft supply costs	$____	$____
3. Non-craft supply costs	$____	$____
4. Printing costs	$____	$____
5. Advertising costs	$____	$____
6. Audio/visual costs	$____	$____
7. Postage costs	$____	$____
8. Food costs	$____	$____
9. Equipment costs	$____	$____
10. Team development costs	$____	$____

SUB- TOTALS: _____

Priority #3:
_____

	Monthly	Yearly
1. Curriculum costs	$____	$____
2. Craft supply costs	$____	$____
3. Non-craft supply costs	$____	$____
4. Printing costs	$____	$____
5. Advertising costs	$____	$____
6. Audio/visual costs	$____	$____
7. Postage costs	$____	$____
8. Food costs	$____	$____
9. Equipment costs	$____	$____
10. Team development costs	$____	$____

SUB- TOTALS: _____

Priority #4:
_____

	Monthly	Yearly
1. Curriculum costs	$____	$____
2. Craft supply costs	$____	$____
3. Non-craft supply costs	$____	$____
4. Printing costs	$____	$____
5. Advertising costs	$____	$____
6. Audio/visual costs	$____	$____
7. Postage costs	$____	$____
8. Food costs	$____	$____
9. Equipment costs	$____	$____
10. Team development costs	$____	$____

SUB- TOTALS: _____

Priority #5:
_____

	Monthly	Yearly
1. Curriculum costs	$____	$____
2. Craft supply costs	$____	$____
3. Non-craft supply costs	$____	$____
4. Printing costs	$____	$____
5. Advertising costs	$____	$____
6. Audio/visual costs	$____	$____
7. Postage costs	$____	$____
8. Food costs	$____	$____
9. Equipment costs	$____	$____
10. Team development costs	$____	$____

SUB- TOTALS: _____

Sub-totals:

	Monthly	Yearly
1. Curriculum costs	$____	$____
2. Craft supply costs	$____	$____
3. Non-craft supply costs	$____	$____
4. Printing costs	$____	$____
5. Advertising costs	$____	$____
6. Audio/visual costs	$____	$____
7. Postage costs	$____	$____
8. Food costs	$____	$____
9. Equipment costs	$____	$____
10. Team development costs	$____	$____

GRAND TOTALS:_____

WHAT TO DO WHEN YOU DON'T HAVE ANY MONEY

There's nothing more discouraging than to have plenty of vision and passion, but have no money to do anything about it! First, remember that we have a very rich God who has promised to provide all our needs! It is God who is supplying your needs, not the finance director!

I'll never forget the lesson the Lord taught me as a children's pastor of a small church that grew into a "mega church." When we were small, we prayed for God to provide for our children's ministry. We watched as he provided everything for us through donations. We would "kill the fattened calf" when we got a tape recorder donated, or when someone would bring in a box of white copy paper they didn't need any more. I remember going to the local elementary schools and asking for broken crayons that they were going to throw away. I would bring those crayon ends back to the church where a lady would melt them down and pour them into crayon molds. We praised God for his provision of "new" crayons! The lesson came when, after 8 years of ministry growth, we no longer melted crayons down, or sought donations for used tape recorders. We simply budgeted for new crayons or CD players. It was like we didn't need God's help anymore because we had a huge budget! What an eternal shame!

When you don't have enough money, get on your knees and thank God! When you have enough money, get on your knees and thank him! If you forget who is providing for your ministry, your efforts will fail. *Psalm 1* is a great example of God's views on trust and reliance on his provision: "Blessed is the man...[whose] delight is in the law of the Lord.... He is like a tree planted by streams of water, which yields its fruit in season, and whose leaf does not wither. Whatever he does prospers." *Deuteronomy 8:11-19* has the same sort of promises along with a warning against forgetting God: "Be careful that you do not forget the Lord your God.... Otherwise, when you eat and are satisfied, when you build fine houses and settle down, and when your herds and flocks grow large and your silver and gold increase and all you have is multiplied, then your heart will become proud and you will forget the Lord your God.... You may say to yourself, 'My power and the strength of my hands have produced this wealth for me.' ...If you ever forget the Lord your God... I testify against you today that you will surely be destroyed."

Once you have this perspective, you can ask him for help through the following ideas:

Fund Raising

Inside the word "fund" is the word "fun." Yes, fund-raising can be fun! Remember, our God is creative, and you are made in his image, so go for it! What kinds of money-making ideas can you and your team generate? Remember two important rules: (1) ask permission from the "powers that be" before you embark on any of these adventures and (2) never let children go out without supervision. Consider some of these suggestions for adding the much-needed funds to your budget.

Ten Fund Raising Ideas

1. Chore Teams: Organize your children into supervised Chore Teams that are hired out to members of your congregation to perform specific chores such as: house cleaning, yard work, painting, pet care, etc.

2. Car Washes: Transform your church parking lot into a car wash and detail shop. Advertise well, and add a bake sale to the day for waiting customers.

3. Newspaper Drives: Contact your local newspaper and embark on the great American pastime of raiding garages, libraries, and gas stations. All of these are arsenals of old newspapers.

4. All Church Skate Night, Pizza Night, or Miniature Golf: Invite the members of your church to participate; your ministry will get a portion of the proceeds.

5. Children's Recipe Book Sales: This is a wonderful idea! Children bring in their favorite recipes, which are then uniformly typed, bound into books, and sold. Everybody wants one!

6. Christmas Box Sales: Pre-wrap Christmas boxes, complete with lids. Sell them at church after Thanksgiving.

7. Flower Sales and Frozen Candy-bar Sales: The flowers are for Mother's Day and the frozen candy bars are for Father's Day.

8. Church Concessions (Bake Sales): Offer flavored coffees, teas, goodies at church events such as: Bible studies, movie nights, special guest services, regular week-end services.

9. Professions Fund Raising Organizations: Many organizations will link with your ministry and equip your children to sell popcorn, Christmas cards, candy-bars, etc.

10. Scholarship Donation Funds: Make the needs of special events known—things like camps, VBS, and retreats and the equipment and supplies for them.

Seeking Donations

The vendors and craftsmen in your community are able to provide a wealth of resources; all you have to do is ask! Remember, James says, "You do not have, because you do not ask God" *(James 4:2)*. Consider asking as good stewardship of resources. Here are some suggested strongholds for freebies.

Sources for Donations

1. The Entire Church: If your have a need, publicize it in the church bulletin, place large bins in the foyer, and wait for the Spirit to move in the hearts of your congregation. You will be amazed at how many craft supplies, toys, books, diapers, games, and play equipment can be generated by your own church body.

2. Local Artists: Photographers, video technicians, singers, dancers, directors, writers, clowns, magicians, singers, actors, and many more skilled men and women may be delighted to donate their services to your ministry; simply ask them.

3. Construction Workers: If you need something built, ask the builders—first, those in your congregation, then start down the phone book. Also, these folks have a wealth of building materials available: lumber, chicken wire, fencing, wire. Ask for it!

4. Local Merchants: Craft stores are a treasure house! After the holidays, ask for clearance items:

Christmas, Easter, etc. Paper goods, groceries, and many more items are easily donated.

5. Printing Companies: Ask for the end of the rolls at printing companies. They will gladly donate those, and they make excellent banners, posters, or paper for art projects.

6. Advertising in Programs: Vendors will advertise in performance programs when your children do a special production: musicals, Christmas programs, Easter pageants, etc. This will help defray the cost of the production.

OVERSEEING THE BUDGET
Purchase Order and Record-keeping

I have found that it is vitally important to clarify the process of spending money, and then to properly communicate that process with those who will be spending the money. You must delegate spending money! If you try to control the budget so tightly that you make yourself the only person who can ever spend money, you will be miserable! I know, I have a "frequent member" card in the local Lone Spender's Anonymous recovery group! If you are the only spender, you will find yourself running to the grocery store to buy crackers and masking tape instead of furthering your ministry vision. Create the plan to spend money, and then delegate it!

Meet with your business or finance director to clarify the process of spending money. Take notes, and review those notes with him or her before you go and type it up for those to whom you will delegate the joy of buying things.

Here are a couple of definitions that may be helpful to you:

Purchase Order: A form that proves that the purchase has been approved by those who oversee the budget. This form is also "good as money" to the vendor for whom the church has an account. The Purchase Order lets the buyer purchase the goods without any money being transferred. The vendor bills the church monthly.

How to Spend Money

When You Want to Shop At
Wal-Mart
Do This
(We have an account there.)
1. Get a Purchase Order from _____.
2. Shop
3. At the check-out, show the purchase order to have the amount charged to our account.
4. Bring the receipt and one copy of the Purchase Order back with you.
5. Give the copy of the Purchase Order and receipt to _____.

When You Want To Shop At
Smith's Copy Center
Do This
(We don't have an account there.)
1. Call the Copy Center to get the exact amount of the bill beforehand!
2. Get a Purchase Order from _____.
3. Request a Check Request for the exact amount from _____.
4. Fill out the Check Request and submit it to _____.
5. Once the check is written, leave your job at the copy center.
6. Pay for the job with the church check.
7. Return the receipt to _____.
8. You may also get a Purchase Order from _____ beforehand, then:
9. Pay for the copying with your own money.
10. Turn in the receipt and Purchase Order to _____.
11. A Check Request will be written for reimbursement back to you.

Check Request: A form that the overseer of the budget fills out to request a check for purchase or reimbursement. The finance officer is the one who writes the check and then charges the church account requesting the check with the amount. (There is usually a number of days required from the receipt of the request until the check is actually written.)

Above is an example of what you might produce for your ministry buyers. This system includes the use of Purchase Orders. If your church doesn't use Purchase Orders, you can adjust the wording to fit your particular system (which you should do anyway).

Summary: Goals for the Children's Ministry Budget

1. Clarify your core values in relation to your ministry vision.
2. Become aware of the past expenditures and learn from the mistakes and successes.
3. Become aware of the children's needs in your church and community.
4. Become aware of the parents' needs in your church and community.
5. Prioritize your "Top Five" ministry efforts or areas for the coming year.
6. Set financial costs based on your vision, core values, needs, and goals.
7. Propose the budget to the church leadership.
8. Adjust the budget based on feedback from the church leadership.
9. Operate the ministry within the budget.
10. Keep detailed records of spending for the year.
11. Reevaluate the ministry budget based on this year's spending and ministry success.
12. Begin working on next year's budget early!
13. The budget process is not just about numbers, it's about faith! Don't let the financial overshadow the spiritual. Focus on God's provision, and "all these things" will be yours as well! (See *Matthew 6:33*.)

Garden Pest:
Hopeless Grass

Evidence

This grass is not really the kind of grass you imagine when you hear the word "grass." It is a weed that slowly creeps through your whole garden. Its negative, visionless, hopeless comments will soon choke out your plants. A person with this condition usually makes comments that begin or end with "We can't do that because...." or "We just don't have the money...." To this person, there is no hope in God's provision, just an unhealthy focus on the lack of money. Even ideas of fund raising, scholarships, or donations don't seem to slow this weed down.

Sources of Infestation

A spiritual problem. Lack of awareness or focus on God's provision. Fear of failure. Pride that prevents asking for donations or support.

Treatment

1. Spray on liberal amounts of children's ministry vision.
2. Teach about God's desire to provide.
3. Involve the person in a small group Bible study or fellowship with other team members of faith.
4. Highlight God's provision thus far. If the condition persists, pull the weed. Remove the person from the team.

## chapter 7

Adding Amendments:
Program & Curriculum Goals

"*Compaction is the most troublesome (soil condition). Soil compaction can restrict free entry of air, penetration and drainage of water, and activity of all soil organisms. Breaking up compacted soil is the first step in counteracting this condition; adding soil amendments keeps the soil from becoming compacted again*" (Vegetable Gardening, Menlo Park, CA: Lane Publishing Co., 1975; page 18).

Just as organic amendments keep the soil from becoming compacted and unusable, the correct use of curriculum and programming will soften the children's hearts and make them open to God's love and leading. The problem with today's society is that it encourages us all to become tough or hardened. We are told at an early age to stand up for ourselves and not to let others affect us. These messages, in the right context with godly perspective and wisdom, can be good, but all too often these messages are taken literally by innocent children who soon become hardened to life and to God. The purpose of curriculum and any program in children's ministry is to break up the hardened soil of the children's emotions so they can drink in God's Word.

In this chapter, you will evaluate your current programs and curriculum. Then you will set goals for creating and evaluating your curriculum. We will only deal briefly with programs in this chapter. The design and evaluation of programs will be dealt with in detail in chapters 10-12. The first thing we need to do is look at your current programs and curriculum.

EVALUATE YOUR PROGRAMS

On the chart on page 91, simply list all the information for all the programs currently offered for this year. Check the column closest to the general goal of the

program. Feel free to check more than one column. In the column labeled "Success," mark "Yes" or "No" (based on the goal), and add any comments directly related to the "Goal" column. After you have finished listing and evaluating your programs, you can take this information on into chapters 10 and 11 for further revisions.

For the sake of this evaluation, the definition of "Program" is any gathering of children under the umbrella of the children's ministry. This includes Sunday school. It is important to include Sunday school as a program for the sake of evaluation at this point. Your curriculum producers should include goals for each class. In your evaluation of the success of the Sunday school, you can consider the reaching of these goals as a test of the success of the class or program.

We will look at program success in depth later, but for now make some notes on your own based on what you discover. You will have to talk with those in charge of the programs to complete this chart. If those who are in charge are not available, you can speak with anyone who is involved with the program.

Evaluate Your Calendar

Now that you've listed all your programs, and made notes regarding their success, let's look at your overall calendar. Fill in the yearly calendar on page 92

Program Evaluation Chart

Program	Program Dates	Goal* E B D F	Attend. Yes No	Success Notes

*Program Goals: E = Evangelism, B = Bible teaching, D = Discipleship, F = Fun/fellowship

with the number of programs for each goal. You will have to choose only one goal for each program. This chart will show you a snapshot of your year's programs and their goals.

We will look at the placement of programs in chapter 10, but this chart should show you how your current programs are placed, and where you have holes in your programming. A well-balanced year is the goal. "Well-balanced" refers to both the timing, and goals of the programs. If all your programs are focused toward evangelism, you will not be fulfilling the commission to make disciples and teach. If you have a program emphasis in Bible teaching and discipleship with no clear evangelistic programs, you may also be falling short of the Lord's design for your ministry.

Evaluate Your Curriculum

The design and placement of a program has a significant effect on the curriculum. The curriculum must be chosen, or created, to suit the program goal, not vice-versa. "Curriculum" can be defined as anything that is part of a lesson. We usually only think of printed material (such as a student book or teacher's book) as being curriculum. I believe a video, song, object lesson, or even a field trip should be included in the category of curriculum. When you broaden

your definition of what is the curriculum, you also increase the creativity, variety, and attraction of the lesson.

Criterion #1: Magnetic Teachers

The most effective curriculum is you and your team! I believe that a godly person, whose walk with the Lord is intimate and growing and who is actively studying God's Word, can lead children to the Lord with the daily newspaper or a menu from a local restaurant! Children do not give their lives to God because of a tremendous lecture or an eye-catching PowerPoint presentation. Children give their lives to the Lord because someone has taken the time to become a significant example to them. Evangelism and discipleship have always been critically linked to a personal relationship with a mentor or teacher.

The greatest Sunday school teachers I've ever known have been people who view the lesson as being carried out outside the classroom. Two examples of this perspective come to my mind:

• John and Kelli taught fourth grade together. Kelli cooked her way into the children's hearts by bringing cookies or home-made bread to class every week. The children looked forward to class for the simple, human reason of liking to eat good food that was prepared with them in mind. Kelli's message of love and

Calendar Evaluation Chart
Yearly Programs by Goals

Months	Goal:	E	B	D	F	Total # of this Month's Programs
January						
February						
March						
April						
May						
June						
July						
August						
September						
October						
November						
December						
Total Programs						

concern was shouted loudly as the children enjoyed her goodies each week. Her husband, John, spent time with the children outside the classroom. He would take those who were interested out to the basketball court and shoot some hoops with them before and after class. Those who spent that time with John came to appreciate this Christian man's honest, genuine love for them. John and Kelli also made arrangements to take the children up to their mountain cabin for a day of fun and horseback riding.

• Dave and Carol taught our fifth and sixth graders together as well. Dave and Carol didn't attract the children with cookies or basketball; they had an airplane! As part of their class, they challenged the children to memorize verses and even whole sections of the Bible. They created a contest that lasted a whole year. The prize was a ride in their airplane! They caught the attention of the children and their parents with this challenge. When the contest was over, Dave and Carol treated a group of children, and their parents, to an experience they'll never forget. The experience that will stay with them for their whole lives was not the airplane ride; it was Dave and Carol's investment of time on their behalf.

In the two stories above, what was the curriculum? The curriculum used was chocolate chip cookies, basketballs, and airplanes. But the living Bible curriculum was Dave, Carol, John, and Kelli! You can't find that curriculum in some catalog. That curriculum comes from God.

Criterion # 2: Four-part Lessons

Your curriculum is the tool that must fulfill four essential requirements. Ask yourself these questions:

1. Does it attract the children to the lesson with a relevant attention getter?

2. Does it confront them with new information and challenges, which causes them to consider salvation during a Bible content time?

3. Does it permit them to participate in the learning during an activity time?

4. Does it challenge them with discipleship as they grow in the Lord during an application time?

These are the steps of ministering to children that were covered in chapter 2. Your curriculum must be a tool that works for you. You have to know how to use it and make it work for you. A tool doesn't control the user; the user controls the tool!

What Do You Think of Our Lessons?

Yes! Maybe No!

For the Children

1. Do you like the crafts in Sunday school? ❏ ❏ ❏
2. Do you like the music we sing in Sunday school? ❏ ❏ ❏
3. Do you like the stuff we talk about in Sunday school? ❏ ❏ ❏
4. Does the stuff we talk about in Sunday school help you be more friendly? ❏ ❏ ❏
5. Does the stuff we talk about in Sunday school help you stay out of trouble? ❏ ❏ ❏
6. Does the stuff we talk about in Sunday school help you make God happy? ❏ ❏ ❏
7. Do you look forward to coming to Sunday school each week? ❏ ❏ ❏

For the Parents

8. Do you like the subjects we teach in Sunday school? ❏ ❏ ❏
9. Do you like the way we teach the lessons? ❏ ❏ ❏
10. Do you like the comments your child makes about Sunday school afterward? ❏ ❏ ❏
11. Do you like the crafts your children enjoy at Sunday school? ❏ ❏ ❏
12. Do you like the materials we provide that help you apply the lessons at home? ❏ ❏ ❏
13. Do you feel the lessons we teach help your child grow spiritually? ❏ ❏ ❏
14. Do you feel the lessons we teach help your child make wise decisions? ❏ ❏ ❏
15. Do you feel the lessons we teach apply to your child's everyday life? ❏ ❏ ❏

Comments or suggestions:

Please return this survey to the children's ministry office at the church. Thanks!

Criterion #3: Varied Teaching/Learning Methods

Each child is a one-of-a-kind, unique, never-to-be repeated creation, so look for curriculum that presents the truth of God's Word using a variety of teaching modes (methods) that appeal to the multiple learning styles of children. Children learn many different ways. Four of the most common learning styles are:

1. AUDIO, learning by hearing (20% retention after 3 days). Look for curriculum that contains:

- discussions
- memory-verse games
- oral quizzes
- recordings
- songs
- testimonies
- sound effects
- stories

2. VISUAL, learning by seeing (30% retention after 3 days). Look for curriculum that contains:

- demonstrations
- displays
- maps/charts
- pictures
- skits
- time lines
- object lessons
- videos

3. TACTILE, learning by making things (70% retention after 3 days). Look for curriculum that contains:

- baking
- building models
- clay sculptures
- crafts
- letter writing
- mobiles
- murals
- posters

4. EXPERIENTIAL, learning by experiencing (90% retention after 3 days). Look for curriculum that contains:

- charades
- drama
- evangelism
- field trips
- nature walks
- service projects
- simulations (fasting)
- sports

Curriculum must be chosen with the overall ministry vision, as well as the specific program goals, in mind. There are many good curriculum sources available today. With a little searching, you can probably find printed curriculum for just about any topic or program. It is up to you to decide for what you are looking.

Criterion #4: Parent and Child-Friendly

When you are evaluating your curriculum, it is wise to survey those who use the curriculum (your teaching team), as well as the children and parents. It would be great to compare the team members' evaluation of the curriculum with yours, using the same "Curriculum Checklist." The parents and the children need something a bit less formal. On page 95 is a take-home curriculum evaluation that families can fill out together. (Feel free to substitute "Sunday school" with another program's name.)

Criterion #5: The "Curriculum Checklist"

Evaluating your own curriculum can be difficult because you are so close to it. Unless you've just switched to a new curriculum, you may be comfortable with your purchased curriculum. You may not be able to evaluate your curriculum without the help of a set of standards produced by someone else. Here is a checklist of those standards just for you! Using the checklist on page 95, evaluate your curriculum by checking the boxes to the right for each area. If you use more than one curriculum source, evaluate them separately. After you fill out the checklist, evaluate your findings.

There is obviously no perfect curriculum. Every curriculum will have some "OK" or "Poor" evaluations. These evaluations may be affected by your own perceptions, or they may be accurate. Now, go back and look at the areas that are marked with "OK" or "Poor." For each of those areas, ask yourself these questions:

1. Does the low grade in this area affect the ministry to children significantly enough that I might consider changing curriculum to another source?

2. Can we work around this weakness? (Create our own solutions through training, etc.)

3. Can we supplement another curriculum to strengthen this area?

4. Is this weakness due to poor usage of the curriculum?

CHILD-TARGETED CURRICULUM

In a perfect world you would be able to purchase the perfect curriculum. It would perfectly match your ministry vision. You wouldn't have to change a thing. You wouldn't have to add any of your own personal touches to suit your children's needs or ministry vision. That would be nice, but it would also be boring! Can you imagine just opening the box of your curriculum and never seeking the Lord for its application or use in your children's lives? I personally like customizing the curriculum, with the Lord's guidance, to the needs of our church and children. That forces me to look at the curriculum as only a starting point, and not the final destination.

I'll never forget the really bad feelings I had one Sunday morning as I walked around our facility as Sunday school was beginning. I used the "management by walking around" style every Sunday morning. I would stick my head in the rooms, greet the team members, and encourage them in their ministry for the morning. Just before the service started, and while the children were still arriving, I walked by a third grade classroom to see something I will never forget. As the children were entering the room, both teachers were facing away from the children and looking down at the countertop. I stopped short of going into the room. I couldn't believe what I was seeing. Both of the teachers were ignoring the children for the sake of reviewing the lesson plan for the morning! I fought the urge to yell at them, calmly walked into the room, and said, "Good morning, is there anything you need?" They both jumped! I think they knew what they were doing was not good. They both quickly said, "No, we're fine," and turned to face the children who were roaming aimlessly around the room. I said, "Great, God bless your ministry to the children this morning," and then left before I said something I would regret.

Those two teachers might as well have put signs on their backs for the children to read that said, "We don't care about you; we only care about completing the lesson." No longer can we, in children's min-

Curriculum Evaluation Checklist

	Excellent	Good	OK	Poor

THEOLOGICAL CONSIDERATIONS

1. Are the materials based on the Scriptures as the major instructional source? ❏ ❏ ❏ ❏
2. Do the materials encourage the learner to commit him/herself to Jesus Christ? ❏ ❏ ❏ ❏
3. Do the materials connect the learner's relationship with Jesus and his/her relationship with other people? ❏ ❏ ❏ ❏
4. Do the materials support, and teach, the major doctrines of the Christian faith? ❏ ❏ ❏ ❏

SUBSTANCE AND ORGANIZATION

5. Do the lessons include clear, attainable, age-appropriate, objectives that can be measured? ❏ ❏ ❏ ❏
6. Do the lessons contain a four-part process similar to the "Program Regions" 1-4? ❏ ❏ ❏ ❏
7. Do the lessons employ an adequate number of modes? ❏ ❏ ❏ ❏
8. Do the lessons employ some sort of review of past lessons periodically (chaining)? ❏ ❏ ❏ ❏
9. Do the lessons build on one another as the learners' knowledge increases? ❏ ❏ ❏ ❏
10. Do the lessons include strong "application" suggestions? ❏ ❏ ❏ ❏

TEACHER SUPPORT

11. Does the material provide the teacher with adequate background information for the scriptural passage? ❏ ❏ ❏ ❏
12. Does the material provide several options for the teacher to choose in teaching the lesson? ❏ ❏ ❏ ❏
13. Does the material provide supplementary teaching aids, such as maps, pictures, overhead projections, audio recordings, etc.? ❏ ❏ ❏ ❏
14. Does the material provide the teacher with evaluation tools such as tests, etc.? ❏ ❏ ❏ ❏
15. Are the lessons time-appropriate for the average class period? ❏ ❏ ❏ ❏
16. Are the lessons written with the inexperienced teacher in mind? ❏ ❏ ❏ ❏
17. Do the lessons contain specific teacher-talk and guidelines for each phase of the lesson? ❏ ❏ ❏ ❏
18. Are the student books easy to use by the teacher? ❏ ❏ ❏ ❏
19. Does the material require an unrealistic amount of teacher preparation? ❏ ❏ ❏ ❏
20. Are the extra lesson supplies, not included in the curriculum, listed clearly? ❏ ❏ ❏ ❏
21. Are the extra lesson supplies "common" craft supplies which every church has? ❏ ❏ ❏ ❏
22. Does the curriculum include parent support, such as letters, family activities, etc.? ❏ ❏ ❏ ❏

Garden Pest:
Lesson-targeted Leaf Eaters

Evidence

These dangerous pests are not easily seen by the average gardener. They camouflage themselves to blend into the colors of the garden. To the untrained eye, they appear to be committed, faithful team members, but in reality they only care about completing the lesson perfectly. You will never find these pests outside of the church facilities. They will never venture out into the real world with the children. You won't find them at soccer games, drama performances, or local elementary schools. The most obvious sign that a Lesson-targeted Leaf Eater is present is the lack of laughter coming from the room. In the later stages of infestation, the attendance in that room or ministry environment will drop significantly.

Sources of Infestation

Lack of compassion for children. Belief that knowledge is more valuable than relationships. Failure to recognize that healthy relationships with godly mentors ultimately leads to a greater hunger for knowledge.

Treatment

1. Make sure you have cast your ministry vision clearly to your team.

2. Personally invite this person to accompany you to a soccer game in which your children are playing. As an added treatment, sit by the parents of the child, or go out to lunch afterward with the family of a child from your ministry to talk about the game.

3. Team the person with others who are child-targeted.

4. Train the person in guided conversations and lesson adaptation techniques.

5. If no change is evident after all of the above treatments, remove the person from the team.

istry, be lesson-targeted. We must be child-targeted! Does it really matter what the curriculum says if you have a child whose parents just got a divorce, and he enters the room crying and lonely? Does it really matter what the lesson is about the day that a third grade child raises his hand and asks, "Teacher, why did God let my dad die?" We must remember that our commission from the Lord is not to teach curriculum, or to complete some lesson plan in the allotted time. We are commissioned to go and make disciples! We are commanded to touch lives and

love people in such a way that makes them turn and ask us about the One we serve. Jesus was an excellent example of a teacher who set aside the lesson book for the sake of the needs of others. He knew that caring for the needs of others was the true curriculum! Here are just three examples of Jesus being student-targeted.

• "A large crowd gathered around him while he was by the lake. Then one of the synagogue rulers, named Jairus, came...and pleaded...'My little daughter is dying. Please come and put your hands on her so that she will be healed and live.' So Jesus went with him" *(Mark 5:21-24)*.

• "A large crowd followed and pressed around him. And a woman was there who had been subject to bleeding for twelve years.... She came up behind him in the crowd and touched his cloak.... He said to her, 'Daughter, your faith has healed you. Go in peace and be freed from your suffering'" *(Mark 5:24-34)*.

• "Jesus entered Jericho and was passing through. A man was there by the name of Zacchaeus.... So he ran ahead and climbed a sycamore-fig tree.... When Jesus reached the spot, he looked up and said to him, 'Zacchaeus, come down immediately. I must stay at your house today'" *(Luke 19:1-6)*.

If you train your team to be child-targeted, they will have no other choice but to use the curriculum as a starting point and seek the Lord for wisdom in adapting and adding to it. Here is a list of ways to strengthen your purchased curriculum to be more effective in fulfilling your ministry vision.

Five Ways to Strengthen Purchased Curriculum

1. Write clear objectives. After the lesson is over, you have to determine if the children learned what you set out to teach. A clear, measurable, observable objective is vital! (Example: The children will be able to correctly choose the right choice from a list of ten options.)

2. Design clear, current, real applications to the children's lives. You may have to add these on your own! Knowing your children helps tremendously!

3. Create a balance of Bible study, worship, and prayer. All study with no worship and prayer may produce children who have dry relationships with God.

4. Include challenges for service. Children who simply hear about the Christian life are only half as powerful as those who are challenged to do something! Add your own service projects periodically. Let the children anticipate the experiences, then debrief after.

5. Challenge children to be salt and light!

Evangelism and discipleship are two of the most vital amendments that we can add to our garden soil! Add some teaching about this if it isn't already there. Young children can understand the concept of being an example.

Curriculum and Multiple Services

If you are serving at a growing church, you will face the challenge of multiple services. Besides the thrill of multiple teams, you also are forced to consider the implications of multiple services on curriculum. At first, you may think, "Great, I'll save some money by doing the same lessons at every service." That is true. You would save some money, but you can't do that if you are truly child-targeted. You have to consider the children who will stay for both services, those whose parents serve in the church, and who will serve one service and go to worship the next. Those children will be left in your care for both services! Unless you have an amazingly creative team who adds so much individual flavor to each lesson, the child will basically get the same lesson twice. That's not good. It goes against your basic ministry vision to attract and inspire children to God!

The two options for multiple services are: Two different curriculum sources, or a children's church at one service, and Sunday school at the other. Either way, you have to rethink your curriculum design. Here are some thoughts on the multiple service issue.

Multiple Service Curriculum Considerations

1. Children's Church? Does your current Sunday school offer a balanced program which includes Bible teaching, powerful worship, and meaningful prayer times? If not, a children's church session could add that balance (at least for those "multiple service" children).

2. General Session? Are your services long enough to add a general session in which the children meet together for worship and prayer before going to their Sunday school classes?

3. Special Options? If you purchased only one curriculum for both services, could you offer a special class or experience for those "multiple service" children (service projects, special studies, games, mentoring, etc.)?

4. Auxiliary Programs? Could you start a scouting type program on Sunday morning as an option for "multiple service" children?

A SAFEGUARDED VISION

Your vision, inspired by God, and born of passion for bringing children into an intimate relationship with Jesus Christ, is what drives absolutely everything you do in your children's ministry.

This part of the book has been filled with good advice for evaluating "what is" and setting goals for what "could be." To better assist you in setting goals for your ministry, I have listed 28 realistic ministry goals that relate to the five parts of the "Great Commission Vision" in chapter 3. Human beings are deeply relational creatures, so each of these goals is translated as something we hope to hear people say about the children's ministry.

For this section, each vision category leads to a goal; each goal has a rationale; each rationale has operational objectives through which we intend to make this goal a reality. Before we continue, here are some helpful definitions of those terms.

Definitions for Successful Goal-setting

Vision Categories: The divisions of your vision that can be stated in goals, each of which can be accomplished through implementing operational objectives.

Goals: Statements within a specific category regarding a visible or real expression of your vision for children's ministry.

Rationale: A list of reasons why this goal is important and worthy of budget dollars and team attention.

Operational Objectives: An operational plan for meeting the goal. Many objectives can come under

one goal. Together they develop a strategy by which the goal can be accomplished and evaluated.

THE "GREAT COMMISSION" CHILDREN'S MINISTRY VISION

Since vision is a difficult thing to describe or visualize, here are some tangible "footprints" of vision that we can look for in our ministry as translated in the statements we hope to hear our children, our parents, our teachers, and our pastoral staff say about the children's ministry (translated into goals and operational objectives).

Vision Category: "Go"

#1: We will GO into the world of today's children with trained, well-organized, passionate, godly adults who carry the message of the Gospel.

Goal 1.1 Before they come to an event, we want the children of our ministry to say: "I want to go there because I feel safe, welcomed, and valued."

Rationale:

1. Children feel safe when their fragile self-concept is protected, and their feelings and opinions are valued.

2. Children return to where they are personally greeted and not made to feel guilty if absent.

3. Children will return to the place where their presence and ideas are valued equally.

Operational Objectives:

1. Train all team members in affirmation techniques.

2. Expose all team members to positive examples of child-focused behavior.

3. Reward team members for excellence in child-focused behavior.

Goal 1.2 We want the supervisors and teachers on our children's ministry team to say: "I enjoy serving the Lord here."

Rationale:

1. The Lord is not pleased with "duty service."

2. If there is no joy in a person's service, he or she must be challenged to find out why. If it is something that can be fixed, others need to help.

3. Ministering to children needs to match with a

person's gifts or interests. A ministry transfer to another area where the person can experience joy in service may be a possibility.

4. People enjoy serving where their gifts are used and their needs are met. Excellent training, great curriculum, sufficient supplies, and team teaching enhance enjoyment in service.

Operational Objectives:

1. Support and encourage the coordinators to become aware of their team members' happiness and contentment.

2. Continue to develop a placement process which targets a team member's gifts and personality.

3. Continue to develop the initial orientation process.

4. Continue to develop the training process which includes on-the-job training.

5. Develop a supply system, and supply coordinator.

6. Continue to recruit actively to develop a team-teaching environment ministry-wide.

Goal 1.3 We want the supervisors and teachers on our children's ministry team to say: "I feel a part of a team effort here."

Rationale:

1. Strong, sensitive, dedicated coordinators are the beginning point to a healthy team.

2. Having multiple team members in each room serving different functions adds to the enjoyment.

3. People are drawn to a team in which master teachers apprentice new volunteers.

4. Periodic team meetings (department and all-team) enhance unity.

Operational Objectives:

1. Pray for and seek out master teachers in each area and service.

2. Pray for and seek out supervisors for each area and service.

3. Continue to develop the ministry vision in the entire team.

4. Continue to develop a "one team" mindset throughout the entire ministry team.

5. Continue to develop the individual areas' team identity (nursery, preschool, elementary).

6. Continue to develop the all-team meetings with area small group meetings afterward.

7. Continue to enhance communications within the team (email, newsletters, letters, etc.).

Goal 1.4 We want the supervisors and teachers on our children's ministry team to say: "I want my friends and neighbors to join this team."

Rationale:

1. The greatest recruiter in a ministry is a contented team member! (Healthy sheep reproduce healthy sheep.)

2. Inviting friends to serve with us should be a natural thing to do.

3. Friends serving together is the best way to develop relationships.

4. Every person has a circle of friends who need to be invited to join the team.

5. Hundreds of recruiters is better than just one!

Operational Objectives:

1. Create a "minister with a friend" crusade to encourage team members to invite friends to join the team.

2. Thank those who recruit new team members, during area meetings.

3. Create a recruiting contest, with a great prize, to raise the awareness of the need for more adults.

Goal 1.5 We want every children's ministry team member to say: "I am so glad I get to make the contribution I make with my talents."

Rationale:

1. No matter what part a person plays on the team, they must feel valued and vital to the success of the process.

2. Not everyone needs to be a teacher. We need greeters, restroom helpers, craft experts, etc. to balance our team. Teachers need to focus on the process of teaching.

3. People will want to continue doing what makes them comfortable and fulfilled.

4. People like to be a part of something big.

5. There are people who don't want to be "in front of the curtain," but would rather be behind the

scenes and let others get the applause. We need every member of the body.

Operational Objectives:

1. Create a list of small jobs and publicize in adult worship.

2. Create a promotional video of people serving in small jobs.

3. Plan a "behind the scenes" person appreciation party.

4. Create a "behind the scenes" award.

5. Create a list of the entire team according to each person's function. Use this list to aid in supporting and appreciating each person.

6. Match each team member with another team member's name for prayer and support (verbally, via email, etc.).

Goal 1.6 We want the Lord to say: "Well done, my good and faithful servants."

Rationale:

1. Faithfulness is the greatest quality of anyone who serves on a team!

2. When people in ministry stop serving Jesus and start complaining about the conditions, it's time for them to step aside and let someone else serve in their place.

3. The focus of any ministry team member is to serve the Lord. If someone is serving to impress another person, or to become a big ministry, those motives will produce failure.

Operational Objectives:

1. Continue emphasizing the Great Commission in everything you do (written communications, meetings, etc.).

2. Continue publicly encouraging faithful behavior in your team members.

3. Continue bringing specific prayer requests to your team.

4. Continue teaching your team members what "faithful service" means through Bible studies, tapes, meetings, printed communications, etc.

5. Continue growing in your own personal, intimate relationship with God.

#2: We will GO into the church, community, and the schools with a children's ministry image that attracts children.

Goal 2.1 Before they come to an event, we want the children of our ministry to say: "I want to go there because I have friends there."

Rationale:

1. Friends are developed through interaction.

2. Children must be encouraged to interact in groups, pairs, teams, etc.

3. Friendships are sealed through experiences (especially service).

4. Approved field trips and outings are great enhancers to friendship-building.

5. We should encourage child-to-child contacts outside of church.

Operational Objectives:

1. Develop and approve policies on field experiences.

2. Train all team members in interactive education.

3. Encourage all team members to think outside the box regarding child-to-child interactions.

4. Develop class-level email pals or other outside class networks.

5. Encourage class invitations to child events (parties, games, etc.).

Goal 2.2 When people visit the children's ministry division, we want them to say: "These people look like a team with a purpose."

Rationale:

1. Everybody wants to have a sense of belonging.

2. Unity is developed with common logos and graphics.

3. Team spirit is contagious when people can identify with a cause.

Operational Objectives:

1. Present the children's ministry vision positively before the church body and before the leadership.

2. Develop inspirational media that gives your church an inside look at the heart of your children's ministry.

3. Project your image at church with excellent

printed material that reflects your vision as well as excellent program content.

4. Publicize that team members minister in the "Happiest Place in the Church" on a rotating schedule.

5. Revitalize facilities so parents see that the ministry has pride and takes seriously its responsibilities of caring for the needs of their children.

6. Design vision logos that are placed on team-wear (caps, jumpers, shirts, etc.) that reflect the identity of the children's ministry as well as the identity of specific programs within the ministry.

7. Reinforce your ministry vision with posters, murals, and identifying signs in the children's ministry department.

8. Assure your congregation that teachers are screened and well-trained in emergency responses.

9. Heighten community awareness by designing children's ministry community-wide programs.

10. Use every form of church and community advertising available to you.

#3: We will provide a safe, nurturing environment so that parents can rest assured that our children's ministry is a positive place to which their children can GO.

Goal 3.1 When they leave an event, we want the children of our ministry to say: "I'm sad it's over."

Rationale:

1. Home may not be a happy place for children.

2. Children need, and want, to have fun.

3. Adults who become significant mentors for children can support the parents' function at home.

Operational Objectives:

1. Acquaint all team members in the needs of today's children.

2. Train all team members in how to connect with children through small talk.

3. Train all team members in the art of having fun with children. (Study what makes children laugh.)

4. Train all team members to remember children's prayer needs week to week.

5. Divide the children up into small groups with one or two consistent adults as mentors.

6. Plan for child-targeted fun during each ministry session.

Goal 3.2: When parents think of the children's ministry, we want them to say: "They really understand what I'm looking for in a children's ministry."

Rationale:

1. The best way to guarantee continued ministry to the children is to care for the needs of the parents.

2. Children only come when their parents bring them.

3. Parents will go where their needs are being met.

4. Today's parents face extreme fears and insecurities; they need more help in raising their children spiritually than ever before.

Operational Objectives:

1. Train all team members in the use of and value of the take-home materials provided in the curriculum.

2. Train all team members in effective parent communication.

3. Pray for more time between services for a more relaxed check-out period during which parent communication can take place.

4. Develop a hallway-ministry mindset in which someone greets and talks with parents during check-in or check-out times.

5. Conduct regular parent surveys and then publish results and plans to implement suggestions.

6. Share children's ministry success stories with the parents through a parent newsletter or weekly handouts.

Goal 3.3 About any children's ministry class or event, we want the parents to say: "I feel safe leaving my child there."

Rationale:

1. Parents notice the safety of environments.

2. Steps taken to protect the children must be made public through signs, newsletters, etc.

3. Parent complaints regarding safety procedures must be responded to with, "We're doing this to protect your child."

Operational Objectives:

1. Continually update the children's ministry safety policies.

2. Create a parents' handbook with parent versions of the safety policies and procedures.

3. Train all team members in the safety policies and procedures.

4. Design team member identification badges to be worn during ministry times.

5. Create safety signs for walkways and outside doorways.

Vision Category: "Make Disciples"

#4: We will MAKE DISCIPLES by drawing children into the presence of God through dynamic worship.

Goal 4.1 We want to see a growing number of children engaged in worship. We want children to say, "I want to sing to God because I love him."

Rationale:

1. Children can't be expected to follow God if they don't know him.

2. One of the ways of knowing God comes through worshiping him.

3. Children are naturally ready to worship with innocent faith, trust, belief, and love.

4. Adults can be examples of how to worship, but the children need to worship on their own.

5. Use caution with traditional children's songs; pay close attention to the words. Today's child is very sophisticated; however, active songs for little children are precious and important for your young children. Consider some contemporary worship songs, even though they are written for teens and adults, when selecting music for elementary-aged children.

6. Children must be introduced to deep, heart-felt worship, so gradually wean them off of "little kids'" songs and move them into deeper intimacy with God.

7. Children worship more deeply when led into worship with children as worship leaders, and while listening to worship songs sung by children.

Operational Objectives:

1. Recruit adult team members who have an obvi-ous, growing, intimate relationship with God.

2. Train adult team members in the value of worship.

3. Encourage adult team members to worship openly in front of the children.

4. Develop a library of children's worship music that incorporates children's voices in worship.

5. Develop a library of live worship music (the same that the adults worship with).

6. Invite children to lead worship in front of the other children as a worship team.

7. Encourage the children to focus on the Lord even if they don't know the words to the songs yet.

8. Develop an adult worship leader who encourages the worship by focusing the children's thoughts on God as the songs are sung.

Goal 4.2 We want the parents to say: "My child sings these songs at home. Where can I buy the music?"

Rationale:

1. The true sign of children being drawn into deeper intimacy with God is their conversations and actions at home.

2. If a song follows the children home, it is firmly and permanently planted in their hearts.

3. Parents want to invest in their children's spiritual growth. Music is an excellent investment.

4. A song's presence in the child's memory will have an effect on the child's personal relationship with God.

Operational Objectives:

1. Make the music you use in children's worship available to the parents (a list of CD's, actual CD's for sale, or CD giveaways as prizes).

2. Sing the same basic library of songs from week to week. Introduce new songs slowly, only after the children know the basic library.

3. When new songs are introduced, display the words only for the first few times, then let the children sing the song without the words displayed.

4. Encourage the children to focus on the Lord, not on the words.

Emily's Prayer

One of the most beautiful examples of the significant effects of a prayer-focus in our ministry came over a period of several months, and it involved one 4th grade girl. My assistant was teaching a lesson in children's church on the power of prayer and how to pray as the beginning of a series of lessons. As she asked for children to express their needs for prayer, a girl named Emily raised her hand. Little did we know that that simple, child-like act of raising her hand would begin a series of events that would transform Emily's life.

Emily stood to tell her need for God's help with bullies at school who were making fun of her. We had other children encircle her, lay their hands on her, and pray for God to protect her from the hurtful abuses of others. Emily came back the next week glowing as if she had been on the mountain with Moses! She stood and told the rest of the children that nobody picked on her during the whole week! She was bouncing with joy! The whole room applauded! God had proved his personal care for her. This was only the beginning of Emily's encounters with the caring Father.

At the end of that series on prayer, my assistant taught the children the value of keeping a record of their prayers in a prayer journal. We passed out prayer journals to nearly 250 children with the challenge to write their prayers down and then highlight the answered prayers with a highlighter. For months the children brought their prayer journals to children's church excitedly, wanting to show us the highlighted prayers. Then Emily brought hers.

Emily's prayer journal was full of prayers. She meticulously wrote down the exact words and then signed each prayer with the words, "Your daughter, Emily." She hadn't highlighted any prayers, so my assistant asked her if any of them had been answered. Emily said that she knew many of them had been answered, but she didn't have time to highlight them. My assistant laid aside the lesson while she called Emily up to the front and went through the journal one prayer at a time. After reading each prayer, she stopped and asked Emily, "Did God answer this one?" At first Emily's responses were a simple "yes," but as the time went on, she grew more and more excited. The children witnessed a significant moment in Emily's life as she realized that EVERY prayer had been answered. We were in tears as the lesson for the morning was taught by God himself!

The little girl who once asked God for help with bullies as her first introduction to personal prayer was now a prayer warrior! Any time we have prayer times now, there is Emily right in the middle. God knows what he's building in her, but for now all we can do is pray.

#5: We will MAKE DISCIPLES by teaching children how to pray and providing opportunities for them to experience God's presence and provision.

Goal 5.1 We want the children to say: "Praying is fun!"

Rationale:

1. "Fun" is anything that causes pleasure.

2. Pleasing the Lord is the greatest fun possible.

3. Children need to learn the fun of praying.

4. Prayer is not just talking with God, it is being with God, and hearing from him.

5. Once children get a taste of the power and fun of prayer, they will want more.

Operational Objectives:

1. Teach the children how to pray.

2. Teach the children that prayer is not just a list of "Give me" requests, it is talking and spending time with God.

3. Lead the children to appreciate the power of prayer by encouraging them to create Prayer Journals in which they record their prayer requests and then the answers.

4. Provide time for the children to share their answered prayers (Prayer Journals) with the other children.

Goal 5.2 We want the children to become involved

in the prayer needs of others so people will say: "These children are praying for each other without being told to do so!"

Rationale:

1. The highest level of learning is when a lesson becomes a natural part of a person's life.

2. If the children only pray at church, or when they are told to, we've only created prayer robots.

3. If a child stays in the "all about me" phase of prayer, he or she is not advancing toward maturity.

4. God will bless those who care for the needs of others.

Operational Objectives:

1. Provide time for the children to express prayer needs to the rest of the group, and then encourage the children to pray for those children and their needs (lay hands on the child to focus attention).

2. Adults on the team will be examples of praying for others as they stop the lesson whenever a prayer need is mentioned, and pray for that child.

3. Create prayer partners within the children's ministry (adults to children, children to children).

4. Publicize church-wide prayer needs and ask the children to pray for the people (protect anonymity).

5. Publicly reinforce and compliment those children who are praying for others (caution: don't encourage the child's motivation to get recognition from people!).

#6: We will MAKE DISCIPLES by teaching children the truths contained in the Word of God, and by providing opportunities for them to explore these truths for themselves.

Goal 6.1 We want the supervisors and teachers on our children's ministry team to say: "I enjoy learning right along with the children."

Rationale:

1. Our own personal times with the Lord will make our times with the children fresh and real, not packaged.

2. No one likes to feel stagnant.

Operational Objectives:

1. Develop regular communications with the entire team (email, newsletters, taped messages, etc.).

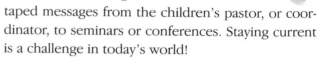

2. Develop team member mailboxes.

3. Develop on-going training and enrichment available to all team members. These will range from taped messages from the children's pastor, or coordinator, to seminars or conferences. Staying current is a challenge in today's world!

Goal 6.2 We want the Lord to say: "Because you are faithful in the small things, I will lead you to large things."

Rationale:

1. We have been placed in the "mother lode" of ministry potential (the children).

2. Our community is growing, strong, and wanting help in the tasks of life.

3. Our job is to be faithful in the small things (tens) and then watch God give us the big things (hundreds or thousands of children each week).

Operational Objectives:

1. Don't plan new bigger programs unless the ones you are currently running are healthy.

2. Focus on the specific children's needs of your community, and do your best with what you have to care for those needs as much as possible.

3. Teach the children how to discern right from wrong instead of just saying, "Don't do that."

4. Create role play situations in which the children must choose the choice that pleases God.

5. Encourage those children who are making godly choices (awards, articles in the newspaper, etc.).

Vision Category: "Baptizing Them"

#7: We will develop a process of child evangelism which leads children to salvation, BAPTIZING THEM into Jesus Christ.

Goal 7.1 We want the supervisors and teachers on our children's ministry team to say: "I cherish the process of preparing, planting, watering, and harvesting."

Rationale:

1. Teachers minister to a wide range of children. It is impossible for a printed lesson to deal with all of

the levels of spiritual growth in your class. Personal prayer for sensitivity is vital.

2. As our ministry grows, the class sizes may fluctuate from small to too big. Remember that the farmer threw seeds out and trusted God to cause the growth. We must all pray for his Spirit to work with us!

3. Personal attention is the greatest fertilizer to growth.

Operational Objectives:

1. Train all team members in the process of evangelism and leading a child to the Lord.

2. Design spiritual growth classes to help children grow in the basics of their Christian life.

3. Create a conversion and baptism class for parents and children.

4. Communicate the process of leading a child to the Lord to the parents.

5. Teach the significance of baptism to the team members, children, and parents.

Vision Category: "Teaching Them"

#8: We will train our team members in effective TEACHING methods based on the interests and needs of today's children.

Goal 8.1 When they leave an event, we want the children of our ministry to say: "I can't wait to come back again."

Rationale:

1. Children will not return to a boring or insulting environment (even if they are physically there).

2. Today's children are surrounded with fun, exciting, fast-moving environments. The Church needs to get with it!

3. Children like to experience things—they don't like to only hear about them!

Operational Objectives:

1. Create fun events on Sunday morning to surprise the children both in and out of the classroom (recruit someone for this area).

2. Train all team members in the use of and value of outside activities, and how to use the facilities we have.

3. Train all team members regarding the dangers of joking with children.

4. Train all team members to recognize signs of embarrassment or withdrawal in children.

Goal 8.2 We want the supervisors and teachers on our children's ministry team to say: "I feel supported and appreciated here."

Rationale:

1. Whether you are a greeter, teacher, or coordinator, you need to be given the right environment in which to serve.

2. Team-wide commitment and faithfulness will produce a healthy environment.

3. The right people using the right tools and supplies produces the right environment.

4. We all like cards, calls, and hugs. There can never be too many!

Operational Objectives:

1. Develop a plan for regular team appreciation events.

2. Continue to develop email communication.

3. Send coordinators to other churches and conferences to learn techniques in team development.

4. Create area team fun events (bowling, pot lucks, variety shows, etc.).

Goal 8.3 We want the supervisors and teachers on our children's ministry team to say: "I want to try new approaches to learning."

Rationale:

1. Every teacher needs to add personal touches to the lesson experience. These additions to the curriculum don't need to be approved unless they are major variations of the lesson topic, or activities that might be unsafe or risky.

2. Team members need to share success stories with each other. These will be done via email or during ministry team rallies.

3. People like to feel like they are advancing in their abilities.

4. Trying new things is risky. A healthy all-team mentality of "Try It" with no fear of criticism if things don't work out as planned, is good.

Operational Objectives:

1. Develop a rotational plan for sending team members to local children's ministry conferences.

2. Let team members, who supplement the curriculum successfully share their techniques during area meetings (or even during all-team meetings).

3. Highlight team members who "Try It" in the newsletters, emails, etc.

4. Provide subscriptions to children's ministry magazines for team leaders.

#9: We will TEACH THEM with relevant curriculum which emphasizes both biblical content and fun!

Goal 9.1 Before they come to an event, we want the children of our ministry to say: "I want to go there because it's fun."

Rationale:

1. Nobody likes to sit and listen to a lecture.

2. Children need activity and challenges.

Operational Objectives:

1. Make CDs and tapes of music, game books, dramas, stories, and object lesson books available to your teachers in a Resource Lending Library.

2. Train all team members in supplementing the curriculum, in activity-based education, and in how to evaluate the curriculum based on activity and application.

3. Train all team members in classroom management.

4. Do all you can to reduce class size or increase times of interaction and "guided conversation."

5. Train the teachers in the teaching methods of Jesus, and help them model his style.

Goal 9.2 Before they come to an event, we want the children of our ministry to say: "I want to go there because I learn more about God there."

Rationale:

1. Children will recognize their need for God only after we show them how important he is to us. Their desire to learn grows with ours.

2. A teacher is one who teaches something he or she believes in, or lives.

3. The best way to teach children is through natural, informal conversations.

Operational Objectives:

1. Place priority on resources and personnel for Sunday programming.

2. Encourage Scripture memorization among the team and the children.

3. Develop ministry team mid-week Bible studies or fellowships.

4. Train all team members in the use of personal daily experiences to enhance the curriculum and lesson.

5. Train all team members in small group discussion strategies that communicate to the children the teacher's own deep, personal relationship with Jesus Christ.

6. Train all team members in the value of informal conversations, guided conversations, and other teaching techniques that make the lesson come alive for the children.

#10: We will establish a variety of child-targeted programs that TEACH THEM how to apply the truths of God's Word in their daily lives.

Goal 10.1 When a parent asks a child, "What did you learn today at church?" we want the child to say: "I learned how to be a better friend," or "I learned how to be a better student," etc.

Rationale:

1. Bible stories are filled with powerful lessons for children, but they have to be "mined" by adults who know the world of the child and who can translate God's Word into the children's world and situations.

2. Children's ministry must never become a place for good, moral lessons apart from the Bible.

3. God's Word is living and active and very valuable to the children of every generation.

Operational Objectives:

1. Train the adult team members to stay current with the world of today's child by viewing the television programs, web sites, and music videos they enjoy.

2. Train the team members to adapt the curriculum to suit the needs of today's children as they find

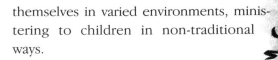

themselves in varied environments, ministering to children in non-traditional ways.

#11: We *will inspire and challenge adult team members to TEACH THEM by becoming role models and by developing significant relationships with the children.*

Goal 11.1 About any children's ministry class or event, we want the parents to say: "I know the teachers care for my child."

Rationale:

1. "Care" means a deep, real, love for children. Class size and class management affect this greatly. Even with large numbers of children, each child should feel cared for.

2. The current condition of children in our community should affect our treatment of the children.

Operational Objectives:

1. Design and print parent letters to be given out on Sunday (topics include parenting, partnering with our ministry, etc.).

2. Train all team members in classroom management.

3. Do all we can to reduce class size or increase the number of team members per children.

4. Train all team members in the application of the results of the parent survey.

Goal 11.2 We want the supervisors and teachers on our children's ministry team to say: "I want to connect with the children beyond the classroom."

Rationale:

1. Involvement with the children outside the classroom is vitally important and effective!

2. Policies and procedures for such involvement will determine the team's preparation for this activity.

3. Team members' attendance at soccer games, recitals, etc. needs no permission or policies.

4. Children love it when adults surprise them with their support outside of church functions.

Operational Objectives:

1. Publicize children's involvement in nonchurch events to the area team members (recruit a volunteer "child-event snoop" for each department).

2. Encourage team members who successfully engage children outside the classroom to share those stories during team meetings.

#12: We *will support the parents in TEACHING their own children through printed materials, seminars, and conferences.*

Goal 12.1 About any children's ministry class or event, we want the parents to say: "I feel like my church is a partner with me in raising my child."

Rationale:

1. In the rush of check-in and check-out, we must greet the parents and make them feel valued.

2. We must view the lesson as a continuing story at home.

3. We must provide parents with assistance in raising their own children in the Lord.

Operational Objectives:

1. Train all team members in parent communication.

2. Provide all team members with a list of creative parent-loving techniques to use during check-out.

3. Create enhanced take-home family application activities for each lesson (recruit a volunteer for each department for this).

Goal 12.2 When the parents think about our support of them, we want the parents to say: "The children's ministry gives us valuable tools in raising our children."

Rationale:

1. Today's parents are busy, confused, and frightened of the world that their children will grow up in.

2. God's Word offers stability, security, and hope to today's parents.

3. The children's ministry must provide parents with real help from God's Word.

Operational Objectives:

1. Provide parent resources (both free and at a minimal cost) at a central location at church.

2. Provide parent classes on specific topics throughout the year. (Sunday mornings are best.)

3. Provide a parent newsletter with articles, stories, testimonies, etc.

4. Provide a parent support component to the church's web site (news items, community events, studies, networking, etc.).

Goal 12.3 We want the supervisors and teachers on our children's ministry team to say: "I enjoy being a partner with the home."

Rationale:

1. Parents need support and help today. If we can influence and support the parents, we can double the influence on the children!

2. Phone calls to the children's home or personal notes and letters draw the parents closer and closer.

Operational Objectives:

1. Encourage team members who do successfully communicate with the home to share those stories during team meetings.

2. Provide team members with note cards printed with the children's ministry logo to be used for parent communication.

Vision Category: "To Obey"

#13: We will teach children TO OBEY the commands of God by participating in supervised service projects.

Goal 13.1 When offered an opportunity to become involved with a service project, we want the children to say: "I want to help others."

Rationale:

1. Involvement in service projects is the greatest way to grow spiritually and emotionally.

2. Children in today's "me first" world need to be directly challenged to serve others.

3. Once children experience the deep joy of helping others, they will want more.

4. Serving others opens the doors for further interest in God's Word.

Operational Objectives:

1. Design a "scope and sequence" for developing a servant's heart in children from the nursery to the sixth grade.

2. Design a service project calendar with projects available for each age group or department.

3. Plan a service project cycle into your curriculum:

Prepare for the project, do the project, debrief from the project.

4. Involve parents and children in the planning of the projects.

5. Publicize the projects beforehand, and share the results afterward.

#14: We will teach children TO OBEY Jesus' command to be "salt" and "light" to others through their words, actions, and choices.

Goal 14.1 We want the church pastoral staff to think or say: "The children's ministry inspires me."

Rationale:

1. The church needs inspirational team spirit and pride!

2. We serve an awesome God by doing an awesome task.

3. The children's ministry is the foundation for the health of the entire church!

4. Our unity and faithfulness will inspire others.

5. We must always ask, "What can we do for you?" What we do in our children's ministry can greatly assist the other ministries.

6. There will come a time when the children's ministry needs support (emergency personnel help, etc.) from other ministries.

7. The Body of Christ works together, not separately.

Operational Objectives:

1. Create a pastor appreciation day during which the children's ministry team brings notes, cards, etc. to the pastors.

2. Be more intentional in sharing, among the pastoral staff, the work the Lord is doing in building the children's ministry team.

3. Always invite the other pastors to children's ministry events. If they come, celebrate their presence publicly.

4. Schedule meetings with each ministry to explore ways to increase the support and teamwork from the children's ministry.

5. Encourage area teams to adopt another ministry for prayer and support similar to the treatment a missionary might receive.

Goal 14.2 When asked, "Do your friends at school know you're a Christian?" we want the children say: "I am not ashamed to take a stand for God at school."

Rationale:

1. Children find it easy to be different people at school than they are at church. We need to encourage, and teach by example, the power of faithful consistency.

2. God's people are too quiet. We need to teach the children how to speak up for God's standards without being obnoxious or weird.

3. Sometimes the greatest inspiration for growth is persecution.

4. The greatest deterrent to growth is complacency or apathy.

Operational Objectives:

1. Weekly compliment and publicly support those children who are taking a stand at school.

2. Teach the children how to be truthful, honest, and righteous without being offensive.

3. Train the children in lifestyle evangelism through role plays.

#15: We will expect the children TO OBEY Jesus' Great Commission by volunteering to help in the children's ministry.

Goal 15.1 When asked to help a fellow child, we want children to say: "I like to help."

Rationale:

1. Children need to learn that serving in the church is part of growing as a Christian.

2. Cross-age ministry is good for all involved.

3. When a child serves, he or she learns.

4. Serving other children can be a habit that is taught beginning in the nursery department.

Operational Objectives:

1. Create a "scope and sequence" for church service that begins in the nursery.

2. Create a multi-age service plan for children in the elementary grades.

3. Publicly support and compliment those children who help other children.

## chapter 8

Putting Up Fences:
Personnel Policies and Procedures

A wise gardener knows how to protect the garden he has worked so hard to create. Knowing the threats to your garden ahead of time will give you an advantage when those threats do come.

We take precautions for all sorts of things these days. We give our children cell phones "just in case." We teach our preschoolers how to recognize bad people, and how to get help if needed. We install smoke detectors in just about every room of our houses. Fast food companies print warnings on cups of coffee to try to prevent any lawsuits from people who are burned from spills. We are even discouraging our youth from helping others along the freeway because of the risk of being killed by those who may pretend to be in trouble. This world is not getting safer. It is becoming more and more complex and dangerous.

Today, when we think about child safety, we must also think about protecting our children's ministry from lawsuits. Recently, one of our nursery rooms was used by a theater production team as a dressing room. The next morning, I did a walk-through of the room to inspect it prior to the day's use as a room for our "MinistryCare" (childcare for a mid-week Bible study) program. As I inspected the floor, I found several small safety pins lying opened on the floor. Having had some experience with theater, I knew that safety pins were a vital tool in costuming. I wasn't surprised to find them on the floor. I began picking them up and throwing them away. As I did this, I thought about how dangerous these opened pins could be to a child who might pick one up, crawl on one, or put one in his mouth. My very next thought was, "If a child got hurt by one of these, we would be sued." I then struggled with deciding what was my motive for picking up the pins. Was it because I cared for

children, or was it because I didn't want to be sued? I came to the conclusion that it was both. I care for children, and I care for the children's ministry at this church. The children's ministry could be damaged by a lawsuit. If the children's ministry is damaged, hundreds of children could be negatively affected. I continued to pick up the pins and asked God to sort out my motives.

The enemy comes to your ministry garden in many forms. He could take the form of poor planning, disorganization, faulty procedures, lack of training, errors in recruiting or in screening team members, poor supervision of children, or poor supervision of team members. It is against these threats that we must erect fences around our ministry garden.

THE VALUE AND FUNCTION OF POLICIES

I like to compare the policies to the fire blocks in your walls. Behind the drywall on your walls are vertical wood boards stretching from the floor to the ceiling. These are called studs. These studs are placed about sixteen to twenty inches apart. Between the studs are horizontal wood boards. These are called "fire blocks." There are one or two of these fire blocks between every stud. I used to think that these horizontal wood boards were just places to climb up the wall, like a ladder, for the construction guys. I was wrong. These fire blocks are critical pieces of equipment that are designed for a specific purpose. Their placement in the walls is governed by the local building codes. They are designed to slow down the fire in the wall if the

The Church Policy House

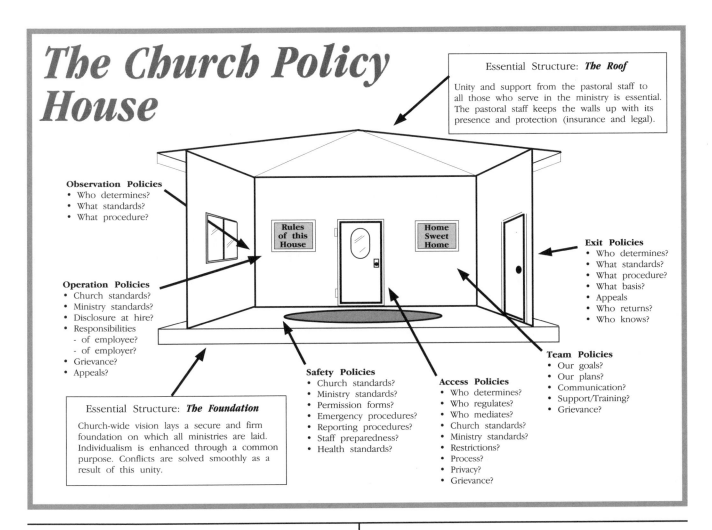

Essential Structure: *The Roof*

Unity and support from the pastoral staff to all those who serve in the ministry is essential. The pastoral staff keeps the walls up with its presence and protection (insurance and legal).

Observation Policies
- Who determines?
- What standards?
- What procedure?

Operation Policies
- Church standards?
- Ministry standards?
- Disclosure at hire?
- Responsibilities
  - of employee?
  - of employer?
- Grievance?
- Appeals?

Essential Structure: *The Foundation*

Church-wide vision lays a secure and firm foundation on which all ministries are laid. Individualism is enhanced through a common purpose. Conflicts are solved smoothly as a result of this unity.

Rules of this House

Home Sweet Home

Exit Policies
- Who determines?
- What standards?
- What procedure?
- What basis?
- Appeals
- Who returns?
- Who knows?

Team Policies
- Our goals?
- Our plans?
- Communication?
- Support/Training?
- Grievance?

Safety Policies
- Church standards?
- Ministry standards?
- Permission forms?
- Emergency procedures?
- Reporting procedures?
- Staff preparedness?
- Health standards?

Access Policies
- Who determines?
- Who regulates?
- Who mediates?
- Church standards?
- Ministry standards?
- Restrictions?
- Process?
- Privacy?
- Grievance?

house is on fire. I can hear you say, "What's he talking about? I thought this was a chapter on policies?" Stay with me, this will help you understand the purpose of policies.

Fires generally begin low, near the floor. They begin with a cigarette tossed in a trash can, a spark at an outlet, or a child playing with matches. As the fire burns up the wall, it burns up alongside the studs inside the wall. If there's nothing stopping the flames, they go right up to the ceiling and on to the roof. Any firefighter will tell you that once the roof is on fire, the structure is doomed. If we can slow the fire's travel up to the roof, firefighters have more time to save the building. Fire blocks are placed between the studs to slow the fire down. The flames stop at the fire blocks and have to burn through the block before they resume their travel up the studs toward the roof. The local building department determines if the wall should burn ten minutes, fourteen minutes, etc. The more fire blocks placed in the wall, the longer the wall will burn before the roof catches fire.

Now, with that lesson in construction completed, let me tell you that your ministry policies are designed to slow the "fire" of a lawsuit as it burns up the church administrative structure. If you think of a fire as an accusation of neglect or abuse, the wall as being your church staff, and the roof as being your senior pastor or church corporate charter, this analogy will make sense. Most fires (legal problems, accusations, etc.) start low on the church wall: in the children's area. Fewer lawsuits have been filed related to the youth or adult ministries compared with those related to the children's area. If someone accuses one of your team members of touching a child inappropriately, the fire that is started by that lawsuit can climb up the wall quickly. The courts will ask questions about supervision and policies. If you have no fire blocks in the wall, the fire can burn up to you, the children's pastor, and on to the senior pastor or church charter. Churches have been shut down as a result of lawsuits that began as a fire in the children's ministry. A policy can act as a fire block. It can slow the fire down as it burns up the corporate wall.

A policy slows the fire down by providing tangible support to your intent. Here's an example. One of your three year olds goes home and says something about one of your team members touching her that makes her parents concerned. The parents jump to conclusions and file a lawsuit against your church for sexual abuse. The fire begins to burn up the wall. In the course of the investigation, the court discovers that your policy manual states, "At no time will any adult be alone with children." Upon further investigation, it is discovered that the three year old teacher was alone in the classroom because of some last minute cancellations by other team members (does this sound familiar?). You were working on the problem, but this incident happened before you could get another adult shifted over to the three year old classroom. The judge may be forgiving or lenient with you because of your "never alone" policy! If the child's story or the parent's accusation is not substantiated, the fact that you had a policy that was designed to protect the children is a definite fire block in your corporate wall! Without that policy, you and your entire administrative wall might be judged as negligent, or even supportive, of the alleged abuse! A policy expresses your intent, and thereby may protect you from harm even if you fail to abide by the policy temporarily.

HOW TO WRITE POLICIES

Writing policies is not that difficult. The hardest part of writing policies is clarifying what you want, or don't want, to happen. I'll help you with that. Then, after you've defined your boundaries, you can write some basic policies. Don't worry about the words at this point. Your feelings, views, and opinions of what needs to happen, or not happen, are the most important thing at this point. You will get help from elders or an attorney for the final crafting of the legal words later. Here are some basic questions to ask as you begin writing policies

Basic Policy Questions

• Identify your enemy—What do you want to prevent from happening?

• Identify the earliest point of contact—Where can you perform your greatest level of prevention?

• What process is needed?—In order to prevent the problem, what needs to be done?

• What happens if the problem occurs?—What is the process to deal with the problem?

• What happens afterward?—What forms of communication, reporting, follow-up, etc. are needed?

• What legal boundaries are present?—What laws pertain to this area?

Keep in mind that a policy is a document that is constantly in revision. You must start somewhere, but the words or processes you put into place in the beginning need to grow and improve as you become more experienced and as the society and the ministry grow.

Know Where to Place Your Policies

Obviously, you can write policies for everything! You can be so afraid of being sued that you even have a policy for behavior at a drinking fountain! Have you ever been involved with people or companies that have a policy for everything? It's terrible. That level of paranoia drives people away. Jesus knew that we would be involved with people who would misunderstand and judge us. He told his disciples: "I am sending you out like sheep among wolves. Therefore be as shrewd as snakes and as innocent as doves" (Matthew 10:16).

When he said to be shrewd while, at the same time, being innocent, he meant that we are to be careful, watchful, and have pure motives. I believe there are critical areas for which to create policies, and the rest has to be given to the Lord. We need to be wise without being paranoid. The "Policy House" on page 111 might help you know where to place your children's ministry policies.

This chapter is focused on policies regarding personnel only. Policies concerning personnel issues comprise the largest block of policies in ministry. We will not deal with policies about child sickness, or other non-personnel policies here. Those will be dealt with in the next chapter. I have to tell you, though, that separating the policies this way is like trying to pull apart a peanut butter and jelly sandwich after it has already been put together. The team members and their actions affect everything in your children's ministry. For the sake of chapter length, I'll do the best I can to separate the peanut butter and jelly.

Nine Categories of Personnel Policies

1. *Recruitment*
What kind of person is recruited to the children's ministry team?

2. *Screening*
What is the team member screening process?

3. *Training*
How are the team members prepared to be with children?

4. *Supervision*
Who supervises the team members while they are with the children?

5. *Access*
How is access to the children protected and restricted?

6. *Removal From Ministry*
How is a person removed from the team, and why?

7. *Reinstatement to Ministry*
Can a removed team member ever return to the team? How?

8. *Touching*
What is the correct way for team members to touch children?

9. *Discipline*
What is the correct way for team members to discipline children?

The Five Step Policy Creation Process

The remainder of this chapter will focus on a five-step process designed to assist you in writing your own personnel policies. At the fourth step, you will be given an example of a policy dealing with that category. In the template, I have written in a "General Belief Statement." There is nothing holy about my words. They are simply a starting point for your own thoughts. Feel free to change those statements to reflect your own church's views, if needed.

Five Steps to Writing a Policy
1. Define the policy.
2. Understand the rationale for the policy.
3. Evaluate your current policy.
4. Consult sample policies from other churches.
5. Work through the "Policy Template" as you tailor the necessary components of each policy to your own church.

Category 1: The "Recruitment Policy"
Definition. A policy for governing the recruiting of people to the children's ministry team.

Rationale. To recruit the people with the character, spirit, and other qualities that match the ministry vision is much easier than dealing with their differences after they are already on the team.

Evaluation. Does your policy regarding the recruiting process protect your team and children from those who would be harmful to the team or to the children? Is it clear that you are seeking a certain kind of person with a certain "heart attitude" or spiritual character?

Sample "Recruitment Policy"

It is the policy of our children's ministry to recruit "those whose hearts are fully committed to him" *(2 Chronicles 16:9)*. We will look for adults who have attended our church for at least six months, and whose relationship with God is growing as evidenced by the responses given on the Children's Ministry Application and the personal references submitted. The people who are invited to serve on the children's ministry team must have been Christians for longer than one year. We will place new team members into areas of service based on the results of the Personality Inventory.

The "Recruitment Policy" Template

General Belief Statement: We believe that those who serve in the children's ministry must be committed Christians whose personal relationship with Jesus Christ is growing and intimate. The fruit of that relationship must be visible in the form of love, joy, peace, patience, kindness, goodness, faithfulness, gentleness, and self-control. We believe people are most effective if they are placed in service areas which match their personality and gifts.

1. How long should a person be a Christian before serving in the children's ministry?

2. Is membership in your church required for those who wish to serve in the children's ministry?

3. Do you require at least six months of fellowship at your church prior to applying? (The "six months" rule is advised by nearly all who deal with the process of screening children's ministry personnel. A child abuser is less likely to wait for six months to gain access to your children!)

4. Is there a certain age limit for those who wish to serve in the children's ministry?

5. Are there any other conditions that pertain to those who wish to serve in the children's ministry?

Category 2: The "Screening Policy"

Definition. The process through which all children's ministry team applicants must pass.

Rationale. The screening process is designed to be a "front door" for all applicants. It will be a deterrent to child abusers or others who may not fit the ministry vision.

Evaluation. Does your policy regarding the screening process protect your children from those who would be harmful to the children? Does the process contain multiple steps, or layers, through which all who wish to join the team must pass?

Sample "Screening Policy"

All who serve in our children's ministry will pass through our application process which includes:

1. The application form (See pages 127-130.)

2. Four personal references (one from a church member)

3. Six months attendance or membership at this church

4. Attendance the "Children's Ministry Introduction" class

5. Background check with law enforcement agency

6. Signing the "Agreement to Serve" (See page 131.)

If the applicant refuses to complete any of the components of the application process, the application will be denied and access to children, on the part of the applicant, will not be permitted.

If the information received during the application process is deemed questionable by those who review the results, the application will be denied and access to children will not be permitted. The senior associate pastor or senior pastor may be consulted by the children's pastor for counsel regarding an application.

We will accept applications from people who are 16 years old and older. People younger than 18 will be considered teens and must be teamed with adults in service.

Teens (12 to 15 years old) who wish to serve in the children's ministry must enter the children's ministry team through the youth-in-ministry supervision process within the youth ministry.

The "Screening Policy" Template

General Belief Statement: We believe that protecting the safety of children is our highest responsibility (equal to their spiritual development). We believe we must protect the trust the parents give us to nurture their children while not permitting any harm to come to them. We believe that those adults who serve in the children's ministry have a significant potential to do good or harm in the children's lives. We will do all we can to screen out those who may desire to do harm.

1. Do you require an application for those who wish to serve in the children's ministry?

2. Do you require personal references for those who wish to serve in the children's ministry?

3. Do you support the "six months rule" for those who wish to serve in the children's ministry?

4. Do you require background checks for those who wish to serve in the children's ministry?

5. Do you require that fingerprints be taken and checked for those who wish to serve in the children's ministry?

6. Do you require that those who serve in the children's ministry sign an "Agreement to Serve" clarifying their responsibilities and your expectations?

7. Do you require that those who serve in the children's ministry sign a statement that they have read, and agree with, your ministry policies?

8. Do you require an apprenticeship period, which is a supervised probationary period as well as a training period, for those who wish to serve in the children's ministry?

9. Are there any other steps in the screening process that your church will require for those who wish to serve in the children's ministry?

Category 3: The "Training Policy"

Definition. The process by which team members are prepared and equipped to fulfill the ministry vision.

Rationale. People are attracted to those areas for which they feel qualified and supported. We will recruit people with good hearts, and then give them the tools they need to succeed. This policy states our plans and resolve to do so.

Evaluation. Does your policy regarding the training process provide those who volunteer with enough support and guidance to guarantee that they will be secure and successful?

Sample "Training Policy"

All who serve in our children's ministry will be required to receive training appropriate for their area of service. We will provide the following training:

1. Age-group characteristics of children
2. Discipline of children
3. Classroom management
4. Lesson presentation
5. Use of curriculum
6. Emergency procedures and reporting
7. Child abuse recognition, prevention, reporting

8. Cleanliness and disease control
9. Parent relations

Opportunities will be made available for specific training in CPR and basic first aid via outside agencies. Training will be accomplished through two required meetings and a mandatory 4 week apprenticeship. The apprenticeship will be served under a mentor for the specific area of service. If, during the apprenticeship, the mentor's concerns are severe enough to question the trainee's suitability for children's ministry service, the mentor will contact the coordinator who will contact the children's pastor. The children's pastor will consult with the trainee, the coordinator, and the mentor to determine the possibility of service. The senior associate pastor, senior pastor, or the children's ministry elder designate may be consulted at the discretion of the children's pastor.

The "Training Policy" Template

General Belief Statement: We believe that people are more successful when they feel equipped to do the task and feel connected to others on the team. We also believe that on-the-job training is the best way to learn.

1. What role does the apprenticeship period play in the screening process?

2. Who supervises the apprenticeship process?

3. Who will be the apprenticeship mentors?

4. How long will the apprenticeships be?

5. What determines if the apprenticeship is successfully completed?

6. What happens if the new team member fails the apprenticeship?

7. Can a failed apprenticeship be repeated?

Category 4: The "Supervision Policy"

Definition. A policy regarding the supervision of team members while children are present.

Rationale. This policy identifies the chain of command for the children's ministry as well as guidelines for adults interacting with children. It is designed to protect the children, team members, administration, and church from accusations of negligence or abuse.

Evaluation. Does your policy regarding the supervision of team members while they are with the children protect the children, you, and the church from any accusations of negligence?

Sample "Supervision Policy"

At no time, will any one who serves in the children's ministry be alone with children. All who serve in the children's ministry will serve as part of a team of at least two adults. It is our desire, whenever possible, to create teams of three or more. The addition of an approved youth assistant to a classroom does not equal the addition of an adult. One adult with one approved youth assistant is still considered an adult alone with the children. This situation must be corrected.

Approved adult/child ratios for children's ministry classes and events will change with each setting. In addition to the "never alone" clause stated above, the children's ministry will work toward the following adult/child ratios:

Nursery—1/3
Toddlers—1/4
Preschool—1/7
Elementary—1/10

If, due to unforeseen circumstances, a team of at least two adults cannot be guaranteed for a children's ministry event or program, the coordinator or supervisor for that event will decide which of the following options are best for the situation, and then act on that situation. The options are:

1. Join the children in two classes or areas to guarantee a team of two or more adults.

2. Borrow adults from the teams in other classes or areas.

3. Do not accept children for this class or area until at least two adults can be placed.

All of these options, by their nature, may not be the best choice for either the church or the children. If options 1 or 2 above cannot be done without raising the adult/child ratios beyond our approved limits, then the only option is to close the class. Considerations must also be given to the maximum occupancy of the room being used. Child safety and church liability must take priority over convenience or programming.

Married couples will be permitted to serve together only when they are joined by a third adult.

The "Supervision Policy" Template

General Belief Statement: We believe in the value of a team. A team, two or more, serving together is good for the children, the ministry, and the team members themselves. A team also protects the children's ministry and the church from false accusations about team member behavior.

1. What do you believe about adults being alone with children?

2. What should be done if a "lone adult" situation arises?

3. Who is responsible for the supervision of team members while in service?

4. Are there any other team members who will supervise other team members?

5. What happens if a team member is doing something wrong?

Category 5: The "Access Policy"

Definition. A policy to restrict access to children while they are under the children's ministry's care.

Rationale. Parents entrust their precious, priceless children into our care, believing that we will do all we can to protect the children from any form of harm. Today's world has many people who would like to harm children. This policy restricts access to the children only to those who have been approved by our screening and application process.

Evaluation. Does your policy regarding the access to the children while in your care protect the children from bad people who might want to harm them? Does the policy protect you and the church from accusations of negligence?

Sample "Access Policy"

No adult will ever be permitted to be with the children except those displaying the children's ministry photo ID badge and lanyard. Those parents who wish to experience the children's ministry with their children will be given guest badges which will be turned in after the service. Team members who lose their ID badges will be permitted to serve with a guest badge until theirs is replaced. All intruders without approved photo ID badges will be viewed as potentially dangerous and will be dealt with seriously by the children's pastor or other children's ministry or church administrators.

The "Access Policy" Template

General Belief Statement: We believe that it is our responsibility to restrict access to the children while they are under our care. We will accomplish this at all costs in support of the parents' trust. Only those who have been cleared through our children's ministry screening process will be granted access to the children.

1. How will you identify children's ministry team members who have been cleared to be with the children?

2. Will others ever be permitted to visit or observe?

3. Under what conditions will non-team members be permitted to visit or observe the children's ministry?

4. Who monitors the access to the children's ministry?

5. Do you restrict access to the children's ministry facility areas?

6. What happens if a cleared team member isn't properly identified (see #1 above)?

7. What is the process for dealing with an intruder who is not cleared for access?

Category 6: The "Removal From Ministry Policy"

Definition. This policy will define the process for removing team members from service.

Rationale. Just as it is critical to determine the process for recruiting and adding people to your ministry team, it is also critical to create a policy for removing them, if needed. In this policy, the rights of the individual in question are balanced against the protection of the children and the team. This policy dictates a process of communication, evaluation, cautions, and rights to appeal. Those who are not supportive of your ministry vision or who may harm children must be removed, but we must do so carefully and in harmony with state and local laws.

Evaluation. Does your policy regarding the removal from ministry of children's ministry team members who may be harmful to the children, your team, or the church clearly state the process required? Does the process protect the children from any harm? Does the process protect you, the children's ministry, and the church from any accusations of wrongful dismissal?

Sample "Removal From Ministry Policy"

It is the desire of the children's ministry that all who serve in the children's ministry be dedicated to that service, and that they take seriously the commitment and related responsibility. We will do all we can to support and equip each team member in the hopes that this will produce a deepening sense of personal dedication. If, however, the children's pastor or the department coordinator have reason to question a team member's commitment, the following steps will be taken to determine the status of the team member's service:

1. The children's pastor and department coordinator will consult together regarding the team member's observed behavior.

2. If the team member's commitment is questionable, the department coordinator will discuss their observations with the team member. The team member will be given an opportunity to explain his or her actions. The department coordinator will reinforce the value of commitment and the correct procedures or policies as well as encouraging the team member. The conversation will be documented on the Children's Ministry Team Member Review Report. A copy of the report will be mailed to the team member and kept on file in the children's ministry office. All personnel reports and forms are considered confidential and are available to only the children's pastor and the coordinator for that specific area. The information may be available to others only at the request of the senior pastor or senior

associate pastor. (If the team member's actions are determined to be physically, emotionally, or spiritually harmful to the children, the team member's service will be immediately terminated. Possible steps for reinstatement will be considered based on the children's ministry "Reinstatement to Ministry" policies.)

3. If the team member's actions or signs of commitment do not change as a result of the meeting with the coordinator, the children's pastor will join with the department coordinator in the next meeting with the team member. At this meeting, the team member will be placed on probation for a period of 3 months. It will be explained to the team member that if his or her signs of lack of commitment don't improve during this probationary period, he or she will be removed from the children's ministry for a period of 1 year. The conversation will be documented on the Children's Ministry Team Member Review Report. A copy of the report will be mailed to the team member and kept on file in the children's ministry office. If the team member wishes to challenge or change the information recorded on the report, he or she must do so in writing within 48 hours. No changes will be made after 48 hours. Copies of this report and any previous reports related to this team member will now be sent to the senior associate pastor.

4. If, after three months of probationary service, the team member's actions fail to indicate an increase in commitment in the area specifically mentioned in the two previous meetings and reports, it will be determined that he or she is unable or unwilling to change. Provisions will be made for replacing him or her immediately. The team member will be removed from service for one year. At the end of that one year period, the team member may apply for reinstatement based on the policies and procedures for "Reinstatement to Ministry" contained in this manual. If, during the probationary period, the team member's actions constitute a direct threat to the unity or health of the entire children's ministry team, the children's pastor, together with the senior associate pastor, and the designated elder, may decide to discontinue the probationary period before its completion and remove the team member from service immediately.

5. If, at any time during this process, the team member wishes to appeal the decisions being made on his or her behalf, he or she may request an audience with an elder designated for the children's ministry. A copy of the Appeals Policy and Process form will be given the team member in preparation for the meeting. Prior to the appeals meeting with the elder designate being scheduled, the team member must sign the statement at the bottom of the Appeals Policy and Process pages stating that he or she has read the policy and agrees to abide by the process. No appeals proceedings will continue without this statement being signed. If the team member refuses to agree to the appeals process, he or she waives his or her right to such an appeal.

6. If a team member is accused of child abuse or neglect, he or she will be removed from service immediately while his or her situation is considered by the designated elder or the legal system. (If the designated elder so desires, the entire elder board may be included in this process.) If a team member's past arrests or convictions for child abuse or neglect are uncovered after he or she begins serving in the children's ministry, he or she will be removed from service immediately while his or her situation is considered by the designated elder or elders. His or her return to service will be governed by the "Reinstatement to Ministry" policies and procedures.

The "Removal From Ministry Policy" Template

General Belief Statement: We believe that only those adults who benefit the children with their presence should serve in the children's ministry. We believe that, if at any time, a team member becomes, in our judgement, a threat to the children or others on the team, that person's involvement in the children's ministry may be at risk.

1. How do you define "being a threat" to the children?

2. How do you define "being a threat" to the other team members?

3. Who decides when a team member is a threat

to the children or other team members?

4. Who confronts the team member with the concern regarding the threat?

5. Do you believe the person should be given a chance to correct the threatening behavior?

6. How much time should the threatening team member be given to correct the behavior?

7. Does the supervision of that team member change during the probation period?

8. What documentation is made of the confrontation and probation of the team member?

9. Does the team member sign the documentation and receive copies?

10. Where is the documentation kept?

11. Who has access to the documentation?

12. How is the team member's right of confidentiality protected?

13. What happens to the documentation if the problem is corrected?

14. What happens if the problem is not corrected?

15. What is the process for removing a team member from service?

16. What are the legal standards for removing a team member from service?

17. Are there any threats for which the team member is removed instantly, with no probation?

18. Is there an appeals process available to the team member?

19. What communication is required with the senior pastor or other church administrators, and when should that communication take place?

20. If parents are involved, what can or can't you tell them about the process?

Category 7: The "Reinstatement to Ministry Policy"

Definition. This policy will define the process by which a removed team member may be reinstated to service.

Rationale. Once a team member is removed from service, he or she may be reinstated if the church or children's ministry administration deem him or her fit for service. This policy clarifies the process by which that reinstatement may occur. It also identifies any conditions for which reinstatement is not possible. At all times, the protection of the children and the unity of the children's ministry team must be the primary focus.

Evaluation. Does your policy regarding the reinstatement to ministry of children's ministry team members who have been removed from service clearly state the process necessary to protect the children from any harm? Does the process guarantee that the reason for the removal is now not present? Does the process guarantee that the reinstated person will be closely supervised? Does the process protect you, the children's ministry, and the church from any accusations of negligence?

Sample "Reinstatement to Ministry Policy"

When faced with the choice between guarding a team member's feelings or reputation and guarding the safety of the children, we will always act in favor of the children's safety. When a team member is removed from service, he or she may be reinstated based on the following policies and procedures:

1. No one who is convicted of child abuse or neglect may ever serve in the children's ministry, or be permitted to have contact with any children in any event connected with the church.

2. Any one who has been FALSELY accused or arrested for child abuse or neglect may apply to be reinstated to service only after all of the following conditions are met:

a. All charges are dropped and the team member's record is cleared by the police department or prosecuting agency.

b. A completed Request for Reinstatement form with attached personal statement of growth and commitment from the team member is given to the designated elder of the church.

c. A meeting occurs between the team member, children's pastor, and the designated elder of the church to discuss the situation and the team member's Request for Reinstatement form. (If the designated elder so desires, the entire elder board may be included in this process.) If, after reviewing the team member's Request for Reinstatement form, the children's pastor or designated elder or elders so decide, a mandatory leave of absence of 6 to 12 months may be required prior to reinstating the team member to service. At the conclusion of such a mandatory leave of absence, the team member may be required, at the children's pastor's or designated elder's discretion, to submit an updated Request for Reinstatement. Prior to being reinstated, the team member must meet with the children's pastor and designated elder. If, after reviewing the team member's situation, the children's pastor, or designated elder or elders decide that reinstating the team member may place the children or children's ministry at risk, they may choose to refuse to reinstate the team member to service in the children's ministry. The team member may or may not be invited to become involved in service in other areas of the church.

3. Any one who has been removed from service in the children's ministry based on an apparent lack of commitment or dedication to the children's ministry may apply for reinstatement only after all of the following conditions have been met:

a. The completion of the mandatory 1 year leave of absence.

b. A completed Request for Reinstatement form with attached personal statement of growth and commitment from the team member is returned to the children's pastor for review.

c. A meeting occurs between the team member, the department coordinator, and children's pastor to review Request for Reinstatement. This can only take place after the completion of the mandatory 1 year leave of absence.

d. If it is determined by the children's pastor and the department coordinator to reinstate the team member, the team member will be placed on a 3 month probationary period. During this period, the team member's actions, which would indicate improvement in commitment or dedication to the children's ministry, will be evaluated.

e. If, after the 3 month probationary period, the team member's commitment or dedication is no longer in question, the team member must meet with the department coordinator and the children's pastor to discuss what was learned during the reinstatement process. After this meeting, the team member will be returned to full, non-probationary status and will be given equal support and encouragement as other team members.

f. If, during the 3 month probationary period, the team member's commitment or dedication is still in question, the team member will be removed from service immediately and permanently. The team member may never re-apply to be reinstated to any service in the children's ministry.

The "Reinstatement to Ministry Policy" Template

General Belief Statement: We believe the Bible clearly teaches that we have a responsibility to offer forgiveness to a brother or sister who is repentant. We also believe that God has commanded us to be shepherds of the children in our ministry. In the case of a team member who has been removed from service, we are willing to reinstate him or her only under certain conditions.

1. Are there any situations for which a team member has been removed that warrant a non-reinstatement policy?

2. After removal from ministry, how long must a team member wait before applying for reinstatement?

3. How can you be sure the team member has corrected the problem?

4. What is the process for applying for reinstatement?

5. What communications are made to the senior pastor or other church administrators in considering the reinstatement application?

6. Who supervises the reinstatement process?

7. Will there be another probation period?

8. How long will the reinstated team member be on probation?

9. What will you tell the other team members who

serve with the team member during the probation period?

10. If the probation period proves that the problem is corrected, what happens to the documentation of the original situation?

11. What happens if the probation period proves that the problem is not corrected?

Category 8: The "Touching Policy"

Definition. This policy defines appropriate and inappropriate touch, and also clarifies the consequences of the inappropriate touching of children.

Rationale. Children of this impersonal world of today need to be touched. This policy clearly describes appropriate and inappropriate touching. Unless we describe both in detail, we cannot expect the team members to know the difference. Unless we train and communicate the team members in the appropriate forms of touch, we cannot correct those who touch inappropriately.

Evaluation. Does your policy regarding touching allow for appropriate touch? Does your policy define what is appropriate and inappropriate touching? Does it explain the difference clearly? Does the policy define the necessary training to explain the policy and to help teachers and leaders know how to express God's love through appropriate touch?

Sample "Touching Policy"

It is the policy of the children's ministry to train those who serve on the children's ministry in the appropriate forms of touching children, and then to encourage the team members to use the "tool" of touch freely in developing relationships with children. We believe that touching children appropriately will further the Gospel by increasing the ministry to the children. We also believe that inappropriate touching can severely damage the child and thereby impede the spread of the Gospel in that child's life for many years. We also believe that those who willfully touch children inappropriately, or permit children to be touched inappropriately, will face judgement from God, as it states in *Matthew 18:6-8*: "But if anyone causes one of these little ones who believe in me to sin, it would be better for him to have a large mill-stone hung around his neck and to be drowned in the depths of the sea. Woe to the world because of the things that cause people to sin!...woe to the man through whom they come!"

Appropriate touching is any touching that occurs on the child's shoulders, arms, hands, back, or head. Inappropriate touching is any touching that occurs in areas that the swimsuit covers. The inappropriate areas are: the chest, buttocks, pelvis, or lower back.

It is also not appropriate for team members to permit children to sit on their laps. The appearance of evil is not healthy for the team member or the children's ministry. If a child climbs up onto the lap of a team member, the team member should briefly hug the child and then either get up and let the child sit on the chair, or ask the child to sit on his or her own chair. The team member should be careful not to jump or otherwise negatively react to the child's innocent desire for closeness. Strong reactions may scare the child or give the child the message that the team member doesn't like him or her.

Other inappropriate touching is:

1. Giving a child a back rub, or massage.

2. Frontal hugging (sideways hugs are appropriate).

3. Tickling a child (inappropriate touching may occur unexpectedly).

4. Kissing a child on any part of the body.

5. Licking a child on any part of the body.

A team member who has been accused of inappropriate touching will be asked to take a break from service while the accusation is investigated. Those involved in the investigation can include the other team members present in the room at the time of the alleged touching, the children's pastor, the senior pastor, and any other assistant administrators who are invited to be a part of the investigation. If, after the investigation, it is determined that the team member did intentionally touch the child inappropriately, he or she will be removed from service. It will be the decision of the investigating members and the senior pastor whether or not a report should be made to the police. A formal apology will be made to the parents of the child. The church attorney should be contacted regarding preparation for any legal proceedings that may be filed by the parents. If, after the investigation, it is determined that the team member did not touch the child inappropriately, he or she will be returned to service as usual.

The "Touching Policy" Template

General Belief Statement: We believe that children today need to be touched. We believe that touch is a God-created way to express love and encouragement. We recognize that touch can also be harmful if done incorrectly or carelessly.

1. What do you define as "good touching"?

2. What do you define as "bad touching"?

3. How will you teach "good touching" to your team members?

4. What is the process for dealing with accusations of "bad touching"?

5. What will happen to the team member who touched a child inappropriately by mistake?

6. What will happen to the team member who touched a child inappropriately on purpose?

7. How will you abide by the law to report child abusers if a team member touched a child inappropriately on purpose?

8. What communications will be made to the senior pastor or other church administrators?

9. What communications will be made to the parents of the child who was touched?

10. How will you document all the facts and conversations regarding the accusations of inappropriate touching by a team member?

11. Who has access to the documentation?

12. Where will the documentation be kept?

Category 9: The "Discipline Policy"

Definition. This policy defines the procedures for managing the learning environment and for controlling the children's behavior in appropriate, child-targeted ways.

Rationale. Today's children are less controlled, and less disciplined than ever before. It is the growing challenge of the children's ministry team members to create a learning environment that attracts the children to the lesson and keeps the children interested through real-life applications and enjoyable experiences that are appropriate to their age group. If this is accomplished, there will be fewer discipline problems. Those discipline problems that do arise must be handled with the emphasis on discipline and not on punishment. The discipline measures must be gentle, yet firm. We must focus on the child needing discipline while not neglecting the other children.

Evaluation. Does your policy regarding the discipline of children protect the children from harm? Does the policy protect you, the children's ministry, and the church from accusations of negligence? Does the policy clearly state the process for dealing with disruptive children through classroom management, building relationships, and positive reinforcement?

Sample "Discipline Policy"

It is our desire to create and preserve environments in which children feel safe, secure, and loved. Because of this goal, we believe we must do all we can to maintain control in every children's ministry class or area.

We believe that children need boundaries which are created and reinforced with gentleness and understanding. We also believe that there will be certain children who need extra attention and encouragement in the area of discipline. It is the focus of our policy to protect the ministry environment while still being sensitive to the needs of each individual child.

We believe there are three critical components to an effective discipline process: the teacher's personal relationship with Jesus, the classroom environment (classroom management), and the treatment of the children. Our discipline policy/procedures will be divided into these three areas.

1. The Teacher's Personal Relationship With Jesus. We believe a person's actions are determined by his or her emotional/spiritual health. Jesus said, "The things that come out of the mouth come from the heart, and these make a man 'unclean.' For out of the heart come evil thoughts" *(Matthew 15:18, 19)*. We believe that, as a person becomes more acquainted with the grace and mercy of Jesus, that person will treat others with more grace and mercy (*Colossians 3:12-17*).

It is the policy of the children's ministry that all those who serve in the children's ministry must attend church services regularly, and be devoted to growing in their own personal relationship to Jesus. This consistent spiritual growth will have a positive effect on the treatment of the children in our ministry.

2. Classroom Management. We believe the classroom environment effects every child in that classroom. A class that is out of control more than likely began that way long before the first child arrived. An effective children's ministry team plans for a controlled, yet enjoyable, classroom environment. The children's lack of discipline problems is simply a result of that planning.

It is our policy that each children's ministry team member accomplish the following:

1. Pray regularly for the children in the class (especially for the challengers).

2. Review the lesson several days before the presentation to become familiar with it and to let the Lord begin to prepare his/her heart.

3. Complete any craft preparation before class time so the children can be the focus of attention when they arrive.

4. Arrive at least 15 minutes before class time so the room and lesson supplies can be arranged.

5. Greet each child as he/she enters. This lays a foundation of love and trust which greatly affects classroom discipline.

6. Be excited about the lesson, the children, and the Lord! Children will mirror our feelings. The more we are into the lesson, the less problems we will have with the children's attitudes as well.

7. Plan for variety in the classroom. Movement, activity changes, the use of audio/visuals, and the use of drama draw the children into the lesson.

8. Give positive rewards to those who behave or participate. Rather than focusing on the problem child, let's focus on the children who are good examples!

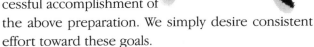

We understand that life isn't always predictable, and that family needs and personal matters may effect the successful accomplishment of the above preparation. We simply desire consistent effort toward these goals.

3. The Treatment of Children. It is our policy that the children who attend our ministry classes or events will leave better than they arrived. It is also our policy not to permit a few children to ruin the learning environment for the rest of the class. The blending of these two policy statements requires a God-given wisdom!

Classroom discipline begins before the children enter the room. The children's ministry team members' and the children's attitudes prior to the class time effect what happens in the class. We cannot control what happens in the children's home before class. We can control how we treat them in class. We must be ready for all actions and reactions.

It is very important to clearly state the rules or standards of the class. Most children want to do what is right. If we do not tell them what we expect, we cannot expect them to do what we want. If we have clearly told them what we expect, and they fail to do it, we can assume it is a choice on their part (unless they are too young to make such a choice). The following is a brief description of our discipline policy/process:

1. Make every child feel loved and welcome. This happens as soon as they enter the classroom. Eye-contact and smiles work wonders!

2. Clearly state expectations. Make sure directions and expectations are clear and understood. Speak slowly and friendly. Give examples if needed.

3. Reinforce positive behavior. Compliment children who do what you expect. Say, "Good job," "nicely done," or "thank you."

4. Correct negative behavior. Verbally correct the wrong behavior, clarify the standards, compliment the positive behavior if/when it happens. Do not touch a child in anger! If you must touch a child to separate him/her from others, be very careful not to squeeze or shake a child. Hitting, squeezing, slapping, pushing, or shaking a child may result in the children's ministry team member's immediate removal from ministry. See the "Removal From Ministry" policy section. Reinstatement to ministry may be accomplished through the process outlined in the "Reinstatement To Ministry" policy section.

5. Separate disruptive children from others. If a child continues to misbehave, regardless of all attempts to positively encourage the right behavior, separate the child from the rest of the class. No child will ever be sent outside the classroom alone. Children may be separated within the classroom only. Children must always be within the direct supervision of the children's ministry team members. No team member will be permitted to be alone with a child outside the classroom.

6. Communicate with the parents regarding the child's behavior. Remain positive and hopeful while still being truthful. Make sure another team member is present when a parent is talked to about the child. If the child is an extreme, consistent challenge, the team member may refer the matter to the children's pastor.

7. Build relationships with the children! Control, power, and threats are all weak discipline tools compared to a healthy, sincere relationship! Instead of backing away from a disruptive child, move toward him. Get to know what he likes or dislikes. Become interested in his hobbies or sports interests. If you develop a relationship, the child will not want to damage that relationship with disruptive behavior. You will soon be able to communicate with the child through eye-contact from across the room!

The "Discipline Policy" Template

General Belief Statement: We believe that children benefit from secure, realistic boundaries. We believe in reinforcing those boundaries through encouragement and gentle correction. We believe that developing relationships with children is the greatest way to discipline them. If a child chooses not to respond to our attempts at gentle correction, we are forced to protect our ministry to the other children while not giving up on the disruptive child.

1. How will you challenge your team members to develop relationships with the children as a step in the discipline process?

2. What is the effect of a creative, challenging, fun learning environment on children's discipline choices?

3. How will you train the team members in the process of discipline?

4. How can you train the team members in relationship-building?

5. What is the process for dealing with a disruptive child?

6. What is the difference between discipline and punishment?

7. What do you think about touching a child during discipline? What are the dangers?

8. What do you think about putting a child outside, all alone, as a form of punishment?

9. What role do other team members play in the discipline process?

10. What happens to a team member who disciplines a child inappropriately?

11. What communications should be made to the parents of a child who is disruptive?

How to Make Changes

Children's ministry will always have a need for volunteers, and those volunteers need clearly established parameters in order to operate as part of a unified team. That seems to be par for the course. I used to dream of days when I would have to put people on a worker's waiting list because I did not have any openings for new people. I believe that will happen—just after Jesus takes me to Heaven.

The process of applying what was learned from the surveys in the establishing of policies is not too complex, but it is very critical that we follow some needed steps in the initial stages of making the changes that will implement the results of our findings and our policy decisions.

Deciding on the Needed Changes

1. Share the results of the survey with your pastor. Do the best you can to somehow compile the responses into an easily-read, one-page synopsis. Chart or list the responses for the pastor to see without too much reading.

2. Ask for his permission to form a group to discuss possible changes. This group may be your Christian Education Board, if you have one. The group may also be comprised of yourself, the pastor, and an elder. You may want to hand pick the group's members as a result of the relationships you developed during some of your "Turning The Soil" investigations. This group will not enact any changes, but they will brainstorm the possibilities with you.

3. Formulate a list of possible changes, giving careful thought to timing. This list should include some notation system that refers back to the related survey question. Be careful not to suggest that too many changes be attempted at one time. People can only take so much! Pray for wisdom as you consider his timing.

4. Determine the costs involved. This will give the pastor the kind of complete information he needs in order to give you adequate guidance. Be careful not to get bids on any job without telling the person that this has not been approved yet. You don't want word getting back to the pastor that you are beginning on the project without his support. If there are optional ways of doing the job, be sure to price those too. If you have to get the pastor's "yea" on each suggested change, that's OK! You do not want to do any changing without his support. Be ready for him to ask you some questions or make suggestions that will require you to return to your counsel group or survey responses for further data. Pray that Jesus will speak to and through the pastor, and pray for wisdom!

5. Have all policies approved by those leaders who have that responsibility. These policies have serious legal implications, and you want the leaders of your church to be fully informed with regard to any procedures that may ultimately affect them.

Now that you have an approved list of needed changes and some idea of when to make these changes, you can begin to work on the actual changes themselves. Changes are like brownies. If done correctly, with the right ingredients, the correct baking time and temperature, and the right pan size, they are, in my opinion, the only goodie that can compete with hot apple pie a-la-mode. On the other hand, if they are not blessed with the kind of loving care they deserve, they will prove to be excellent paper weights or a protective coating for the underside of your boat. The success of any change, in human terms, is directly proportional to the thought and preparation given it prior to its inception.

Remember that we are all like the animals at the zoo who, according to a folk song some years ago, are "skeptical of changes in their cages." We basically don't like anything that disrupts our comfort zone. Therefore, you must devote a significant amount of time to the preparation of the people prior to the change occuring. Even something as simple as a finger-printing policy could send your teaching staff flying! They may feel like their privacy is being invaded. So move slowly and explain yourself at every turn. If you are confident that the Lord is in favor of this change, and that it will enhance the ministry-potential to the children, you will not have any problem reproducing that vision. Here are some simple steps to making a change a bit easier to swallow.

Preparing for Changes

• Pray for prepared hearts. You can only do so much. With the Holy Spirit's work in the hearts of those affected by the change, what you do will be that much more effective. Pray for unity!

• Provide the people with enough data to see the need for change. You will not please everyone this way, but you may succeed in opening most of their eyes to the necessity for improvement.

• Highlight the positive goals involved. We talked about selling people on your ideas in the first chapter. This is an acceptable opportunity to use any and all techniques the Lord may have blessed you with to excite the people about these thrilling improvements. With Jesus' help, the future is bright!

• Give dissenters an audience. There will be those who disagree with what you are planning. I'm convinced this is their calling! I have found people who seem to be gifted at finding fault no matter what is done. Give them personal attention, listen to their ideas, tell them you understand, thank them for their honesty and commitment to the children's ministry.

• Stand consistently firm. If you have followed the steps I've suggested, you should be able to be fairly confident in what you're doing. You must stand firm behind your goals and vision. This doesn't mean that you shouldn't listen to other people's opinions, and maybe even apply them, but it does mean that you cannot appear wishy-washy. There's a fine line between being bull-headed and being confident. The difference is how you treat others and their ideas. If you have some doubts, there's nothing wrong with contacting your multitude of counselors, or the pastor again, for reinforcement or more wisdom.

• Spread the good news! Once you begin to see some fruit as a result of your change, let the whole children's ministry and the pastor know about it. This will reinforce the fact that God is with you and that he cares enough to help you make decisions. (It will also quiet any noisy lions that are still growling around.)

I wish I could tell you that you will have no trouble making changes or instituting policies and procedures now that you have read these chapters. You will still have trouble, but you also have a friend in him who loves these little children more than you and I can ever imagine. You must put your faith in Jesus, and open your heart to the people who will be affected by your newly-formed policies. Ask yourself these questions:

• "Can I feel the feelings or fears of the people who will be affected by these changes?" "If someone disagrees with my decisions, do I take it personally? Why?" (This is a good reason to have an advisory council; you can share the blame!)

• "Is it easy for me to admit a mistake? Do I plan not to fail?"

• "Is my confidence in the Lord, those who counsel me, or in myself?" Remember who you are and who he is: "I am the vine; you are the branches. If a man remains in me and I in him, he will bear much fruit; apart from me you can do nothing" *(John 15:5)*.

Children's Ministry Application

Name: _____

Address: _____

City: _____ Zip: _____

Phone: _____ Email address: _____

Age: (Check one) ❏ Over 18 ❏ Under 18 Driver's license number: _____

Marital status: _____ Spouse's name (if applicable): _____

Children's names and ages:

Current occupation: _____ Employer: _____

How long have you been attending this church? _____

Are you a member of this church? _____ Membership date: _____

It is our desire to provide a safe, consistent, and spiritually-nurturing environment for the children who come to our church. To accomplish this goal, we ask that you fill out the following information. Thank you for the time you will devote to this application.

When completed, please mail this form to the church or bring it to the church office. Someone from the children's ministry will contact you soon. *Thanks!*

PREVIOUS MINISTRY EXPERIENCE

Have you served in a church before? _____ If so, please describe your last service.

Position: _____ Dates of service: _____

Church name: _____ Address: _____

Church city: _____ State: _____ Phone #: _____

Ministry supervisor: _____

Desired Age Group	**Desired Service Time**	**For Office Use**
(Check one)	(Check one)	
❏ Nursery/Toddler (birth-2 yrs.)	❏ Sun. 8:30 am	Background _____
❏ Preschool (3-5 yrs.)	❏ Sun. 9:45 am	References _____
❏ Elementary (first-sixth grade)	❏ Sun. 11:00 am	Orientation _____
	❏ Sun. 6:00 pm	Fingerprint _____
	❏ Midweek	Name Badge _____

CHRISTIAN TESTIMONY

When did you become a Christian? Date:

Briefly describe the events that led up to your becoming a Christian. What "condition" is your spiritual life now?

SCRIPTURAL / SPIRITUAL BELIEFS

Because we in the children's ministry have a significant influence in the shaping of a child's spiritual life, we believe we should agree on the "basics" of our Christian faith. Below is a brief statement of what our church believes and teaches. If you agree with these beliefs, please sign your name below to verify that agreement. If you differ with these beliefs, and do not wish to sign the agreement, please contact someone in the children's ministry to discuss your views.

We believe in God the Father, God the Son, God the Holy Spirit. We believe they are distinct personalities with distinct roles, but one God, the Creator of the universe.

We believe Jesus Christ is the Messiah, the Savior, the Son of God who was born of a virgin, lived a sinless life, died on a cross, and was raised from the grave. He will return as our victorious Lord.

We believe our salvation comes only through Jesus Christ and cannot be earned. It is a gift of God.

We believe faith in Jesus requires repentance, confession of that faith before witnesses, and obedience to his Word. Baptism by immersion demonstrates our faith and obedience while it depicts our union with Christ in his death, burial, and resurrection.

We believe everyone who accepts Jesus has the indwelling presence of the Holy Spirit who acts as a comforter, guide, and advocate.

We believe the Bible is the divinely-inspired Word of God in its entirety and that it does not contradict itself. It is our guide.

We believe the Church, as the body of Christ, is the extension of Jesus Christ's character, attitude, behavior, and mission in our world today.

We believe God gives gifts to both men and women through the Holy Spirit for the benefit of the Church's ministry.

We believe that humility in prayer is the foundation for all we do and that celebrating communion together weekly is beneficial for all Christians.

I agree with the above beliefs. I understand the importance of unity among the children's ministry team. If, at any time, I question or disagree with the teaching of this church, I will make an effort to speak with the children's pastor in an attempt to clarify my concerns.

Applicant Signature _____

PREVIOUS CHURCH ATTENDANCE

List the churches you have attended regularly over the past seven years. Use an additional page to list more churches if needed.

Church name:_____

City _____State: _____

Phone number: _____

Pastor:_____

Dates attended: _____

Church name:_____

City _____State: _____

Phone number: _____

Pastor:_____

Dates attended: _____

PERSONAL REFERENCES

Please give four nonfamily character references. One must be a member of this church.*
All references will be contacted. No application will be accepted without reference information fully completed.

1. Name:_____

   Address:_____

   City: _____

   State: _____ Zip:_____

   Phone: _____

   Relationship: _____

   Years known: _____

2. Name:_____

   Address:_____

   City: _____

   State: _____ Zip:_____

   Phone: _____

   Relationship: _____

   Years known: _____

   *Church Member

3. Name:_____

   Address:_____

   City: _____

   State: _____ Zip:_____

   Phone: _____

   Relationship: _____

   Years known: _____

4. Name:_____

   Address:_____

   City: _____

   State: _____ Zip:_____

   Phone: _____

   Relationship: _____

   Years known: _____

PERSONAL BACKGROUND

Have you ever been arrested for, convicted of, or pleaded guilty, or "no contest," to a criminal act?

Have you ever been accused, arrested or convicted for any sexually-related crime?

Have you ever been accused, arrested or convicted for any abuse-related crime?

Do you use illegal drugs?

Have you ever been hospitalized or treated for alcohol or substance abuse?

Have you ever, to your knowledge, been investigated by Child Protective Services, or any other governmental agency involved with the protection of children?

If you answered "yes" to any of the above questions, please explain each one separately (use an additional page, if needed):

Why do you want to work with children?

PERMISSION TO CHECK BACKGROUND

I give this church permission to check my references, church history, personal or criminal background using the information I've provided in this application. I understand that by submitting this application I am willfully permitting to this background check process. I understand that the personal information learned from such background checks will be held confidential by the church staff.

Applicant Signature _____ Date _____

VERIFICATION OF TRUTHFULNESS

I affirm, to the best of my knowledge, that the information on this application is correct.

Applicant Signature _____ Date _____

Children's Ministry Agreement to Serve

We on the children's ministry team believe that unity among the children's ministry team members is a critical part of a successful ministry to the children. In order to do all we can to create and further that team unity, we have made this Agreement To Serve a part of the children's ministry application process. Please read the attached Children's Ministry Team Job Descriptions, and complete and sign the agreement. A copy of the completed agreement will be returned to you, and the original will be kept in the children's ministry office. This agreement is valid for one calendar year (Jan. - Jan.). Thank you for being a valuable part of our team!

VERIFICATION OF RECEIPT AND UNDERSTANDING

I have received a copy of the documents listed below. My initials beside the documents verify that I have read, understood, and agree with the intent and contents of these documents.

Document	*My Initials*
1. Children's Ministry Team Job Descriptions	_____
2. Children's Ministry Policy Manual	
a . "Team Ministry" policy	_____
b. "Sickness and Disease Control" policy	_____
c. "Child Discipline" policy	_____
d. "Emergency Response" policy	_____
e. "Events" policy/procedure	_____
f. "Removal From Ministry" policy/procedure	_____
g. "Appeals" policy/process	_____
h. "Absence From Service" policy/procedure	_____
i. "Reinstatement to Ministry" policy/procedure	_____
j. "Child Abuse Recognition and Reporting" policy	_____
k. "Bodily Fluids / HIV" policy	_____

AGREEMENT TO SERVE FAITHFULLY

I agree to serve the Lord, Jesus Christ, as a part of the children's ministry team. I agree to abide by the policies contained in the Children's Ministry Policy Manual. I agree to attend the monthly children's ministry team meetings, even if I am not serving during a rotation period. I understand that my service on the children's ministry team is voluntary, and I willfully place myself under the authority of the children's ministry leadership staff. I understand that I may choose to change my position on the children's ministry team if the opportunity is offered, but that change in my position does not change this agreement to serve faithfully. I understand that my service may be discontinued if I so desire, or if my faithfulness is questioned by the children's ministry leadership staff as outlined in the "Removal From Ministry" policy/procedure. I agree to do all I can to be a productive, faithful part of the children's ministry team.

Children's Ministry Applicant _____ Date _____

## chapter 9

Building the Trellis:
Program Policies and Procedures

"*Shade-giving garden structures, from a simple canvas awning to a delicate gazebo to a leafy arbor, can give welcome, refreshing protection to tender, shade-loving plants and people alike*" (Shade Gardening, San Francisco, CA: Chevron Chemical Co., 1982; page 31).

The importance of child safety was brought home to me again recently. Our children's ministry team had worked for several weeks designing a new program for our Sunday evening children's ministry. When we launched it, it was a fantastic success. We had planned for somewhere around 80 children. We had planned our whole program around that number. We got our first hint that this program was going to be well-attended when the parents and children began lining up 30 minutes before the program was scheduled to begin. We were overwhelmed with the attendance! We had 217 children and 57 adults for a total of 274 people! Everyone was thrilled and the children enjoyed all we had planned for them.

We had used the check-in/security system that we use on Sunday mornings: matching number stamps on the hands of the parents and children. Everything went well, and when the parents came to pick up their children, we thought every child was present and accounted for. We were surprised when a frantic mother came to pick her children up, and they weren't there! This successful program that had produced so many compliments from the parents was suddenly a tragedy for this one mother. In an instant, the mother's attitude shifted from, "Thank you," to "What have you done with my children?" We found her children in another building. They had gotten mixed up with another age group. They were reunited with their mother, and they all went home "happy."

I tell you this story to illustrate the importance of child safety and security during events. You can create the most amazing program and spend millions of dollars on special effects or equipment, but if the children's safety or security is not protected, your program is a miserable failure! Nothing else can have this kind of affect on the success of a program. If your refreshments are not good or you run out of glue, that's fine. If your lesson is boring or you run out of time, no problem. If you lose a child or a child is injured by your neglect, you're in deep trouble!

Parents want us to develop their children's spiritual lives, but they also trust that we will place their children's safety on the highest level of importance. This chapter will help you evaluate, and update or create, safety policies that affect your children's health and safety. This is not a fun chapter. You probably won't want to curl up with a cup of tea, some nice music, and savor this chapter. Sorry. This may not be pleasurable reading, but it is perhaps the most critical chapter in the whole book from the perspective of giving the parents the level of peace of mind that will draw them, and their children, back week after week.

PARANOIA OR WISDOM?

If you let yourself, you can become very worried about doing anything wrong with children. We serve in a very "lawsuit happy" world. Everybody is suing everybody for the silliest little things. Parents are more sensitive to what happens to their children than ever before. I suppose that's a good thing. Parents should care what happens to their children. The challenge to us all is to find the middle ground between paranoia and wisdom regarding child safety.

If you are too afraid of being sued, you probably won't want to touch a child, or even be in the same room with children. Your paranoia actually stops ministry from happening. In order to minister to children, we must touch them and definitely be in the same room with them. On the other extreme, if you think that nothing bad ever happens to good people who are serving God, you might be a little

Nine Categories of Safety Policies

1. Health Concerns
How should we deal with cleanliness and bodily fluids?

2. Sick Children
How should we deal with sick children and their parents?

3. Child Protection on Campus
How should we check children in and out of programs?

4. Adult/Child Ratios
How many adults do we need to be safe?

5. Program Development
How are programs organized to protect the children?

6. Event Development
How are events planned to protect the children?

7. Emergency Procedures
What should be done during emergencies?

8. Child Abuse
How should we recognize and report possible signs of child abuse?

9. Communication With Parents
How should we communicate with parents?

naïve, and you might be in danger of not being careful enough.

The goal of this chapter is to move you toward the center "wisdom" area. I don't want you to get so paranoid about child safety that you quit the ministry, but I also don't want you to be naïve and never take any steps to protect the children, yourself, and the church.

God has promised to be present with us when we ask him. He has promised to take care of our needs when we seek him first. He has promised to give us the desires of our hearts when we delight ourselves in him. He is very able to keep any harm from coming to us, our children, or the church. Yes, he performs miracles. Yes, he protects us and his children. But there is no magic guarantee that the evil of the world won't spill over onto our worlds. That's why he cautioned us to be "wise as snakes and gentle as doves," and why he said that he sends us out as "sheep among wolves," and why he says that "in the world you will have tribulation." We need to constantly beg him to protect the children and our ministry, but at the same time, we need to do all we can to be wise. Wisdom means that you are aware of the dangers, you take steps to protect yourself, and then move forward in faith with what he has called you to do. I will use the same approach I used in chapter 8. It is a simple, five step process of writing your own policies.

Category 1: The "Health Concerns Policy"

Definition. A policy for the correct handling of sick children, and blood or bodily fluids.

Rationale. No matter what we do, children will get sick. This policy clarifies the procedure for protecting the other children or the team members from infection through exposure to blood or bodily fluids.

Evaluation. Does your policy regarding health concerns protect the children and team members from contracting sickness or disease from others? Does the policy clearly state the process for dealing with blood or bodily fluids? Does the policy protect you, the children's ministry team, or the church from accusations of negligence?

Sample "Health Concerns Policy"

It is our intention to protect children from all harm while they are in our care. This includes protection from sick children, sick adults, or dirty surfaces and toys.

All surfaces and toys in the nursery/toddler classrooms will be disinfected at the end of every use period. Those who serve during that use period are responsible for this cleaning. Duplicate toy supplies will be provided for convenience during check-in/out periods. Linens and bedding used in the nursery will be changed after each use and washed prior to being used again.

All those who serve in the nursery/toddler areas will use latex gloves when changing diapers or handling soiled clothing, sheets, or bedding which may contain bodily fluids.

All used latex gloves, dirty diapers, dirty sheets, dirty bedding, or children's dirty clothing items must be disposed of or stored in protective containers away from the children. Children's dirty clothing must be returned to the parents in plastic trash bags.

Every children's ministry team member must use caution when exposed to children's blood or bodily fluids. Whenever possible, latex gloves must be used in these situations. Hands must be washed with disinfectant soap immediately after changing diapers, assisting children with the toilet, or handling clothes or other materials containing blood or bodily fluids.

Latex gloves must be changed after every diaper change or after handling blood or bodily fluids.

General Policies/Guidelines. After a thorough review of current medical research and in consultation with health professionals and legal advisors, we have established the following policy guidelines.

1. All contact with bodily fluids or blood must be treated as potentially dangerous. All children's ministry team members who change diapers or come in contact with blood or bodily fluids must use latex gloves, dispose of dirty gloves and diapers correctly, wash hands thoroughly afterward, and disinfect all related surfaces immediately after a diaper change or exposure to blood or bodily fluids.

2. The parents of children who are exposed to

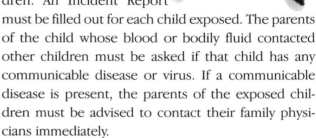

another child's blood or bodily fluids must be advised of such an exposure when they come to pick up their children. An Incident Report must be filled out for each child exposed. The parents of the child whose blood or bodily fluid contacted other children must be asked if that child has any communicable disease or virus. If a communicable disease is present, the parents of the exposed children must be advised to contact their family physicians immediately.

3. Gloves must be changed after each diaper change or exposure to blood or bodily fluids.

4. Hands must be washed with disinfectant soap after the removal of gloves before touching another child or surface.

5. All used latex gloves, dirty diapers, dirty sheets, dirty bedding, or children's dirty clothing items must be disposed of or stored in protective containers immediately away from the children. Children's dirty clothing must be returned to the parents in plastic trash bags.

6. No children's ministry team member who has an exudative or weeping skin sore shall be permitted to serve in the children's ministry unless the sore is covered completely. The children's pastor may request that the team member refrain from service until the sore is healed.

7. Those who assist children with using the toilet must use latex gloves and wash their hands with disinfectant soap after removing the gloves.

HIV/AIDS. It is not our intention to discriminate against any person with HIV/AIDS. We desire to avoid reactions based on exaggerated fears and prejudice. We do, however, have the responsibility to be wise and protect the health and safety of the children who attend our classes and events, our children's ministry team, and all who attend our church.

We believe education is the greatest tool to use not only in protecting those who are not infected with HIV, but also in making sure the "doors of ministry" are open to those who are infected with HIV.

To this end, we will include HIV awareness sessions as part of our on-going children's ministry training process.

In the event that a child who has the HIV virus expels bodily fluid or blood, this situation must be dealt with seriously, as with all exposures to blood or bodily fluids. The presence of the HIV virus should not change how we treat such a situation. All exposures to blood or bodily fluids must be treated as potentially dangerous for all involved.

Children with the HIV virus who do not have open skin lesions should be permitted to participate in children's ministry events or classes. Any child with open skin lesions should be restricted from such participation until the lesions have healed or are adequately covered to prevent exposure to others.

Adults with the HIV virus who do not have open skin lesions should be permitted to participate in children's ministry events or classes. Any adult with open skin lesions should be restricted from such participation until the lesions have healed or are adequately covered to prevent exposure to others.

Any restrictions to participation suggested by the children's ministry team may only be in the best interest of the infected person (to prevent contact with other illnesses).

The "Health Concerns Policy" Template

General Belief Statement: We believe that there is no such thing as a germ-free environment. We believe we can take some active steps toward slowing down the spread of germs or preventing other children from contracting a sickness. We know we are required by law to present a clean environment to children and their parents.

1. How should the surfaces in your nursery/toddler areas be cleaned? How often?

2. How should the soiled diapers, gloves, or bedding be dealt with?

3. How often should your team members wash their hands in the nursery?

4. What should be done if a child or adult is exposed to blood or bodily fluids?

5. How are the parents told about their child's exposure to another child's sickness?

6. How will your team members be trained in these procedures?

Category 2: The "Sick Children Policy"

Definition. A policy to protect healthy children from exposure to sickness brought in by other children.

Rationale. Sick children need to be home with loving parents. They shouldn't be at church where other children can catch their sickness. This policy defines the procedure for keeping sick children out of our ministry environments.

Evaluation. Does your policy regarding sick children protect other children and team members from contracting sickness from other children? Does your policy clearly state the process for dealing with sick children and their parents before, during, and after the class or event? Does the policy protect you, the children's ministry team, or the church from accusations of negligence?

Sample "Sick Children Policy"

No sick children will be accepted into any children's ministry event. It is the responsibility of the children's ministry team member checking in the child to recognize the sickness symptoms and graciously ask the parent to care for his/her child elsewhere until the child is well. If the parent desires to discuss the policy further, the children's ministry team member will refer the parent to the coordinator, supervisor, or children's pastor. It is not appropriate to debate the policy or the decision not to accept the child during check-in in front of other parents.

If a child's sickness is discovered or he/she becomes sick after check-in, the children's ministry team member will consult with another team member in the classroom, and together they will decide on one of the following options:

1. Page the parent to come and check the child out immediately.

2. Isolate the child from the other children.

3. If possible, send one team member to get the parent.

4. Let the child remain, and give the parent a

"We're Sorry Your Child Is Sick" flyer explaining our sick child policy.

The "Sick Children Policy" Template

General Belief Statement: We believe that children who are sick need to be home with the parents. We also believe that parents of healthy children do not appreciate their child getting sick while in our care.

1. What can you do to stop sick children from entering your ministry environments?

2. What should your team's response be if a child is discovered to be sick while inside the ministry environment?

3. What are the indications of the various sicknesses, and how will you treat those that are communicable?

4. How do you communicate with the parents regarding a sick child?

Category 3: The "Child Protection on Campus Policy"

Definition. A policy to protect the children from abuse, neglect, or abduction while in our care.

Rationale. If we protect our system of check-in and check-out, we will guarantee that only those adults who dropped the children off will pick the children up.

Evaluation. Does your policy regarding child protection on the church campus protect the children from harm? Does the policy clearly state the process for guaranteeing that the approved adults pick the children up from class or an event? Does the policy protect you, the children's ministry team, or the church from accusations of negligence?

Sample "Child Protection On Campus Policy"

All children must be checked-in to their classroom by an adult. The following procedures will be followed to protect children from abduction:

1. Adults who check-in children aged three years and younger will be given a parent pager whose number matches the number on the child's label. No adult will be permitted to check-out a child without a parent pager with a matching number on the child's label.

2. Adults who check-in children aged four years old through sixth grade will be given a number stamp on their hand to match the stamp on the hands of the children they are checking in. Only those adults whose stamped numbers match the numbers on the child's hand will be permitted to check-out a child. No child will be permitted to leave a classroom without being checked out or picked up by an adult.

The "Child Protection On Campus Policy" Template

General Belief Statement: We believe that we are responsible to protect the safety of the children that are in our care during ministry times. We believe we must protect the safety of children at all costs.

1. What system of protection do you have to guarantee that children are not abducted?

2. What will you do to guarantee that the adult who picks up the child doesn't have a restraining order preventing him or her from doing so?

3. Where will you conduct your check-in process? (At a central location? At the classroom?)

Category 4: The "Adult/Child Ratios Policy"

Definition. A policy to regulate the number of children per adults in a ministry environment in order to protect the quality of ministry as well as the safety of children. (This policy is nearly identical to the "Supervision Policy" in chapter 8, although it does have a slightly different focus.)

Rationale. It doesn't matter how great a teacher is if he or she is alone. Being alone is dangerous and draining. When a teacher is alone, there is no defense for any accusation. The more adults you have in a ministry environment, the more enjoyable the ministry is for both the children and the adults. More adults mean more fruit!

Evaluation. Does your policy regarding adult/child ratios protect the children from any harm due to overpopulation or neglect? Does the policy protect you, the children's ministry, or the church from harm or accusations of negligence? Are your ratios set correctly to guarantee a productive ministry environment?

Sample "Adult/Child Ratios Policy"

At no time will any one who serves in the children's ministry be alone with children. All who serve in the children's ministry will serve as part of a team of at least two adults. It is our desire, whenever possible, to create teams of three or more. The addition of a youth volunteer to a classroom does not equal the addition of an adult. One adult with one youth volunteer is still considered an adult alone with the children. This situation must be corrected.

Approved adult/child ratios for children's ministry classes and events will change with each setting. In addition to the "never alone" clause stated above, the children's ministry will work toward the following adult/child ratios:

Nursery—1/3

Toddlers—1/4

Preschool—1/7

Elementary—1/10

If, due to unforeseen circumstances, a team of at least two adults cannot be guaranteed for a children's ministry event or program, the coordinator or supervisor for that event will decide which of the following options are best for the situation, and then act on that situation. The options are:

1. Join the children in two classes or areas to guarantee a team of two or more adults.

2. Borrow adults from the teams in other classes or areas.

3. Do not accept children for this class or area until at least two adults can be placed.

All of these options, by their nature, may not be the best choice for either the church or the children. If options 1 or 2 above cannot be done without raising the adult/child ratios beyond our approved limits, then the only option is to close the class. Considerations must also be given to the maximum occupancy of the room being used. Child safety and church liability must take priority over convenience or programming.

Married couples will be permitted to serve together only when they are joined by a third adult.

The "Adult/Child Ratios Policy" Template

General Belief Statement: We believe that a healthy children's ministry environment is one in which two or more adults are serving in a team. We believe the adult/child ratios must be guarded to prevent overcrowding and loss of ministry effectiveness. We believe that protection of the adult/child ratios will prevent the children and children's ministry team from harm.

1. Does the local building and safety code describe acceptable adult/child ratios?

2. If you set adult/child ratios, what happens when those ratios are not met? Do you close the class?

3. What does your pastor and board think about setting adult/child ratios?

4. Are the ratios applicable for all children's ministry events (on and off campus)?

Category 5: The "Program Development Policy"

Definition. A policy regarding the procedures for creating, planning, and executing a program safely. A program is defined as a reoccurring (weekly, monthly, etc.) ministry experience.

Rationale. If a program is planned carefully, it will be safe. If a program is planned carelessly or quickly, it can be a high risk event with regards to child safety. The tighter the guidelines on program development, the more secure the parents will be about this, and other, children's ministry programs.

Evaluation. Does your policy regarding program development protect the children from any harm due to poor planning? Does the policy protect you, the children's ministry, or the church from harm or accusations of negligence due to poor planning?

Sample "Program Development Policy"

Programs are ways to accomplish our ministry vision. A program will be approved for development only after the following process has been carried out, and the program has been agreed-upon by the children's ministry leadership team.

Program Evaluation Process

1. The program idea is presented using the

"Program Presentation Form."

2. The program's connection to the ministry vision is evaluated.

3. The program's cost (financial, personnel, time, curriculum) is considered.

4. The program's relation with other programs and ministries is considered.

5. The program's potential fruit is considered.

6. The program is approved for development or rejected.

The program must be given at least two months for development. No program will be approved with a development period shorter than two months.

The adult team members who will serve in the program must be recruited and trained at least one month prior to the program's launch. No program will be permitted to launch with fewer adults than the approved adult/child ratio dictates, or without those adults being trained one month prior to launch.

Advertisement for the program must be readied at least one month prior to the program's launch. No program will be permitted to launch without adequate advertising begun at least one month prior to the launch.

Child protection and safety considerations must be finalized at least one month prior to the program's launch. No program will be permitted to launch without adequate child protection and safety considerations being finalized one month prior to launch.

Program curriculum must be decided upon at least one month prior to launch, and prior to the start of advertising. No program will be permitted to launch without curriculum being decided upon one month prior to launch.

The "Program Development Policy" Template

General Belief Statement: We believe that a well-designed and well-staffed program can literally be an event that changes a child's life forever. We also believe that a poorly designed and poorly-staffed program can trip up children or offend parents who will refuse to bring their children to us for ministry. Program planning is critical to the fulfillment of the Great Commission and our ministry vision.

1. What do you believe about the timing of program development prior to the launch?

2. What steps do you want to require in the program approval process?

3. What do you think makes a successful program?

4. What do you think makes a failed program?

5. Who supervises the program development process?

6. When is a program approved?

7. When is a program ready to launch?

8. What happens if a program's development is too late, or not adequate?

Category 6: The "Event Development Policy"

Definition. A policy regarding the procedures for creating, planning, and executing an event safely. An "event" is defined as a one-time occurrence.

Rationale. Events are much like programs, but more intense. If a program's failure can be bad for the children or your ministry team, an event's failure can be disastrous for all of those, and your church's reputation in the city as well. An event usually involves more children and more first-time visitors. An event captures more attention (good and bad). Therefore, the safe development and planning of an event is vitally important!

Evaluation. Does your policy regarding event development protect the children from any harm due to poor planning? Does the policy protect you, the children's ministry, or the church from harm or accusations of negligence due to poor planning?

Sample "Event Development Policy"

It is the policy of the children's ministry that we offer a variety of events for the children and families to enjoy. We believe that communication, team work, and advanced planning are essentials to a safe, successful event. All events held during Sunday morning or Sunday evening must be approved by the children's pastor; all others must be approved by the family ministry pastor. All events must be approved at least 2 months prior to being advertised. This approval process includes clearing the dates on the church calendar. The earlier the clearance, the more likely the date will be approved. If printing is involved, 3 months' advance notice is required! No letters, phone calls, or notes will be sent out prior to the event being approved by the children's pastor. The Event Planning Guide will be followed by the event planner. Any variance from this guide must be approved by the children's pastor or family ministry pastor.

All those who serve in any event involving children must be approved by the children's ministry through the application process. No one may serve in the event or come in contact with children as a volunteer, without being approved through the application process.

All those who drive children must be approved through the children's ministry application process. In addition to the children's ministry application process, those who wish to transport children in private vehicles must fill out the Children's Ministry Driver Application Form. Background checks will be conducted through the Department of Motor Vehicles (DMV) for all those who wish to drive children. Anyone who has had an accident or moving citation within a year prior to the event must give the details of the accident or citation to the children's pastor prior to being approved to drive. The children's pastor may, based on the details, refuse to permit the person to drive children.

All children under the age of 18 who attend an event must have submitted an Event Release form for that specific event and have an Emergency Release form on file with the children's ministry office. Both forms must be signed by a parent or legal guardian. No child will be permitted to attend an event without both forms being submitted and signed by a parent or legal guardian. Copies of both forms must be carried by a children's ministry team member who attends the event with the children. Complete rosters of the children attending the event must also be carried by the children's ministry team member who carries the copies of the "Event" and "Emergency" forms. If the children are divided into groups, a children's ministry team member who stays with a group of children must carry the copies of the "Event" and "Emergency" forms for the children in that group. If the groups rejoin, all forms must be returned to a single children's ministry team member who will carry the forms for all the children.

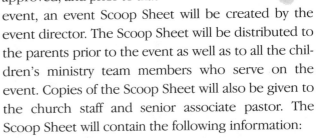

After the event has been approved, and prior to that event, an event Scoop Sheet will be created by the event director. The Scoop Sheet will be distributed to the parents prior to the event as well as to all the children's ministry team members who serve on the event. Copies of the Scoop Sheet will also be given to the church staff and senior associate pastor. The Scoop Sheet will contain the following information:

1. Date of event
2. Ages/grades of children involved
3. Location of event with map in relation to church
4. Event times
   a. Child drop-off time (at church?)
   b. Departure time from the church
   c. Actual event times
   d. Departure time from the event location
   e. Arrival time back at the church
   f. Child pick-up time (from church?)
5. Emergency contact information
   a. Pager number for church-based person
   b. Cell phone number for church-based person
   c. Pager number for person at event location with children
   d. Cell phone number for person at event location with children

The "Event Development Policy" Template

General Belief Statement: We believe that an event captures more attention than a program. We believe that the large number of children and the potential for significant numbers of first time visitors demands that every precaution be taken to guarantee a safe event. We believe that there cannot be too much planning and forethought given to an event.

1. What does your pastor believe about the seriousness of an event's safety?

2. How far in advance do you want to force the planners of the event to work?

3. How far in advance do you need to plan the advertising?

139

4. How far in advance do you need to plan the security/safety measures?

5. How far in advance do you need to recruit and train your team members?

6. What could go wrong? How can you counteract those possibilities in advance?

Category 7: The "Emergency Procedures Policy"

Definition. A policy that contains basic procedures for dealing with emergencies safely.

Rationale. Emergencies are not planned, but the responses to those emergencies can be rehearsed. Negligence can be described as not doing what should have been done. The parents and courts will determine if we are negligent based on what was done. People don't think clearly in emergency situations. Training and repetition can help in emergency situations. Policies and procedures are a starting point. Practice is the final touch in preparation.

Evaluation. Do your policies regarding emergency procedures protect the children from harm as much as possible during the various emergencies listed? Does the policy clearly state the procedures that should be followed by team members to protect them, you, or the church from accusations of negligence? Does the policy clearly define the process for communicating with the parents after an emergency?

Sample "Emergency Procedures Policy"

The policies for emergency procedures are too long to quote here. Here is a list of things that emergency procedures need to include:

1. A brief description of the emergency.

2. A clear "first response" behavior recommended for all team members.

3. Recommendations for dealing with the immediate needs of the children.

4. Recommendations for contacting help.

5. What to do while waiting for help.

6. What to do when help arrives.

7. How to assist the paramedics, fire, or police personnel in caring for the children.

8. How to help others.

9. How to communicate with the parents.

10. What forms or reports should be filed and stored.

The "Emergency Procedures Policy" Template

General Belief Statement: We believe that emergency situations can be worsened by adults who are unprepared. Being prepared means that there is some process or behavior that has been taught and practiced. We believe that the welfare of the children is the primary concern. Every emergency is unique. Training and adults acting in the wisdom of the Lord will help protect the children.

1. What sorts of emergencies might your children experience at church? (natural disasters, weather-related, people-caused, facility-caused, etc.)

2. Does your city offer any printed preparedness booklets or training?

3. For each emergency, what is the best way to protect the safety of the children?

4. What forms of communication will you have available during emergencies?

5. Who is in charge during each emergency?

6. What are the team members' rights in making decisions during emergencies?

7. Who calls for professional help (fire, police, medical personnel)?

8. How are the parents contacted?

9. What happens when the professional help arrives?

10. How are the parents united with the children?

11. Are there emergency release forms for the children?

Category 8: The "Child Abuse Policy"

Definition. A policy that describes the legal procedures for recognizing and reporting suspected child abuse to the local child protective agency.

Rationale. We are bound by law to report any suspected signs of child abuse. This law is designed to protect the children. It is not created to be an evil law to harm the families. Those who serve in the agencies that deal with child abuse want to partner with us to do all we can to stop children from being abused. The law describes every step in the process. We abide by the law.

Evaluation. Does your policy regarding the recognition and reporting of child abuse protect the children from harm? Does your policy clearly state the process for reporting any signs of abuse? Does the policy protect you, the children's ministry team, or the church from accusations of negligence?

Sample "Child Abuse Policy"

It is the desire of the children's ministry to create an environment which is safe and secure for all children. We must be prepared to take an active role in recognizing and reporting possible signs of child abuse if we should encounter them. We also realize that we are bound by the law to report suspected child abuse within a limited time. We will operate within the reporting standards set forth for our county as stated in *Child Abuse & Neglect Reporting Law Handbook*. The required time for reporting is immediately (or as soon as practically possible) by phone, with a written report forwarded within 36 hours of receiving information about, or observing, the alleged abuse.

In conjunction with the above state law, the children's ministry has the following policies regarding the procedures for reporting suspected child abuse:

1. No one may report a suspected child abuse situation without first notifying the children's pastor. This is for communication purposes only and to prevent unwarranted reports to Child Protective Services. The children's pastor cannot deny anyone access to Child Protective Services.

2. The person who first observes the suspected abuse or sign of abuse must contact the service supervisor or department coordinator immediately. The service supervisor must contact the department coordinator who will then contact the children's pastor. Details of the suspected abuse must only be shared with these people who are directly responsible under the children's pastor. No information about the suspected abuse may be shared with any other members of the children's ministry team.

3. It is the responsibility of the person observing the suspected abuse or stories of abuse to report such observations to Child Protective Services. This reporting will be made with the use of the Suspected Child Abuse Report provided by the County Social Services Department. We are bound by state and county law to make a phone report of the observation or suspicion to Child Protective Services immediately (as is practical) and to file a written Suspected Child Abuse Report within 36 hours of observing or receiving information about the suspected abuse. If the person observing or receiving information about a suspected abuse refuses to file the report within the time limit, it is the responsibility of those church officials who are aware of the matter to file such a report. In the event that a teen volunteer observes or receives information about a suspected abuse, he or she must also abide by these procedures. It is recommended that the children's pastor be contacted prior to a report being filed.

4. Prior to filing the Suspected Child Abuse Report, the following process must be followed:

a. Immediate discussion regarding the situation between the team member who observed or received the information, the service supervisor, the department coordinator, the children's pastor, and the senior associate pastor. Not all of the above people must be present at the meeting, but all must be briefed and consulted prior to reporting. The senior pastor may also be invited at the senior associate pastor's discretion.

b. Phone consultation with Child Protective Services will be considered for clarification or counsel regarding our observations, procedures, etc.

c. Detailed records of observations, conversations, and meetings will be made using the Sensitive Situation Report. These forms will be kept locked in the children's ministry office. Access to these reports will be restricted only to those directly involved in the situation (as listed in 4a above).

5. The parent or guardian of the child victim will not be notified or consulted with prior to reporting

unless we are otherwise counseled by Child Protective Services.

6. Relatives or friends of the child victim will not be notified or consulted with prior to reporting unless we are otherwise counseled by Child Protective Services.

7. Other church pastors or staff will not be notified or consulted with prior to reporting unless we are otherwise counseled by Child Protective Services, or unless those other ministries or positions are directly affected by the suspected abuse or abusers.

8. The identity of the person making the report to Child Protective Services is protected. At no time will that identity be made known to the alleged abuser unless we are instructed to do so by Child Protective Services or other prosecuting agencies.

9. Someone from the children's ministry may remain in close contact with the child and families connected with the abuse throughout the process unless otherwise advised by Child Protective Services.

The "Child Abuse Policy" Template

General Belief Statement: We believe that child abuse is an offense that needs immediate, professional help for the sake of the children involved. We believe the trained personnel employed by Child Protective Services must be involved in order for the children to be protected. We believe that the spiritual protection and support for the children and families comes through us.

1. What are the local laws regarding reporting suspected child abuse?

2. What are your pastor's views on the laws, and how does he suggest abiding by them?

3. Who oversees the reporting process?

4. At what point does your church board become involved?

5. What forms and records are kept, by whom, and where?

Category 9: The "Parent Communication Policy"

Definition. A policy to protect the vital partnership between the parents and the children's ministry through planned and purposeful communication.

Rationale. Parents are vital to the children's min-istry because they can either choose to involve their children in our ministry, or not. Our support of the parents through clear communication with them will keep them "on our side" no matter what.

Evaluation. Does your policy regarding communicating with parents support the vital unity between church and home? Does the policy clearly describe the process in dealing with upset parents? Does the policy protect you, the children's ministry, and the church from accusations of negligence?

Sample "Parent Communication Policy"

We will make every effort to keep the parents informed about events and programs, as well as provide them with support in their ministry to their own children. We view the parents as partners in ministry with us. Therefore, we will fulfill the following commitment to communicate with the parents:

1. We will provide the parents with weekly communication regarding their children's lessons through the use of the "Let's Face It" papers.

2. We will provide the parents with communication about monthly events through our monthly newsletter.

3. We will provide the parents with communication about any injuries their children received while in our care with the Incident Report forms.

4. We will provide the parents with communication about any serious injuries their children received while in our care with the Serious Injury forms.

5. We will provide the parents with communication about an event or field trip with the use of the Event Scoop Sheet.

The "Parent Communication Policy" Template

General Belief Statement: We believe that parents want to support our ministry. We believe that the parents can't support what they don't know about. We believe that most parents will be supportive if they feel their needs have been considered through communication.

1. What do you think your parents need to know about Sunday school?

Garden Pest:
Policy Hoppers

Evidence

These insects jump over any fence or barrier you put up in your garden. They refuse to be controlled! No matter what you do, they will not abide by your policies or standards. Evidences of these Policy Hoppers existing in your garden are parent complaints, poorly run programs, or last-minute emergencies.

Sources of Infestation

Ego, or pride. This person doesn't want to be controlled. A lack of respect for you or any other authority.

Treatment

1. Face-to-face, immediate reactions from you regarding the policy infringement.
2. Support the person, but control the action.
3. Reinforce the value and purpose of the policy.
4. Place the person under the direct supervision of a trustworthy team member for the next event or program.
5. Give clear, written and signed, warnings with clear consequences.
6. Support correct behavior if corrections are made.
7. If necessary, remove the person from the team.

2. What do you think your parents need to know about events?

3. What do you think your parents need to know about injuries or their child's safety?

4. What do you think your parents need to know about monthly plans?

5. What do you think your parents need to know about the curriculum you use?

6. What do you think your parents need to know about emergency situations?

COMMUNICATE THE POLICIES

Once you have written the policies pertaining to your team members and child safety, you need to publish them. Policies are only as valuable as their distribution! If nobody knows about your policies, you haven't really accomplished anything by creating them. Here are two great ways to communicate your policies.

Children's Ministry Team Handbook

This is a great tool for training and team development. Nothing demoralizes a team faster than feeling unprepared or unqualified. Producing and distributing a Team Handbook gives your team a sense of security. Training them to apply all that is in the handbook is another story. We'll talk about that in chapter 15.

This booklet should include the following sections:

1. The ministry vision.
2. Goals for the ministry.
3. The value of the team.
4. The application/screening process.
5. The apprenticeship/training process.
6. The value of the parents.
7. Protecting the children through the check-in/check-out process.
8. Protecting the children through adult/child ratios.

Your Policy Checklist

Check here if your church has this policy in place:

- ❏ Our church has a volunteer "Recruitment Policy."
- ❏ Our church has a "Screening Policy."
- ❏ Our church has a "Training Policy."
- ❏ Our church has a "Supervision Policy."
- ❏ Our church has an "Access Policy."
- ❏ Our church has a "Removal From Ministry Policy."
- ❏ Our church has a "Reinstatement to Ministry Policy."
- ❏ Our church has a "Touching Policy."
- ❏ Our church has a "Discipline Policy."
- ❏ Our church has a form called "Children's Ministry Application."
- ❏ Our church has a form called "Children's Ministry Application: Youth Version."
- ❏ Our church has a form called "Children's Ministry Driver Application."
- ❏ Our church has a form called "Request for Reinstatement to Ministry."
- ❏ Our church has a form called "Team Member Review Report."
- ❏ Our church has a form called "Agreement to Serve: Paid."
- ❏ Our church has a form called "Agreement to Serve: Volunteer."
- ❏ Our church has a form called "Appeals Policy & Process."
- ❏ Our church has a "Health Concerns Policy."
- ❏ Our church has a "Sick Children Policy."
- ❏ Our church has a "Child Protection on Campus Policy."
- ❏ Our church has a "Adult/Child Ratios Policy."
- ❏ Our church has a "Program Development Policy."
- ❏ Our church has an "Event Development Policy."
- ❏ Our church has an "Emergency Procedures Policy."
- ❏ Our church has a "Child Abuse Policy."
- ❏ Our church has a "Parent Communication Policy."
- ❏ Our church has a Children's Ministry Team Handbook.
- ❏ Our church has a Children's Ministry Parent Handbook.
- ❏ I have an advisory council to assist me in formulating policies.
- ❏ The board and/or the elders have approved the Children's Ministry Policies.

---

9. Protecting the children through sanitary classrooms.

10. Protecting the children through refusing sick children.

11. Protecting the children through the "never alone" rule.

12. Protecting the children through well-planned programs.

13. Protecting the children through well-planned events.

14. Protecting the children through careful touching.

15. Protecting the children through positive discipline techniques.

16. Protecting the children through child abuse recognition and reporting.

17. Protecting the children through emergency plans.

18. Removal of team members from the ministry

19. The appeals process.

20. Reinstating team members to the ministry.

21. Advancement in the team.

Children's Ministry Parent Handbook

This Booklet should include the following sections:

1. Our children's ministry vision.

2. Our respect for parents.

3. An overview of our team members.

Emergency Release Form

WE / I, _____, the parent(s) or legal guardian(s) of _____, certify that we / I have been informed that, as members of the church, our/my child will be participating in a number of activities which carry with them a certain degree of risk. These activities might include swimming, boating, hiking, camping, field trips, sports and other activities offered by the church. We/I consent for my child to participate in these activities. I affirm that my child is physically fit and has the necessary skills to safely participate in these activities. He/she is able to swim.

MEDICAL TREATMENT AUTHORIZATION

I understand that the church will attempt to notify me in case of a medical emergency involving my child. If the church cannot reach me, I authorize the church to hire a doctor or other healthcare professional to provide the medical services he or she may deem necessary. I will pay for any medical expenses incurred in this treatment.

I will notify the church if I feel there are any health considerations that would prevent my child's participation in any of the activities listed above. I also give my permission for church leaders to restrict my child from participating in any activity if they should doubt my child's ability or safety while participating.

_____   _____
Parent/Guardian Signature   Date:

Parent/Guardian Phone # (Work) _____   (Home): _____

Parent / Guardian Pager #: _____   Pin #: _____

Medical Ins. Co: _____   Policy # _____

Doctor's Name: _____   Dr. Phone #: _____

---

4. A review of what we offer to you and your children.

5. Our plans for this year.

6. We're protecting your children through our team member screening process.

7. We're protecting your children through our check-in/check-out process.

8. We're protecting your children through our adult/child ratios.

9. We're protecting your children through our sanitary classrooms.

10. We're protecting your children through our concern for sick children.

11. We're protecting your children through our "never alone" rule.

12. We're protecting your children through our well-planned programs.

13. We're protecting your children through our well-planned events.

14. We're protecting your children through careful touching.

15. We're protecting your children through our positive discipline techniques.

16. We're protecting your children through our emergency plans.

17. A map to your child's classroom.

Children's Ministry Incident Report

It is the policy of the Children's Ministry to do all we can to protect the safety of all children who participate in church-sponsored classes or events. It is also our policy to communicate, as best we can, with the parent(s)/guardians of those children regarding their children's needs, behavior, etc. while in our care. This Incident Report is simply a reporting of facts and does not imply any guilt or liability associated with this incident.

Child's Name: _____ Date: _____

Description of incident: _____

Location of incident: _____

Was there an injury? (check one) ❏ No   ❏ Yes
(if yes, check "Minor" or "Serious" and describe below)

❏ **Minor**
"Minor" injuries are scratches, bumps with no swelling, carpet burns, pinched skin, fingers or toes, etc. Bleeding is considered "minor" if it is only from the top layer of the skin and stops in 2 minutes with little pressure.

❏ **Serious**
"Serious" injuries are injuries to the eyes, bumps with swelling, cuts beyond the top layer of the skin, burns, broken bones, muscle sprains, bruising, internal or relentless bleeding, severed fingers, toes or limbs, etc. Complete a Serious Injury Report.

Description of the injury: _____

Action taken: _____

Action taken by: _____
                    (Print name)   Signature of team member

Incident Checklist
   (Completed by ministry team member)
   ❏ Child's needs cared for
   ❏ Incident Report filled out completely
   ❏ Coordinator or children's ministry director informed
   ❏ Parent(s) informed
   ❏ Parent(s) signed Incident Report
   ❏ Parent(s) given copy of Incident Report
   ❏ Incident Report original to children's ministry director

I verify receipt of a copy of this Incident Report.

_____
Signature of parent/guardian   Date   Home phone number

To discuss this incident further, contact: _____

Children's Ministry Sensitive Situation Report

It is the desire of the Children's Ministry to create an environment which is safe and secure for all children. We must be prepared to take an active role in recognizing and reporting possible signs of child abuse if we should encounter them. We also realize that we are bound by the law to report suspected child abuse within a limited time. The church's Children's Ministry will operate within the reporting standards set forth by the state. The required time for reporting is immediate (or as soon as practically possible) by phone, with a written report forwarded after receiving information about, or observing, the alleged abuse. This report is designed to serve as an ancillary account of conversations between children and adults related to an alleged abusive act, and is not intended to replace the required state forms and interviews. All conversations and contents of this report must be kept confidential and restricted to the team member who encountered the report, the area coordinator, the children's pastor, the senior associate pastor, and the senior pastor of the church. Additional people may be included in the above list as directed by the senior associate pastor or senior pastor.

Child's name (first, last): _____

Date of report: _____

Situation category (check which apply):

❏ Suspicious marks or bruises   ❏ Child-reported abuse
❏ Observed parental "harshness"   ❏ Child sex-related words
❏ Adult comment   ❏ Nutrition concern
❏ Hygiene concern   ❏ Neglect concern
❏ Other

Details of situation (what was heard or seen, by whom, where, when):

Action taken:

Name of person filing report:

_____   _____
Printed name   Signature

This report must be locked in the children's ministry office.

## chapter 10

Choosing the Seeds:
The Design of Programs

"*Seed racks are usually stocked with everything a given company produces for the year. But just because a package of seeds is there doesn't mean you can run home and plant the seeds. Don't buy anything until you read the directions on the package*" (Basic Gardening Illustrated, Menlo Park, CA: Lane Publishing Co., 1975;. page 47).

I love Chinese food! When we visit a great Chinese buffet, I feel like I'm doing something naughty! Being surrounded with all this good food, just for the taking, couldn't be good for me! I soon find myself in a "feeding frenzy." My eyes roll back into my head as I pile the different favorite foods onto my plate. When I make my way back to the table, I'm dizzy with anticipation. About halfway through the meal, I always have the same regret: I wish I hadn't taken all this food! I think to myself, "I wish I could just take a reasonable helping of one or two kinds of food and then totally enjoy those, rather than getting a plate full of stuff that mixes together and overwhelms me."

Planning programs in children's ministry is much like eating at a Chinese buffet! The challenge is to fight the temptation to load your plate with too many programs. When this happens, you and your team, and even the children, begin to get too full and the value of each individual program gets mixed in with all the busy rushing and doing. The end result is a lot of burping and regrets.

The trend in church ministry today is for fewer, more focused programs. It is much more effective to have one or two programs that really advance your ministry vision, rather than a dozen that simply keep the children busy. This trend is the result of busy families and the fast-paced world in which we live! In the church, we need to do all we can to offer the families quality programs, but we need to pace these programs in such a way that the families are able to enjoy the fewer, more effective programs while still being busy with soccer, piano lessons, and gymnastics.

PROGRAMMING FOR A NEW GENERATION

The world is changing rapidly in every way imaginable. Technology is leading us down paths that few have the skills to maneuver. Families are bearing the brunt of faster, better, newer, and the list goes on. The programs you design must meet both the felt and the real needs of the children and families in your community. (Review chapter 2.) Spend some time as a children's ministry staff brainstorming ideas for programs you would want to offer at your church if you had all the money and all the staff in the world.

You have to think big or you'll never get there! This is a good idea to do once each year as you "blue sky" your way into the future.

The programs you generate from your "blue sky brainstorming" session will give rise to all kinds of programming questions, but the first one addresses the Chinese buffet dilemma: How much will fit on our church plate?

Remember Your Vision

Plants can't grow without water. Your ministry can't

grow without programs which are designed with the proper purpose. Your purpose for every program must be the fulfillment of the Great Commission. This purpose is the "water" that softens the hard places around the children's hearts and makes them ready to receive the love of God.

Asking, "Why are we doing this?" about every program before it is begun, is an excellent habit. Even those programs whose main purpose is to have fun must be viewed as fitting into the Great Commission because fun attracts children, and because in the middle of having fun, relationships with Godly mentors are built. Let the water of God's love and restoration of a corrupt creation flow through the "particles of soil" that walk through the doors of your programs. Design purposeful methods of watering, and don't let any water be wasted!

From this point on, to the end of the book, we will be taking a closer look at the 15 "Great Commission Vision" goals that ended chapter 7. Each one of these goals leads the children's ministry to realizing some aspect of the commission our Lord gave his church. We will begin with the command to make disciples.

We may plant the seeds of conversion, but the Holy Spirit does the watering. The Spirit of God is often compared to water, "the living water." We in children's minister bathe these children in the word of God and refresh them with the water of the Holy Spirit. God will bring them into his kingdom when they are ready, but we must be faithful and do our part.

All our programs, our goal-setting, our surveys, our political campaigning, and our fancy lessons, are for nothing if they do not further the "Great Commission." It is our supreme command, and all we do bows to its importance. Let's take up the cause of Christ and continue to develop spirit-filled adults who will attract children to God, to establish a salvation relationship with Jesus Christ, and who will then teach them to become significant role models, teaching the children to obey all that he has commanded us. It's not about anything else!

As you go about your delightful job of brainstorming new ideas, always ask: "Which of the five categories of our "Great Commission Children's Ministry" does this program serve? If it does not directly influence meeting one of the goals in at least one of these five categories, then why are you even entertaining spending the time and the money it would take to make this program a reality? Once your program has passed the "vision test," determine where it will fit in with the rest of the year's programs.

Yearly Program "Scope and Sequence"

In designing your children's ministry's year calendar, here are several questions to consider regarding the scope and sequence of your programs.

Important Questions to Consider

1. Do you understand the busy world of your community?

2. At the end of the year, what do you want to have accomplished?
   a. In your children's spiritual development
   b. In your support of the families
   c. In your ministry team

3. What programs are a definite?
   a. Sunday morning/evening
   b. On-going, successful programs
   c. Programs that worked before and need to be repeated

4. What programs need to be retired?

5. Is there room for more programs when you add the definite ones?

6. Are there seasonal holes in your calendar that can be filled with programs?

7. Are there aspects of your ministry vision that aren't being furthered by current programs?

8. Has the Lord made you aware of needs in your church or community that could be aided by a new program?

9. Is there a way to chain your programs together into a theme or learning process for the year?

10. Do your programs build on each other, or do they exist as separate entities with no cross-over?

11. If you and your family were involved in all the

programs you plan, what would be the effect on your family?

12. What have you learned about the pacing of major programs? How long does it take to prepare, operate, and recover from a major program?

13. Are there programs offered by the city or other local churches that you can support instead of trying to create your own?

14. Do you have a boundary policy for programming, such as, "We will only create two new programs per year." If not, is this a good idea?

Principles of Calendarizing

A student asked me if it was possible to over-plan or to plan too far in advance. That was an interesting question. What do you think? What may happen if you began recruiting for your VBS in September? You do run the risk of losing your momentum and making the people immune to your ideas because they are too far away. You may even lose some of your volunteers. So, yes, it is possible to plan too far in advance. I don't think you can over plan an event, though. I would rather run the risk of over-planning than under-planning.

If you don't already, get in the habit of making "to do" lists. This is a great way of keeping track of your progress toward an event. The wall calendars that use a wipe-off pen are also great to use. Color-code a program's deadlines for easy visualization.

Points to Consider When Creating Your Calendar

1. Is this a season for this event or program? (Consider seasons, holidays, school schedules, etc.)

2. What else is going on at the same time or within weeks of the event? (Other church events, retreats, city events, sports events, etc.)

3. Consider your target audience. With what are they also involved? (vacations, sports events, graduations, taxes, etc.)

4. Consider your volunteer pool. With what are they also involved, or what have they just completed? (Work schedules, other church events or ministries, retreats, crusades, etc.)

5. Consider your leadership team. With what are they also involved, or what have they just completed? (Be selfish. Protect yourselves and your families!)

6. Consider your budget. Do you have enough money at the projected time to create the kind of event you want? Should you wait until you do?

7. Is there a connection between calendarized events that must be carried out?

You did some basic evaluation of the current programs in chapter 7, but we need to go a bit deeper here. The process of evaluating your programs is vitally connected to the designing of new programs. Before you can design new programs, you must look at what has been done in the past and ask yourself the basic question, "Why did the programs in the past succeed or fail, and how are the new programs different?" We need to learn from the past, and then apply it to the future. Church growth experts tell us that becoming comfortable with the present is one of the best ways to guarantee that you'll never enter the future. The "Program Evaluation Form" (page 152) is a brief tool to evaluate your current programs in light of creating new ones.

DESIGNING NEW PROGRAMS

If you've decided to create new programs, it is important to seek God's wisdom and the counsel of others. Be cautious if you find yourself going on your own feelings. You should be passionate about a new program, but you should not let your passion drive out wisdom. Wisdom requires us to slow down, consider our ministry vision, and ask God for help. Consider these Scriptures when developing new programs: "If any of you lacks wisdom, he should ask God, who gives generously to all without finding fault, and it will be given to him" *(James 1:5)* and "Plans fail for lack of counsel, but with many advisers, they succeed" *(Proverbs 15:22)*. With that caution in mind, take a look at the following process of designing a new program.

The Basics of Programming

1. Establish Your Ministry Vision. This will be the foundation for all of your program ideas.

2. Identify the Program Need. What do you plan to do to reach your ministry vision? PRAY!

3. Evaluate the Program Need. Does this program really fit your vision? Is it the best way? PRAY!

4. Seek Counsel. Ask those you respect for opinions and suggestions. PRAY!

5. Set Rough Plans. Based on counsel, establish dates, determine cost projections, facility, and personnel needs.

6. Answer All Questions. (Before you are asked!) Predict questions to be asked by the board and formulate your answers.

7. Make Proposal to Pastor/Board. Be sold on plans by this stage. Provide them with all they need to be sold also. If your plan is not approved, go back to the beginning and rework your plans with the counsel of those you respect. Solve the problems that were brought up. PRAY!

8. Advertise. Personally "sell" the plan to key people. Print flyers, make announcements, etc.

9. Purchase. Develop a shopping list for needed items and purchase within budget limits.

10. Recruit, Train. Advertise openings or personally recruit. Train in all areas of plan: curriculum, procedures, etc.

11. Advertise. Continue to advertise the program. Make sure your "target audience" is exposed to the advertising.

12. Communicate. Remain close with the volunteers for the program through meetings, meals, letters, calls, etc.

13. Invite. Personally (you and your staff) invite those who you want to participate in the program. (Don't forget the senior pastor!)

14. Operate Program. Do your best, care for the people involved! This is not just a program, it's a gathering of people!

15. Support. Compliment your volunteer staff. Recognize them publicly.

16. Evaluate. Meet with your staff either during or after the program. Did you meet your goal? Changes?

17. Repeat? Based on the success of the program (goal-related, people-centered) will you repeat it? Would your volunteers?

18. Advertise. Whether you do it again or not, report to the board, pastor, and church. Highlight success and fruit!

Be careful of the dreaded fork in the road after the "Make Proposal to Board/Pastor" step. You may or may not get approval at this point. You may have the board or pastor tell you to rework your plans and try it again next month. If this is the case, return to "Start." If you do get approval, you can proceed downward toward the "Advertise" step.

Notice the last step is "Advertise." We do so well in the preprogram advertising. We put up banners and make announcements in the worship service. Everybody knows about the event prior to its arrival. Then, after the event has happened, and the Lord has done great things, we neglect coming back and advertising the success! We rob ourselves of the fruit! One of the greatest recruitment techniques I ever began was to advertise the success after the event or program's beginning. (See the "Sandwich Principle" illustration in chapter 13.) If you do this, those who didn't volunteer this time will regret that they didn't when they hear about all the good stuff that happened. Then, you tell the church that you will repeat this again, and tell them to be listening for the announcement. Now, that's a winning plan! You'll have to turn volunteers away!

Planning the Program

The greatest protector of a program's success, apart from the leading of the Lord, is adequate planning. The slogan for children's ministry is too often, "Next time." "Next time" I'll have the food ready earlier. "Next time" we'll get the advertising out sooner. "Next time" we'll keep the three-year-olds home when we go on our desert hike. There seems to be an endless parade of "next times," and we seem to learn too slowly. I was frustrated with this cycle in my

Program Evaluation Form

Every program must be evaluated based on its impact on your ministry vision. Most ministry visions employ four basic components: Evangelism (E), Bible teaching (B), discipleship (D), and fun or fellowship (F). (Service to others is included in discipleship.) For the sake of universal use, this form evaluates programs based on these four basic goals. Your own ministry vision can be divided into these areas or additional areas can be added at the end of the form. Enter your current programs, and then for the area or focus of that program. Then, respond to each question by marking the appropriate rating (1 = poor, 4 = excellent). At the end of the section, total that program's score. Scores lower than 30 points indicate a weak program.

PROGRAM: _____

Evaluation Questions

1. What is the basic program goal (more than one is OK)	**Goal:** E B D F
2. Was the overall program goal met?	**Rating:** 1 2 3 4
3. Did the program meet a need in the children?	1 2 3 4
4. Did the program meet a need in the community?	1 2 3 4
5. Did the program meet a need in the parents?	1 2 3 4
6. Did the program meet a need in the church?	1 2 3 4
7. What was the general response from the team members about the program?	1 2 3 4
8. Were the children challenged by the curriculum?	1 2 3 4
9. Did the attendance grow over the course of the program?	1 2 3 4
10. Was the amount of money invested into the program worth it?	1 2 3 4
11. Was the amount of hours invested into the program worth it?	1 2 3 4
12. Was the date of the program a good choice?	1 2 3 4
13. Was the program's schedule comfortable?	

Overall Program Total Score _____

own ministry, so I created a tool that I'll pass on to you. This little exercise has saved many events from sure failure due to lack of planning. I used to lay awake at nights thinking about the event or program. To deal with that, I would take a virtual walk-through of the event weeks before its launch. I got so good at this, that I would actually feel like we had already had the event! Follow the process of the walk-through on pages 153 and 154 and I'm sure it will become a habit of yours for years to come. Revise and add to it to suit your own event or program.

Ending a Program

A program must have a life span! When a program is created, one of the critical things to determine is what will be the criteria used to determine the program's life span? Above, I gave you a program evaluation tool. You can use something like that to determine a program's life span, or you can simply decide that a program will only last a certain amount of time. In today's busy, changing world, being the same is not a good thing! Change is expected and desired. "New" means better, more exciting, fresh!

We have run a children's church program at our church called "God Squad" for over a year now. We invested quite a bit into camouflage outfits for the team members. We created a theme of being a part of the army of the Lord. The children and parents responded quite positively to the program in its early months. Now, after one year, we are starting to

Children's Ministry Program Mental "Walk-Through"

Take a mental walk through your program long before it happens! Every program is different, but this form has some general prompts to help you along your journey. If you come across something that affects your team training process or an item that needs to be budgeted, mark the appropriate boxes.

❏ 1. How does this program help fulfill the Great Commission?

❏ 2. How does this program fit in your philosophy of children's ministry?

❏ 3. How will this program benefit the church and community?

❏ 4. What have you done to make sure others know your answers to numbers 1, 2, and 3?

❏ 5. Have you reserved the facility far enough in advance?

❏ 6. Is there a cost in using the facility? Do you have keys?

❏ 7. What time are you arriving? How much time do you need to get ready before the children arrive? Have you cleared the time, date, and facility use with the church secretary?

❏ 8. Will you be alone? Are there people who must arrive early to help you? Are they trained?

❏ 9. When and how were they trained?

❏ 10. When did you start the recruiting/training process?

❏ 11. How were these people recruited?

❏ 12. Are these volunteers or paid staff? If paid, how much, and did you get this approved?

❏ 13. Were these people screened through church and legal channels? Were there background checks done early enough to provide time for you to re-recruit if necessary?

❏ 14. Is the room large enough to accommodate the number of children expected?

❏ 15. Are the air conditioners/heaters accessible and working?

❏ 16. Is the facility secure from outsiders? How many entrances/exits are there? Will there be enough staff to monitor these doors?

❏ 17. Is the lighting adequate, both inside and out? Is it working?

❏ 18. Do you have enough tables and chairs? Who will set them up? Are you responsible for putting them away? Will you have help? Are those people expecting to stay?

❏ 19. Are there supplies to get ready? Who bought them? How do they get to the facility? Were they budgeted? Who planned for their purchase and use?

❏ 20. Are there refreshments to get ready? Who bought them? How did they get to the facility? Were they budgeted? Will the refreshments be messy? Are there cleaning supplies available? Are there enough trash cans? Who is responsible for cleaning up afterwards?

❏ 21. Is there audio/visual or other technical equipment required for the program? Whose equipment is it? Who sets it up? Will that person be there early enough? Who runs it? Does that person know how to fix it if it doesn't work during the program? Do you have a backup person who will be ready if needed?

❏ 22. As the children start arriving, do they know where to go, and what time to be there? How do they know this? Have their parents been told clearly, often, and soon enough? Who created this printed material? How much did you budget for this? Was it approved? When did you start distributing printed material?

❏ 23. How are the children getting to the facility? Do you have to organize transportation? What does it cost? Is it budgeted? Is the cost covered by the program or the church? If carpools are used, does the church's insurance cover the cars, drivers, and children? Are the cars pre-approved? Have the drivers been screened? Do the drivers have maps, directions, and any other necessary information? Do the parents know when and where to drop off and pick up their children? Are there maps for the parents? Will the drivers stay for the whole program? Do they know when to return?

❏ 24. Are there signs that point the way from the parking lot to the program area of the facility? Who made them? How much did they cost?

Was it budgeted and approved? Who put them up? Who takes them down after the program?

❏ 25. Is there adequate staff to greet the children in the parking lot, assist in traffic control, and direct the children safely to the program area? Are they easily identified as members of your team (with shirts, badges, etc.)? Who designed the shirts and badges? Was the cost budgeted and approved? Does the staff know where to find a phone in case of an emergency? Can they locate you quickly?

❏ 26. Are the children checked in and out somehow? Who does this? How were the supplies purchased? Is there a check-in/out area? Are the children organized into groups at this time? Is there a list indicating each child's group in case of emergency? Who has the list? Are the permission and emergency release forms distributed, filled out, and collected in advance? Who does this? Who has the forms? Where are they kept?

❏ 27. Is there a registration cost? Can payment be made at the door? Who handles the money? Who has a list of those who have prepaid? Do you have change and a cash box? Are there at least two adults with the money at all times? Where does the money go when the program begins? Is it safe there? Is there are receipt book for those who need receipts?

❏ 28. What do you have planned for the children who arrive early? How early will you be prepared? Will you keep children out until a certain time? Will they be supervised and safe?

❏ 29. Will there be a person leading songs or doing something "on stage" for the few minutes before the program starts? Who is it? Have you asked them to do this ahead of time?

❏ 30. Are there enough adults to be greeters in the program area? Are they trained in discipline techniques? Are they easily identified as members of your team (shirts, badges, etc.)?

❏ 31. As the program begins, what is the program curriculum? How did you choose it? Did you write it yourself? Was the cost budgeted and approved?

❏ 32. Are the adults trained in the curriculum?

❏ 33. Have you planned for enough time for the entire program? Is there a printed schedule?

❏ 34. Will there be restroom breaks? Are the restrooms close and adequate? Are they open early enough? Do you know who to call if a toilet overflows? Are cleaning supplies available? Is there enough soap, toilet paper, and paper towels? Do you have enough staff to supervise restroom breaks? Is this part of your team training?

❏ 35. Will refreshments be served to children in groups? Do you have enough staff to cover the groups? Who sets out refreshments? Who cleans up the mess?

❏ 36. Will there be a craft time? Who planned it? Who purchases and prepares the supplies? Was it budgeted and approved? Will the activity take place in another area? Is that area prepared and supervised? Do you have enough supplies for more kids than you expect? Who will clean up the area?

❏ 37. When the program is over, do you have activities planned to fill extra time? Can your song leader or other volunteers help? Are they planning to stay?

❏ 38. Do you want to take the children to their parents or let parents come to the program area? Which is better for the children's safety? Have the parents been informed of this process? Are there enough staff to help parents in this and to assist with traffic control and check-out?

❏ 39. If check-out is at night, is the lighting adequate? Does your team need flashlights? How were they purchased?

❏ 40. What will you do with children who aren't picked up on time? Where will they be watched and by whom? Who will call the parents? What will you do if you cannot contact the parents? Do the parents know your plan?

❏ 41. Who will help "clean up, put away, and turn off"? Are they planning to do this?

❏ 42. Will you have a team debriefing meeting to discuss the program? Will you have refreshments? Does the team know this? Have you reserved the meeting area?

❏ 43. Who locks up the facility?

❏ 44. How will you say "thank you" to all who helped with the program? Is the cost budgeted and approved?

❏ 45. How will you publicize the fruit of the program? Will you ask the senior pastor for a few minutes to share your testimony or story? Who will do that? Will you show a brief video? Who has prepared it? Will it be ready for the pastor to view ahead of time? Was the pastor invited to the program? Will you print an insert for the bulletin? Who will prepare this? When must it be ready? Do you know the date of the next program so that you can advertise it at the same time you share the success of this one?

hear grumbling about the content, the theme, the look, etc. The children are still responding well to the program, but it's interesting how once the newness wore off, the criticisms increased. We are planning to change the program soon. We think it is time. We will take what we've learned from "God Squad" and inject it into a new program with a new look and feel.

If a program's effectiveness in furthering the ministry vision is slowing, it is time to make a change. I remember years ago when the television show "Seinfeld" ended. It took us all by surprise. The show was very popular. I remember hearing an interview with one of the producers who said, "It is better to go out when the audience wants more, than to be run out by a bored audience who is tired of you." That makes sense. Once a program has peaked in its fruitfulness, and you see signs of the children, parents, or team members being tired of it, retire it soon! It is better to retire a program and move on to a new one than to drag around an old program for the sake of tradition or security.

The best way to end a program is to launch a new one! Don't end a program and have "dead air" in your programming. You will have more complaints than you can ever imagine! Have you ever cared for toddlers? One of the fascinating things about toddlers is that they can be easily distracted. If you want a toddler to loosen up his death-grip on something, all you have to do is offer him something else. He will drop that old thing like a hot rock and latch onto the new thing. If you are planning on retiring an old program, set a date for the end of that program that coincides with the development time needed for the new program. While the old program is slowly sinking in the West, behind the scenes you are developing the new one. Advertise the new program before you announce the old program's end. The folks that might hold onto the old program will become toddlers as they drop the old one and latch onto the new one!

## chapter 11

Planting the Seed:
Options for Programs

"**S**eeds sprout best in a moist, well-drained, well-pulverized soil. You can work up the soil either several weeks or a few days before planting. To an often-used garden soil, simply add a fresh supply of amendments and work them in. You will have to use more elaborate techniques to prepare soil that has never been gardened before"* (Vegetable Gardening, Menlo Park, CA: Lane Publishing Co., 1976, page 32.).*

There are moments in life that God lets you witness just to remind you that you are a part of something eternal. I've had several of those moments in my children's ministry, but this one is on the top of the list. It was a Sunday morning in our children's church program. I don't even know what the lesson was about, but I'll never forget what some of the children learned that day.

We have a sweet, fourth-grade friend who wheels his way into children's church each Sunday morning on his motorized wheelchair. On this day, he wheeled his way into our hearts. His name is Scott. He is quite intelligent and very sensitive underneath his paralyzed body. He can't speak in words, but we can all understand his gentle smile and kind eyes. Toward the end of the service, we noticed Scott moving back and forth with his wheelchair. We thought little of it. We figured that he was just trying to get a better location to see what was going on. A few minutes later, another fourth grade boy joined Scott in working with his chair. Soon, that other boy was frantically going to other children in the back of the room saying, "Something is wrong with Scott's chair. We have to help him!" Within seconds a whole group of "back row, tough guys" were hovering over Scott's chair trying to fix the problem. By this time the first boy who helped Scott was in tears; he said, "We have to pray for Scott!"

And then it happened. It was like one of scenes in a movie where the room spins around and the scene is the only thing visible. I don't remember what else was going on at the time. I can't remember who was talking on stage. The only thing we saw was a group of eight children laying hands on Scott and his wheelchair and praying for God's help.

My assistant and I were in tears as we watched this moment from God. The first boy who helped Scott sank into his chair, still crying, after the prayer was over. My assistant went over to him and encouraged him for responding to Scott's needs. The spontaneous prayer meeting for Scott's wheelchair was our first precious moment of the morning; the next ones came when the parents picked up their children.

During check-out, we complimented the parents of the boy who organized the prayer time for Scott. They began to cry as we told the story. Then, we told the story to Scott's parents who also began to cry. That day, in that one series of moments, God showed us all the beautiful effects of sacrificial compassion and service to others. We will never forget the smile on Scott's face as he wheeled out of children's church knowing that God and his friends cared enough for him to become involved!

The purpose of the programs we spend so much time designing, developing, paying for, and facilitating is for the Scotts of our ministries! The children are listening! They are watching! They are waiting for God to use them! All we need to do is attract them to God, lead them into a relationship with Jesus Christ, and provide the training and opportunities; then, get out of their way!

In the first few weeks of my current children's ministry, I met with the youth pastor and asked him, "What do you want us to 'graduate' into your ministry? What character or qualities are you wanting from the sixth graders?" After a pause, and some discussion, his answer was, "Children who have an intimate relationship with God and who are willing to serve." He echoed the vision the Lord had given me. Developing a heart for God and a heart for service are the two pillars that hold up my Children's ministry vision. This chapter is, once again, about passion, vision, and goals. Everything we do must fit into the big picture of spiritual development.

Throughout this chapter I'll refer back to the "Great Commission Children's Ministry Vision" that was outlined in chapter 7. Remember: program options and their corresponding planting guidelines must always find their reason for existence in your vision. Otherwise, why have them?

CORE VALUES FOR PROGRAMS

As I started to create planting guidelines for the various programs, I noticed that they all contained basically the same core concepts. Rather than repeat them for every program, I'll list those guidelines that are transferable to all programs here, at the beginning, and then I won't mention them again. Programming in children's ministry is much like Mexican food (at least the Americanized versions that we have in this country). If you notice, most Mexican food dishes contain the same ingredients, they're just served differently. For instance, if you layer some beans, lettuce, onions, salsa, cheese, tomatoes, and beef on a flat flour tortilla it is called a "tostada." If you roll that "tostada" up, it is now called a "burrito." If you deep fry the "burrito," it is now called a "chimichanga." If you fold the "tostada" in half, it is called a "taco." All of these forms of Mexican food contain the same basic ingredients; the only difference is in the presentation.

The Basic Ingredients of Every Children's Ministry Program

1. Recruit only those adults who are child-targeted, not lesson-targeted!

2. Apprentice new volunteers under experts in child-targeted ministry.

3. Use the team approach instead of a one-person show.

4. Organize team rotation options (monthly, quarterly, etc.).

5. Train team members in guided conversation techniques.

6. Emphasize application of the Bible concepts to children's real lives.

7. Greet the children even before they enter the room!

8. Create learning environments in which children explore on their own.

9. Replace lectures with interactive teaching. (80% them, 20% you)

10. Utilize audio/visuals (popular songs, music videos, etc.).

11. Incorporate the four-part lesson concept in every lesson.

12. Incorporate out-of-class experiences (field trips, walks, etc.).

13. Plan significant prayer/worship times for the children's needs.

14. Offer opportunities to apply the lesson through organized service projects.

15. Visit the children apart from Sunday (soccer games, karate lessons, etc.).

16. Communicate with the children apart from Sunday (email, cards, phone calls, etc.).

17. Pray for the children and their families daily.

The basic ingredients of children's ministry are all the same. The only difference is in the presentation, or setting of the ministry environment. The basic ingredients of a midweek program are the same as Sunday school, it is simply the setting that changes. On page 159 is a list of the basic ingredients of all children's ministry programs. The following are specific, unique planting guidelines for each program that go beyond this basic list.

REGULAR WEEKLY PROGRAMS

These programs relate to vision category #9: "We will TEACH THEM with relevant curriculum which emphasizes both biblical content and fun!

Goal 9.2 Before they come to an event, we want the children of our ministry to say: "I want to go there because I learn more about God there."

No matter how sophisticated and trendy our children's ministries become, the staple diet will always be the Sunday programs. Give these your best effort in planning and place your most talented teachers in this time slot. Studies have shown that most seekers visit churches on Sunday mornings, and the church they choose to visit has "three minutes to make a good impression" (*Frog in the Kettle*, George Barna). This is the time when we will see most of the children who attend the church, and these children will recognize their need for God only after we show them how important he is to us. Their desire to learn grows with ours. A teacher is one who teaches something he or she believes in or lives. The old adage is true: "More is caught than taught." The best way to teach children is through natural, informal conversations and through excellent curriculum presented by well-trained, spirit-led teachers.

To Reach This Goal:

1. Place priority on resources and personnel for Sunday programming.

2. Encourage Scripture memorization among the team and the children.

3. Develop ministry team mid-week Bible studies or fellowships

4. Train all team members in the use of personal experiences to enhance the curriculum and lesson.

Programs That Develop This Goal:

Planting Guidelines for Sunday School

The concept of Sunday school is changing. It is now viewed as a small group experience in which relationships are built: relationships between the adults and the children, and ultimately, the children and God. Bible knowledge remains critical, but that knowledge must be related to the children's daily life even more than before or it will be viewed as old fashioned or not useful. Here are some planting guidelines to make Sunday school a life-changing experience.

1. Protect the maximum adult/child ratio of 1/10.

2. Create a two-year only maximum age range for each class.

3. Incorporate missions or service projects in each class.

4. Develop a curriculum scope and sequence (provided by publisher?).

Planting Guidelines for Children's Church

Children's Church is a valuable part of a balanced ministry program. Children's Church offers multiple-service children an additional option apart from repeating Sunday school. Children's Church will provide an environment for teaching and enjoying extended times of worship. Children's church can also be the best environment for dramatic productions and unusual guests. Here are some planting guidelines to make children's church a life-changing experience.

1. Rotate team members through a duty roster monthly.

2. Begin with worship music as the children are entering.

3. Greet every child (touched, high 5) as they enter.

4. Use worship songs that are more adult than childlike.

5. Don't display the song's words past the initial learning phase.

6. Let the children see the adults worshiping.

7. Use children worship-leaders, not adults.

8. The lesson is a presentation that actively involves the children.

9. Break up into small groups for adult/child lesson interaction.

10. Prayer times can be included in the small groups.

11. Return to worship during check-out.

12. Provide a Parent Guide which summarizes the day's lesson.

13. Plan service projects, field trips, etc. throughout the year.

14. Rotate your program options

a. Elective Centers "Round Robin"—The children rotate through centers of crafts, games, Bible stories, or worship singing.

b. Sunday School General Session—Children gather together in a larger room for worship singing, prayer times, and a brief skit or puppet show, then go to Sunday school classes.

c. Bible Character Encounter—Children interview a Bible character who is actually a church leader (elder/deacon, etc.) in full costume and make-up. The children must guess who the character is prior to the interview.

d. "Special Forces" Worship—Children come to church dressed in their work clothes. An organized service project would be carried out during the children's church hour.

e. "Worship-on-the-Road"—Children would ride the church bus to a nearby biblical location for a time of worship and a lesson (a river for a baptism study, for example).

Staffing Secret—Rotate workers who specialize in the various programming listed above. Only use them a few times a year as their specialty comes up in the yearly calendar.

Planting Guidelines for Evening Programs (Sunday or Mid-week)

Evening programs, whether Sunday or mid-week, are perhaps the most difficult for which to recruit, but they have the most potential for personal connection with children. There's something about an evening that makes the children more relaxed and contemplative.

So, I view evening programs as extreme. You have extreme difficulty recruiting for an extremely potential program! You must be extremely clear about your vision and plans for these programs. Here are some planting guidelines to make evening programs life-changing experiences.

1. Since Sunday night is more relaxed, plan for longer worship and prayer times.

2. Provide some sort of food or snack.

3. Schedule and utilize guests heavily.

4. Develop curriculum that is different from Sunday morning.

5. Plan more unusual or extreme experiences for the children.

6. Rotate your program options.

7. A "club" environment—Children arrive to music being played, and sit at round tables with an adult at every table. The evening is filled with music, goodies, and guided conversation.

8. A "camp" environment—Children experience everything they could experience at camp! Team members are called counselors, and each night's events include a theme that is expressed in activities, food, guests, crafts, team competitions, or field trips.

9. A "world tour" environment—Children arrive to a different world site or country each night. The music, dress, speech, food, and activities all relate to the location of your tour.

PROGRAMS BEYOND THE WEEKLY OFFERINGS

These programs relate to vision category #10: We will establish a variety of child-targeted programs that TEACH THEM how to apply the truths of God's Word in their daily lives.

Goal 10.1 When a parent asks a child, "What did you learn today at church?" we want the child to say: "I learned how to be a better friend" or "I learned how to be a better student."

Traditional church programs are powerhouses of evangelistic and teaching potential; however, the list of additional programs for children is virtually endless! The work of the Holy Spirit takes place whenever you find children eager to learn and adults who teach the Word of God. These Bible stories are filled with powerful lessons for children, but they have to "mined" by adults who know the world of the child and who can translate God's Word into the children's world and situations. As your imagination runs wild with program possibilities, be careful that children's ministry never becomes a place for good, moral lessons apart from the Bible. God's Word is "living and active" and critical to the children of every generation.

To Reach This Goal:

1. Train the adult team members to stay current with the world of today's child by viewing the television programs, web sites, and music videos they enjoy.

2. Train the team members to adapt the curriculum to suit the needs of today's children as they find themselves in varied environments, ministering to children in non-traditional ways.

Programs That Develop This Goal:

Planting Guidelines for Camps

Camping has always been, and always will be, an exciting experience for children. It is one of the only times that children can be on their own for an extended period of time. Camping creates a heightened sense of anticipation and awareness in children by placing them in an unfamiliar environment. More and more parents are becoming cautious about sending their children to camp for financial, time, and safety reasons. There will always be those who will send their children to a week-long camp, but the need for shorter, less-expensive options is growing. Here are some planting guidelines to make camp programs life-changing experiences.

Day Camps (Local, day trips with no overnights):

1. Become aware of the various visit options around your town (factories, or other unusual sites).

2. Based on the options, create a theme for the camp.

3. Create a schedule that includes a rotation of at-church and on-location experiences.

4. Contact the sites and visit the sites to create the curriculum or purpose for the visit.

5. Organize the transportation. Work the lease of a bus into the cost of the camp—no private cars!

6. Develop a team which includes people who will supervise:
   • The food, or food stops along the way.
   • The craft or other hands-on experiences
   • The location experience (contact, directions, curriculum, details, etc.)
   • Parent communication (itinerary, camp "scoop sheet," debriefing sheets, etc.)
   • The paperwork (emergency release, event release, payments, incident reports, etc.)

7. Design something the children can make or take home to remind them of the day, or camp focus.

Overnight Camps (Get-away camps with overnights at a camp facility, or cabin):

1. Decide on the camp time (seasonal?).

2. Decide on the camp location (based on availability, personal interests, or theme).

3. Order the bus to transport the children to the camp and back.

4. Based on the cost of the bus and the camp costs, set the price of the camp per child.

5. Pursue any scholarship support from your church budget or donors.

6. Verify that the camp organizes the curriculum and sets the theme. If not design your own.

7. Recruit the counselors.

8. Print the registration forms and publicize the camp.

9. Set a limit on number of campers based on number of counselors. (Is there a ratio from the camp?)

10. Design a follow-up program or effort after the camp (letter, reunion, etc.)

Planting Guidelines for Outings and Field Trips

No matter how old you are, the concept of a field trip still causes your heart to jump! There's something about getting on a bus and going somewhere when you should be in a classroom. The scheduling of field trips throughout the year will boost morale and parent support at critical times. A successful field trip can motivate children and unify your parent support while being just plain fun! Here are some planting guidelines to make outings or field trips life-changing experiences.

1. Get permission for the field trip before you tell the children, parents, or team members.

2. If the field trip is to be taken during the regular ministry time, consider these guidelines:

a. Make sure the timing works! (Enough time to organize the children, drive there, experience the place, load the children, drive back, and unload ready for parents to pick-up.)

b. Make sure the parents know at least two weeks in advance of the trip. Publicize the "scoop sheet" that includes the purpose, location, and timing of the trip.

c. Make sure you have on-campus options for the children who won't be going on the trip due to parent decision, lack of forms, or being new that week.

d. Make sure you have adequate adult supervision for those children staying at church.

3. If the field trip is to be taken outside of the regular ministry time, consider these guidelines:

a. Make sure the parents know at least two weeks in advance of the trip. Publicize the "scoop sheet" that includes the purpose, location, and timing of the trip.

b. Make sure the parents know when their children will be ready to be picked up.

c. Make sure you have parent phone numbers for all the children on the trip (Event Release Form).

4. Publicize the event.

5. Distribute and collect signed event forms: Emergency Release Form (keep on file for one year), and Event Release Form (used only for the event, discard afterward).

6. Organize the transportation. Work the lease of a bus into the cost of the camp—no private cars!

7. Recruit adult supervisors (Parents, adult/child ratio?)

8. Protect the safety of the children at all times.

9. Supervise the children until the parents pick them up.

PROGRAMS THAT TEACH SERVICE TO OTHERS

These programs relate to vision category #13: We will teach children TO OBEY the commands of God by participating in supervised service projects.

Goal 13.1 When offered an opportunity to become involved with a service project, we want the children to say: "I want to help others."

Serving others is not something that comes naturally to the children of today's busy, self-centered world, but it is the most effective tool in leading the children to greater depths of spiritual and emotional strength. We may have to lead the children by the hand into service projects, but once they get a taste of the joy of serving others, they won't want to stop!

To Reach This Goal:

1. Design a scope and sequence for developing servants. We need to have a plan for planting the seed of servanthood beginning with the nursery.

2. Design a service project calendar for all age groups.

3. Plan a service project cycle into your curriculum: Prepare, do the project, debrief.

4. Involve parents and children in the planning of the projects.

5. Publicize the projects beforehand, and share the results afterward. (See the "Sandwich Principle" in Chapter 13.)

PROGRAMS THAT TEACH LIFESTYLE EVANGELISM

These programs relate to vision category #14: We will teach children TO OBEY Jesus' command to be "salt" and "light" to others through their words, actions, and choices.

Goal 14.1 We want the church pastoral staff to think or say: "The children's ministry inspires me."

The children's ministry is a vital foundation for church growth. When the vision of being salt and light to others permeates our entire ministry, others will take notice. We can't be an island unto ourselves. Sharing the talents and testimonies of the children in all-church events like children's musicals, choir presentations in the adult services, and short dramas will help others see the joy and the depth the children celebrate in their relationship with God.

To Reach This Goal:

1. Create a pastor appreciation day.

2. Tell the pastoral staff about the work of the Lord in the children's ministry team.

3. Ask for opportunities to have the children share their talents and testimonies before adult audiences.

4. Invite the other pastors to children's ministry events.

5. Increase the support to other ministries from the children's ministry.

Other ministries would be impressed with your children's servant's hearts if you offered a group of children to assist in their cause or event. Children will learn the value of team support while enjoying giving to someone else. Instead of each ministry creating an outreach to the community during Thanksgiving or Christmas, join forces and support one large effort!

Programs That Develop This Goal:

Planting Guidelines for Scouting Programs

Everybody knows about scouting. Whether it's boy, girl, or Christian scouting, it has the reputation of teaching children how to develop into a morally-fit, mature adult who is able to work hard toward a goal. When the church adds the spiritual development ingredient, you have a winning program, and one to which you can easily recruit adults. Some of the options include Awanas, Boy Scouts, and Girl Scouts.

Planting Guidelines for Children's Choirs

Why have a children's choir? It teaches simple notation and rhythmic movement. Music skips over the generation gap and breaks age barriers. Age-group choirs often become Bible study groups as they explore and memorize biblical themes through songs. Music is an outstanding form of evangelistic witness. People love to hear children sing and share their faith. Children grow spiritually as they learn to worship. It provides opportunities for Christian service. It expands their interest in music and talent development.

Some Hints for Choir Rehearsal:

1. Keep them short: for 4 and 5 year olds, rehearse seven or eight different songs or activities in a fifteen-minute period; for 1st and 2nd graders, stay within 45 minutes and use songs or activities with lots of physical movement; for 3rd through 6th graders, you can practice for 60 minutes with a few breaks to refocus concentration.

2. Saturday mornings are good times, unless sports conflict.

3. Specials can be rehearsed on Sunday mornings during the Sunday school hour if the children are going to sing in church on occasional Sunday mornings. This is a great way to "beef up the choir" and show off the kids to the adult congregation.

4. Have an accompanist at rehearsals or play an accompaniment tape.

Planting Guidelines for Children's Seasonal Productions

1. Keep the performance to one hour or less.

2. Be sure the story line is relevant to the experience of the children.

3. Provide practice tapes with words and music to all songs.

4. Call only the children you intend to work with for the scenes to be rehearsed. Don't call all the children to every rehearsal!

5. Have assistant directors who will work on lines, music, and blocking with groups of children while the director works on the main stage.

6. Ask for the involvement of one adult friend or relative for each child involved in the musical: grandparents, aunts, uncles, friends, guardians, moms, dads. These people become your crew, phone communicators, and crowd controllers.

7. Keep the script simple with short speeches by characters. Set the script in large type for ease of reading.

8. Post "cheat sheets" at all stage entrances and exits to help backstage crews move children correctly and quickly.

9. NEVER keep children at rehearsal for more than 2 hrs. or after 8:00 at night. Parents at the rehearsals is a good idea.

10. Keep director's comments positive. Correct children or give suggestions for improvements privately.

(These suggestions are taken from "Ten Keys to Organizing a Children's Production" by Cora Alley, co-author, *SKITuations*.)

NOTE: For the sake of everyone's sanity, assign a roped-off video area at the back in the center of your auditorium. Elevate it slightly, so the videographers can get a good view of the children, up over everybody's heads. This will save you lots of arguments as you try to get those daddies out of the aisles so old Aunt Bonnie can see!

Goal 14.2 When asked, "Do your friends at school know you're a Christian?" we want the children say: "I am not ashamed to take a stand for God at school."

The pressure to conform and be popular is very strong in children today. The misconception is that we have to compromise to be popular. Children need to be taught that to take a stand for what is godly and right will give them something they can't get any other way: dignity and confidence! Children need to be shown that when they take a stand for what they believe in, they are very attractive and will become popular to a whole different peer group. Other children will want to be like them and will be attracted to God because of their confidence.

To Reach This Goal:

1. Publicly support those children who are taking a stand at school. We need to change the definition of popular. Children who take a stand for what is right need to be lifted up to be examples for others. Children want recognition. If we publicly highlight a child who took a stand for God at school each week in our church programs, others will want that same recognition. We can develop a "salt of the earth" award to give to these children. We have to encourage

and support the behavior we want the children to adopt.

2. Teach the children how to be truthful, honest, and righteous without being offensive.

3. Train the children in lifestyle evangelism through role plays.

Programs That Develop This Goal:

Planting Guidelines for Developing a "SWAT Team"

Fifth and sixth grade children who have been Christians for at least one year are ready for greater challenges! The SWAT Team (Students With A Testimony) program is designed to provide older children with the training they need to be salt and light in their schools. This is a specialty class, and not open to all children. The class might be on-going, or it could be a certain length (quarter, etc.). Children will learn how to witness by their thoughts, words, choices, and actions. Here are some planting guidelines to make the SWAT Team program a life-changing experience.

1. Create the purpose for the program and program logo (rendition of police S.W.A.T. team badge).

2. Design the curriculum. Topics might include:

a. How to witness without saying a word.

b. How to talk about God without being weird or "churchy."

c. Control your thoughts = control your actions.

d. How to understand why people do the things they do.

e. Helping your friends see things differently.

f. Persecution is OK, if it's for the right reason.

3. Advertise the program with restrictions on attendance.

4. Create a "train/do/talk about it" cycle in the class.

5. Design a graduation ceremony open to parents and others.

6. Create "Salt of the Earth" awards as gifts to the graduates. These awards can be clear glass salt shakers mounted on wood with nice brass plaques engraved with the child's name, etc. on it.

7. Share the fruit of the class in ministry-wide newsletters, and to the entire church.

PROGRAMS THAT PRODUCE CHILDREN'S MINISTRY VOLUNTEERS

These programs relate to vision category #15: "We will expect the children TO OBEY Jesus' Great Commission by volunteering to help in the children's ministry."

Goal 15.1 When asked to help a fellow child, we want children to say: "I like to help."

Taking responsibility for the ministry of the church is a quality that seems to be disappearing in today's busy world. Those of us in children's ministry are expected to do it all, without much assistance from the other church members. We must change this mindset starting with this generation of children! When a child is encouraged or led to become involved in the children's ministry, he or she will be blessed and develop a habit of service to the church that will benefit other churches.

To Reach This Goal:

1. Create a multi-age service plan for children in the elementary grades. If the children's ministry team members all believe in this concept, they can incorporate this principle into every class or ministry environment. Here are some ideas: having helpers in the class, developing fifth or sixth grade "deacons" in children's church, sending older children into younger children's classes to be helpers.

2. Publicly support and compliment those children who help other children.

Programs That Develop This Goal:

Planting Guidelines for a "Youth Leadership Program"

The Youth Leadership Program for fifth and sixth grade children. These children are trained to serve in the children's ministry as helpers of varying capacities. There is a director who supervises these children, maintains the evaluations, and makes sure the requirements are met. Children who serve in this program must be in children's church or Sunday school during another service. Here are some planting guidelines to make the Youth Leadership Program a life-changing experience.

1. Clearly define the conditions for application to this program.

2. Appoint a director of the program.

3. Define the expectations for each youth's involvement in the children's ministry.

4. Define the steps that each youth will proceed through on his or her way to graduation

5. Design the signs of advancement in the program (name badges, pins, etc.)

6. Define the process of evaluating the youth's involvement in the children's ministry.

7. Design the graduation program.

PROGRAMS THAT ATTRACT PARENTS

These ideas relate to vision category #3: "We will provide a safe, nurturing environment so that parents can rest assured that our children's ministry is a positive place to which their children can GO."

Goal 3.2 When parents think of the children's ministry, we want them to say: "They really understand what I'm looking for in a children's ministry."

The best way to guarantee continued ministry to the children is to care for the needs of the parents. Children only come when their parents bring them, and parents will go where their needs are being met. Today's parents face extreme fears and insecurities; they need more help in raising their children spiritually than ever before. Before we can help them become better parents, we have to make them extremely comfortable at church. They must know that their children are a priority, and their role as parents is honored.

To Reach This Goal:

1. Train all team members in the use of, and value of the take-home materials that are provided in the curriculum.

2. Train all team members in parent communication.

3. Pray for more time between services for a more relaxed check-out period during which parent communication can take place.

4. Develop a hallway ministry mindset in which someone greets and talks with parents during check-in or check-out times.

5. Conduct regular parent surveys and then publish results and plans to implement suggestions.

6. Share children's ministry success stories with the parents through a parent newsletter or weekly handouts.

Goal 3.3 About any children's ministry class or event, we want the parents to say: "I feel safe leaving my child there."

Chapter 9 covered the importance of child safety quite thoroughly, but all those polices and procedures do you little good if parents do not know about them. Steps taken to protect the children must be made public through signs, newsletters, and most of all through the Parent Handbook. If parents complain about your safety precautions, responded to with, "We're doing this to protect your child." In the long run they will be happier and the church will be more secure.

To Reach This Goal:

1. Continually update the children's ministry safety policies.

2. Create a Parent Handbook with parent versions of the safety policies and procedures.

3. Train all team members in the safety policies and procedures.

4. Design team member identification badges to be worn during ministry times.

5. Create safety signs for walkways and outside doorways.

PROGRAMS THAT SUPPORT PARENTS

These ideas relate to vision category #11: "We will inspire and challenge adult team members to TEACH THEM by becoming role models and by developing significant relationships with the children."

Goal 11.1 About any children's ministry class or event, we want the parents to say: "I know the teachers care for my child."

"Care" means a deep, real, love for children. Class size and class management effect this greatly. Even with large numbers of children, each child should feel cared for, and parents must sense that bring their children to you is like bringing their children to a second home. In a society where people are de-humanized, let's take the challenge to make the children's ministry a place where the individual is celebrated.

To Reach This Goal:

1. Design and print parent letters to be given out on Sunday (topics include parenting, partnering with our ministry, etc.).

2. Train all team members in effective classroom management.

3. Do all we can to reduce class size or increase the number of team members per children.

4. Train all team members in the application of the results of the parent survey.

PROGRAMS THAT TRAIN PARENTS

These programs relate to vision category #12: "We will support the parents in TEACHING their own children through printed materials, seminars, and conferences."

Goal 12.1 About any children's ministry class or event, we want the parents to say: "I feel like my church is a partner with me in raising my child."

Parents are vital to our ministry (because they bring their children), and our ministry is vital to the parents (because we further the spiritual development of their children). We need each other. Our ministry to their children either furthers their work at home, or it is the only ministry a child gets. There are parents who view what we do as enough spiritual development for their children. Regardless of the parents' view, we must support the parents through communication and ministry tools they can use at home.

To Reach This Goal:

1. Train all team members in parent communication.

2. Provide all team members with a list of creative parent-loving techniques to use during check-out.

3. Create enhanced take-home family application activities for each lesson (recruit a volunteer for each department for this).

4. Design church programs that involve the entire family, rather than separating them as the traditional Sunday morning programs typically do.

Programs That Develop This Goal:

Planting Guidelines for Family Programs

Pay close attention to the requirements for church events outlines in chapter 9, but the sky is the limit when it comes to organizing family fun. It's impossible to minister outside the church walls unless you minister to the entire family.

1. Family potlucks at the church or at the park across the street.

2. "Take a Teacher Home for Lunch" Sunday.

3. Trips to family friendly restaurants.

4. Take over a miniature golf course for an evening.

5. Service projects with the family.

6. Movie night at church.

7. A special guest like "Bible Man" at church.

8. Guest musician concerts like Jana Alayra at your church.

9. Neighborhood block parties.

10. Family talent night.

11. Family Olympics.

12. Free digital family pictures taken at church.

13. Midweek service projects with family and team members.

14. Saturday morning pancake breakfast.

15. Tours of local interesting, family-friendly sites (dairies, farms, businesses, etc.).

16. Chat room for parents on the church web site.

17. Sunday morning County Fair.

Planting Guidelines for Family Worship Services

Children in an adult worship service means you no longer have a traditional adult worship service. You can't! There are children present, and it is church for them, too. Here are some cautions you must consider before you embark on designing and implementing a Family Service.

1. A *Child-friendly Sermon:* Is the senior pastor willing to adapt his sermon for the children in the audience? This means he has to make it shorter, use lots of graphics, object lessons, physical props, and walk around the audience, up and down the aisles. He cannot stand behind his pulpit like he would for an adult audience.

2. *Family Interaction:* Family discussion questions before, during, or after the sermon, or throughout the service. Interaction with an object, a simple craft, or a physical activity may be appropriate.

3. *Children's Songs:* Be sure that the children's song menu is equally represented in a family service. Although children do fine with adult worship songs, it is fun and refreshing for adults to sing some children's music.

4. *A Child-friendly Bulletin:* Design the bulletin with a picture to color that re-states the theme of the sermon. Put in a few puzzles, brain-teasers, riddles, questions to answer, fill-in-the-blanks from the pastor's message, and some kid-type announcements that would be of interest to children. The bulletin should be a take-home that will help the parents discuss the events and the content of the service with their children.

5. *A Simple Bible Translation:* It is very important that young readers feel comfortable following along in God's word. The NIV (New International Version) is very popular with children. Children's Bibles are also an excellent choice.

Ten Ways to Use Children in Family Worship Services

1. To read the Scripture

2. As ushers

3. As greeters

4. As performers in a skit to illustrate the pastor's message

5. As someone to be interviewed for his/her opinion

6. To collect the offering

7. As special music presenters (solos, ensembles, choirs)

8. To do interpretive choreography

9. To play in the worship band or perform an instrumental solo

10. On the praise team

Planting Guidelines for Baby Dedications

It is important to start parents off on the right track by encouraging them to dedicate their babies to the Lord. This is typically a wonderful, family event, and it gives your Senior Pastor a moment to bless one particular family. Baby dedications are significant times of spiritual focus for the parents and extended family members. There is no right or wrong way of dealing with this process. Each church and pastor will dictate specific conditions for this process.

1. Design a process that is simple for the parent, the pastor, and the personnel overseeing the process.

    a. Parent phones in request to the church

    b. A designated person takes the information

- Parents' names
- Children's names
- Mailing address
- Phone number
- Requested date of dedication
- Requested service time
- Number of family members needing reserved seats

    c. The date and service time are confirmed

    d. Confirmation letter is sent

    e. Notification to the pastor or service director

    f. Parent packet readied at guest relations booth

2. Make the process known to all church staff and ushers

3. Make the process accessible through the church web site (automatic date/service check and confirmation, letter generated, notification to pastor, and packet label printed)

Goal 12.2 When the parents think about our support of them, we want the parents to say: "The children's ministry gives us valuable tools in raising our children."

We have already established that these are turbulent times for parents to be raising children. Values are relative, norms are abnormal, and the Word of God has been either ignored or shelved in most walks of civic and community life. Unfortunately, most of these parents are recovering from damaging experiences in their own childhoods. All the more reason for the church to step in by offering Parent Education Classes that will help parents establish a firm foundation in biblical parenting as well as understand the needs of their own children. Parents, after all, carry the final burden of discipleship when in comes to raising their children in the Lord, so the church must come along side these precious parents and equip them to do their all-important jobs.

To Reach This Goal:

1. Provide parent resources (both free and at a minimal cost) at a central location at church.

2. Provide parent classes on specific topics throughout the year. (Sunday mornings are best.)

3. Provide a parent newsletter with articles, stories, testimonies, etc.

4. Provide a parent support component to the church's web site (news items, community events, studies, networking, etc.).

AFTER-SCHOOL PROGRAMS

After school programs are excellent evangelistic and outreach programs to create and offer to your community. With the increase in the cost of living, and the busy pace of today's world, more parents are working longer hours. The church could ignore the condition and judge the world by saying, "We don't believe children should ever be left home alone, no matter what," or we can recognize the need and fulfill that need with loving, godly, nurturing people. The period after school is a sensitive time for children. They are tired, lonely, and needing supportive companionship. What a great opportunity for the church! Here are some planting guidelines to make after-school programs life-changing experiences.

1. When possible, offer after-school programs at the church facility.

2. Provide transportation or assist in transporting children from the school to the church.

3. Make the cost as low as possible for the parents (the lower the cost, the greater the outreach).

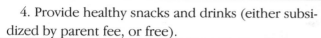

4. Provide healthy snacks and drinks (either subsidized by parent fee, or free).

5. Provide an initial time to transition from the school day which could include:

    a. A free time with games music, books available.

    b. Snacks, drinks.

    c. Adults who are willing to just be with the children.

    d. Art centers.

6. Provide a supervised time to work on homework.

7. Provide free tutoring (from honor roll high school students).

8. Create character-developing options for those who finish homework.

    a. Supervised use of the internet (email encouragement to missionaries, etc.).

    b. Service project ideas (with other children, parents, or alone).

    c. Hobby options (with plans to give away what is made).

    d. Gardening (with plans to give away what is grown).

    e. Cooking (with plans to give away what is cooked).

    f. Reading for the blind.

9. Provide a report to the parents of the activities for the day.

10. Create a connection with the parents for deeper support.

    a. Socials with them and their children.

    b. Trips.

    c. Periodic free meals at the church (that the children cook?).

    d. Written parenting support booklets, etc.

Whether you have hundreds of programs or just a few, do all you can to create environments in which children experience God's love for them. Remember, the purpose of every program is not to fill up the calendar, but to lead children to an intimate relationship with God.

## chapter 12

Garden Signs:
Publicize Your Image

A *garden is a place to relax, restore, and reflect. Those who view your garden should be drawn closer in. Every gardener knows that the design and care of your garden speaks about your view of life, God, his creation, and people. The best garden is the one enjoyed by others.*

If a garden is attractive, it draws you in to enjoy the peace and tranquility. Our children's ministry gardens should draw the parents in. When the parents enter our garden, the children come with them. Making the garden attractive is very important.

We, in children's ministry, are always building, planting, pulling weeds, and rototilling. Much of what we do goes unnoticed by the average garden visitor. It is a wonderful thing when people notice.

We recently refurbished our nursery rooms. We spent large amounts of money and effort to create a great room for both the children and the team members. On the day of the room's Grand Opening, we got many nice comments from parents, but the one comment that stays with me came weeks later. We launched a new Sunday evening program that was themed around a camp experience for children. As a mother was leaving the room during that program, she stopped me, looked me in the eyes and said, "Thank you for all you are doing to make this a fun place for our children." She went on to express her feelings about the nursery room and other things that we had done for the children. I will never forget that moment when God told me, "The parents are watching, thank you."

Creating an image is not about looking good; it's about displaying what is going on inside your garden walls. Be visible with your vision. Let the world know you care about children!

YOUR MOST POWERFUL ADVERTISERS

The greatest image-makers we can have working for us in children's ministry are the children themselves. When they feel welcomed, drawn in with age-appropriate activities that are rich in both content and fun, when they are challenged to go out and change the world, then they will become your greatest spokespersons! They will be little human billboards of happiness. Unfortunately, the reaction of the children is your end result. You must do a tremendous amount of image building, recruiting, and training before those little billboards will start grinning.

These next two chapters will deal with the power of an image. Essentially, image and reputation go hand in hand. Image is how you look, and reputation is what people say. How do people perceive you? It may or may not be the way in which you perceive yourself. Madison Avenue advertisers will tell you, "You have three seconds to make an impression; the mind retains an image 200 times longer than it retains a word." What kinds of slogans, logos, image-wear, and advertising is coming from your children's ministry? Are people attracted to it? Does it seem like working with children would be fun? Will I be successful? Will I have friends who will join me in this?

The Power of Community

We continue now with two important goals: being with friends and enjoying a sense of belonging. in a world that is growing more hostile by the day. These two goals are critical. We will explore strategies by which the perception of outsiders to your ministry is changed, so that more and more of your church body will join the all-important ranks of those who influence his precious little ones.

These strategies relate to vision category #2: "We will GO into the church, community, and the schools with a children's ministry image that attracts children."

Goal 2.1 Before they come to an event, we want the children of our ministry to say: "I want to go there because I have friends there."

Your children's ministry must have the image (reputation) of being a place where children have fun with their friends as they grow spiritually. Children who have friends at church are more likely to want to come back. Develop these child-to-child friendships through interpersonal experiences that bring laughter, fun, and plenty of interaction. Design activities in which children will be encouraged to interact in groups, pairs, teams, etc. Remember: friendships are sealed through experiences. Approved field trips and outings are great enhancers to friendship-building. (See chapter 9: "Event Policies.") Child-to-child contacts outside of church will solidify those inside the church, so encourage sports, scouting, service clubs. (See chapter 11: "Programs.") Those activities become arenas where children can make friends which they will, someday, bring to church.

To Reach This Goal:

1. Develop and approve policies on field experiences.

2. Train all team members in interactive education.

3. Encourage all team members to design creative programs and to think outside the box.

4. Develop class-level email pals or other outside class networks.

5. Encourage class invitations to child events (parties, games, etc.).

Goal 2.2 When people visit the children's ministry division, they will say, "These people look like a team with a purpose."

Believe it or not, your image does most of your recruiting for you. If working on your children's ministry team appears to be a terrific thing to do, then people are more likely to want to do it. Happy workers, dressed in colorful team-wear, sporting attractive logos, distributing quality literature, will ignite enthusiasm for children in their friends, and their friends will bring new friends, and soon you will have waiting lists of people who want to join your "Great Commission force" in children's ministry. (Stop laughing; this is possible!)

To Reach This Goal

1. Present the children's ministry vision positively before the church body and before the leadership.

2. Develop inspirational media that gives your church an inside look at the heart of your children's ministry.

3. Project your image at church with excellent printed material that reflects your vision as well as excellent program content.

4. Publicize that team members minister in the "Happiest Place in the Church" on a rotating schedule.

5. Re-vitalize facilities so parents see that the ministry has pride and takes seriously its responsibilities of caring for the needs of their children.

6. Design vision logos that are placed on team-wear (caps, jumpers, shirts, etc.) that reflect the identity of the children's ministry as well as the identity of specific programs within the ministry.

7. Reinforce your ministry vision with posters, murals, and identifying signs in the children's ministry department.

8. Assure your congregation that teachers are screened and well-trained in emergency responses.

9. Heighten community awareness by designing children's ministry community- wide programs.

10. Use every form of church and community advertising available to you.

Ten Steps to Developing an Attractive Image

Let's take a closer look now at each one of the above statements. The remainder of this chapter will expound on each one of these concepts as we march toward achieving an image that attracts both children and team members.

Step #1: A Positive Public Image

Have you seen the posters that recruit for the military? They show off the handsome, regally clad men and women with swords flashing, gripped by white-gloved hands. Expensive, majestic military equipment is parked in the background, and the expression on the faces of these poster people is one of dignity, strength, and absolute resolve to protect the freedoms you and I enjoy everyday. When they ask for a few good men, you ask yourself, "Could they possibly want me? Can I be a person of such dignity, strength and absolute resolve?" The thought of having your very own set of white gloves and a sword that shines like that is almost intoxicating!

Do you ever wonder why they don't show you the battle-weary, half-starved, blood-stained men and women who wallow in the trenches of real life in the military? Stop wondering. Of course, they won't show you that; you wouldn't want to sign up if that were the image they projected to the public. Well, my dear foot-soldiers in the army of the Lord, we need to take a lesson from Uncle Sam and do our best to get out the white gloves and strike a pose. People want to join a mighty fighting force. We are that mighty force, commissioned to protect the dignity of every child, dressed in the strength of the "full armor of God," and fueled by the absolute resolve to wage a war to end all wars for the soul of every child. Stand tall; "the battle belongs to the Lord."

Present the children's ministry vision positively before the church body and before the leadership. The way you project yourself is 9/10ths of the battle. Be diligent in projecting a positive image and relentless in fighting for the resources to make it a reality.

The Image Projected by the Senior Pastor

In chapter 5, I stated that the senior pastor is your most powerful ally. Ask him to preach on the importance of children's ministry on a Sunday morning. Whatever the pastor says is gold to the congregation, so if he endorses the importance of children's ministry, the congregation will as well.

The Image Projected by the Children

As I said in the opening of this chapter, the children are your greatest image-builders. Show them off! Here are a few ideas:

1. Children's Choirs: Have your children sing before the adult congregation as often as possible. Develop a full Children's Choir program, headed by volunteers who are quality musicians and who are committed to children's ministry. (See chapter 11.)

2. Children's Drama: Have the children perform a short drama that sets the theme for the pastor's message. Children are natural actors, so capitalize on this trait by giving them an audience! (See chapter 11.)

3. Seasonal Performances: Develop seasonal musicals, pageants, and dramas that bring the entire family in to celebrate the faith of the children. Christmas, Easter, 4th of July: These are all great times to show off the talents of your children. (See chapter 11.)

4. Use Children in the Adult Worship Service: See chapter 11 for an outline of the components for a family service. Children can perform many of the functions that at are typically performed by adults in the service. (See chapter 11 for suggested ways to use children in the adult service.)

The Image Projected by the Children's Pastor

If the senior pastor allows you to get up in front of the congregation and speak to them about their involvement in children's ministry, use caution in the words you select. Brainstorm ways to ask for help without making yourself sound too desperate. Begin to change your image by changing the words you use when describing the children's ministry.

The Image Projected to the Board and by the Board

If it is possible to do church board presentations that will strengthen the image of your children's ministry, take advantage of that opportunity. The last thing you need is some "lone elder" waging a private war on you because he thinks you could be doing more for the kids. Keep these important church leadership communication roads open. See the box on the next page for a few ideas.

Step #2: Inspirational Media

Develop inspirational media that gives your church an inside look at the heart of your children's ministry. Few things will bring a tear to the eye of your congregation quicker than a heart-felt look at what's going on with the children. Summarize the success of some of the children's ministry events by showing a highlights video of programs, such as VBS highlights or camp highlights, etc. Use music with children's voices as the background.

11 Ideas for Image-Building at Board Meetings

1. Make a 20 min. presentation quarterly, updating them on what's happening in children's ministry. Include a written summary and/or brochures and printed notices about upcoming programs and events.

2. Present your passion; recognize their support.

3. Dress in children's ministry attire.

4. Provide cookies, etc., with thank-you notes.

5. Decorate the room (balloons, pictures of children).

6. Enter the room to upbeat children's music.

7. Highlight goals, purpose, not facts and figures.

8. Tell a great story from your ministry.

9. Have prayer for the children and ministry.

10. Give them a coffee mug with ministry logo.

11. Remain in contact for mutual prayer, support.

From Jane Larsen, children's ministry consultant, Des Moines, IA.

Step #3: Excellent Publications

Project your image at church with excellent printed material that reflects your vision as well as excellent program content. What you put into print continues to make an impression long after your initial burst of enthusiasm is past. Use your best resources to communicate. Below is a listing of the types of graphic communication you should consider as well as guidelines for its effective use.

Printed Handouts

1. A Parent Guide—A glossy, full-color brochure which clearly communicates our ministry purpose and positively highlights some of our policies and procedures. This contains pictures of children's ministry team members holding, teaching, and enjoying children. This guide also contains a map of the facilities, directions to the classrooms, and a brief summary of how to get involved in the children's ministry. (See Chapter 9 for an outline of the contents of a Parent Guide.) **Desired effects:** "This is a well-organized, safe place for my child to learn more about Jesus. I feel good about leaving my child here, and I'm interested in getting involved as a volunteer." or "I am humbled to be a part of this great team of people who minister, not only to the children, but also to the children's parents. I need to continually remember that the parents entrust their children to me, and to do all I can to support those parents as much as I can."

8 Tips for Making a Good Video

1. Know what you want to communicate.
2. Know your shots before you shoot.
3. Get parent permission to film children.
4. Get close for best shots and sound!
5. Capture faces!
6. Move slowly.
7. Shoot for visual messages! Little or no narration.
8. Keep the video under 3 minutes.

2. "How to Get Involved" Pamphlet— A glossy, full-color brochure which clearly communicates the ministry purpose and the impact our children's ministry team members have on each other, the children and parents, and the community. This pamphlet highlights what we do, and the various jobs people perform as part of this powerful team. Pictures of people serving in these positions communicate both their passion and the effects on those to whom they minister. A clear, easy-to-understand process of how to join the team is given along with the challenge to make a difference in this generation of future adults. *Desired effects:* "I would love to be involved in such an effective ministry, and to serve with this supportive team. The process doesn't look too difficult. This is what I've been looking for. I can do this!" or "I'm proud to be a part of this great team. I need to do more to influence those around me to become involved as well."

3. "Ministry Opportunities" Pamphlet—A glossy, full-color brochure which clearly communicates the ministry purpose and the various ministry positions/opportunities within the children's ministry. Encouragement is given to consider advancing to specific higher levels of leadership within the children's ministry. *Desired effects:* "I like the idea of starting small and advancing in leadership responsibilities as I grow in confidence. Affecting a few children in my particular area is great, but having an affect on several other adults who minister to several groups of children thrills me!"

4. Specific Event or Program Pamphlets—These pamphlets are specific brochures regarding an event or program. If the program is an on-going program, the brochure quality should be glossy and full-color. If the program or event is a one-time event, the brochure can be semi-glossy with less than 4 colors. The brochure clearly communicates the event or program's specific connection to the overall ministry purpose. Information related to the event or program's activities is given as well as the requirements for being an adult volunteer who serves on this event or program. *Desired effects:* "This looks like a well-organized event! I trust my church, and I feel I can trust those in charge of this event. I want my child to be involved in this great experience. I would also like to be part of the volunteer team of adults who serve on this event."

Designing and Creating Brochures and Flyers

For some reason, church publications have the reputation of being silly and as graphically interesting as a hymnbook. It's time for a facelift! Let's show the world, and those concerned parents, that we can produce quality ministries and printed materials. After all, our Lord deserves the best!

It is not that difficult to change a snoozer flyer into one that both children and adults are proud to affix to their 24 cubic-foot, frost-free message-center in the kitchen. All you have to do is learn how to see things through different eyes. Keep in mind that art may not be something that comes to you naturally. If this is the case, practice is the only way to develop this ability. Your first attempts may be humorous or pitiful, but don't give up! Keep working at it. Below are some general principles that will help you get started.

1. Gather Your Data: Make sure you have all the correct information before you design your flyer or brochure. Things such as times, dates, and places are obvious. Try to think like the people who will be reading this for the first time. What kinds of information or questions will you need to provide for them?

2. Is This a Brochure or Flyer? The difference is really not important. A brochure is usually multi-paged while the flyer is more often a single page. A brochure is also designed to be re-used or constantly displayed for an on-going program or ministry. A flyer usually serves a one-time function.

3. Write Your Text: The artwork, borders, and pictures have to enhance the otherwise boring text. You should never rely on the text to capture the readers' attention. Text that is too long or written poorly will find its place in the trash can. Remember that people are generally in a hurry. They don't want to take the time to read long explanations. I've always found that simple, short terminology is the most effective whenever possible. Even though this type of writing can be too sterile to be used throughout the entire brochure or flyer, it sure catches the eye and is easy to remember.

4. *Review Some Samples:* No matter what you may think, Solomon was right when he said, "There's nothing new under the sun." You shouldn't pressure yourself into believing that you can come up with something artistically new. Take the pressure off yourself by gathering as many examples of similar flyers or brochures from as many churches, businesses, etc. as you can. Learn the tricks of the trade by seeing what others have done.

5. *Lay Out Your Text:* If you have to fit everything into one page, you may have to cut your text down or organize it accordingly. If you don't have an overall size limitation, let your text determine how large your flyer or brochure will be. Make sure you aren't telling the reader too much, or superfluous, information. The reader will only stay on a page for a few seconds during the first read through. Make your headings bold and clear. Remember that too much reading all at once scares the average person. Give them small doses of information with plenty of blank space between text blocks.

6. *Choose Your Borders, Pictures, or Other Artwork:* This is perhaps the most difficult step. There are hundreds of clip-art software programs with plenty of borders and general pictures to choose from. Today's computer software is so affordable that it makes designing the artwork easy! Computerized clip art and borders are easy and fun to use. If you don't possess the capabilities to produce your layouts on the computer, seek someone who can! It is amazing how many computer experts there are in our churches who think they can never be used by the Lord. "We have not because we ask not!" Let the church know you need help, and you'll be surprised who you meet! The purpose of artwork is to enhance the text, not to detract from it. Too much artwork will make a busy finished product that confuses the reader. The art should be light and simple. The pictures should coincide with the text. The borders should be far enough from the text and the edge of the paper to simply frame the information, not fence it in. Do some test copies of your work, show them to some friends, and ask for their opinions. Do this until the majority of your friends, not only remain civil, but also enjoy reading what you have to say. If they say, "Oh, look at those pretty pictures," but don't read the text, you may need some balance between the two.

7. *Layout and Print Off the Final Copy Prototypes:* Do your final layout of the project. If you are doing a multi-page brochure, be careful to lay it out correctly. Folded or printed-on-both-sides flyers also require some special attention when laying them out. Make sure everything is straight! (This is not a problem with computers!)

8. *Count the Cost—Color or Black & White?* You may have to take your flyer to a printer for an estimate if you are unsure of the cost for printing it in colored ink. Colored ink will add to the snap of the finished product. You also have the option of only printing portions of the text or pictures in a color. This will call attention to those items. Be careful not to overdo this technique or use an unpleasant color. Remember you want the readers to enjoy the professionalism of the job, not to be bothered by it.

9. *Decide on the Paper:* Plain white or colored bond paper can be upgraded by a thicker stock of paper, a parchment type, or glossy paper. Of course, the best is a colored, thicker, glossy stock, but you may not be able to afford the price of such professional quality. When choosing paper, remember that this paper is going to be the first introduction to the program or ministry it is advertising. It is important that it is appealing. If you can invest more money into the quality of the paper, it may mean more people or children who come to be ministered to.

Step #4: Positive Team Members in a Positive Ministry

Publicize that team members minister in the "Happiest Place in the Church" on a rotating schedule. Chapter 13 will expound on the importance of rotating your team. No one wants to volunteer with no break in sight. In addition to teacher rotation (chapter 13) and effective teacher training (chapter 15), here are twenty-five ideas to stimulate ways to project an attractive image to the members of your congregation.

1. Testimonies from team members or children.
2. Advertise your training/rotation program.
3. Advertise team teaching.
4. Stories, testimonies printed on bulletin inserts.
5. Children's ministry displays in foyer.
6. Walking billboards.
7. "Adopt a class" program.
8. Pot lucks/open house in children's area.
9. Church member guest-visits in classrooms.
10. Children's ministry-sponsored Christmas sales.
11. Children's ministry prayer reminders.
12. Children's ministry tree.
13. "Give your heart to a child."
14. "Adopt a pew" program.
15. Class of children as greeters/ushers.
16. Teachers on rotation as ushers (with ID badges).
18. "Kid's Say the Darndest Things" videos.
19. Video visits to the classroom.
20. Inspirational children's ministry videos.
21. Children's ministry-sponsored events.
22. Children's ministry-sponsored service programs.
23. Classroom open house after Sunday services.
24. Children serve coffee for adult Sunday school.
25. Children's moments with the pastor during the adult message, then excuse kids.

Step #5: Revitalize Facilities to Attract Parents

Revitalize facilities so parents see that the ministry has pride and takes seriously its responsibilities of caring for the needs of their children. Nothing communicates apathy and disorganization more quickly than crumbling facilities that make parents feel like they are leaving their children in a ghost town. (See chapter 4: "Facility Goals" for more details on transforming your facility.) An idea for getting parents and other church members involved in helping you spruce up your facilities is to ask them to serve on a "Home-coming Committee." The task of this committee would be to make classrooms more homey.

Step #6: Vision Logos & Team-wear

Design vision logos that are placed on team-wear (caps, jumpers, shirts, etc.) that reflect the identity of the children's ministry as well as the identity of specific programs within the ministry. (See chapter 3: "The Gardener's Dream" for information that will help you develop a vision statement.)

How to Design the Vision-Reinforcing Children's Ministry Logo

1. Decide what you want to communicate.
2. Do you have a ministry slogan?
3. Decide on a simple picture or graphic.
4. Decide on a simple shape (child-like?).
5. Decide on a few words.
6. Decide on the font (two styles max).
7. Make it simple, not cluttered.
8. Use color.
9. The logo should communicate in 7 seconds.
10. Look at other logos for ideas.
11. Get reactions from others on your design.

Where to Place the Ministry Logo

In addition to printing your logo on all printed materials, brochures, posters, and murals painted on building walls, place it on all team wear.

Children's Ministry Team Wear—Use professional-looking, non gender-specific shirts with further identifiers of the members of the children's ministry team. With either silk-screened or embroidered children's ministry logos on them, these shirts express team spirit and pride. Place logos on caps, nursery-worker smocks, identification tags, jumpers, and anything else you can budget that your team can wear.

What will this communicate to your congregation as well as to your team? It will tell them, "This is a professionally-run ministry! I feel good leaving my child in the care of people who are proud to be a part of such a great team. I wonder if I could ever wear one of those shirts and be so content in my ministry?"

Step #7: Label Facilities with Vision-Reinforcing Signs

Reinforce your ministry vision with posters, murals, and identifying signs in the children's ministry department. Many of us have walked down the carefully manicured rows of plants in a well-loved garden. Each row is usually labeled with an attractive sign that reads "Squash" or "Tantalizing Tomatoes." Sometimes you will see a colorful sign that reads, "Welcome to My Garden," or "Come and Grow With Me." These signs are inviting and useful for identification, but most of all they show that someone cares about the environment you are about to enter. They care enough to guide you through it.

When people enter your children's ministry area, do they feel like they are entering a well-loved environment? Are you guiding them through it? Here are a few suggestions to guide your thinking:

1. A Children's Ministry Area Map: Is there a map that begins at the children's information center with a "you are here" spot?

2. A Parents' Brochure: Do you have a parents' brochure that introduces teachers and helps parents find rooms?

3. Area Names: Name your children's ministry areas according to age and theme, such as "Discovery Land," "Action Figures" (use Bible characters in pictures), "Construction Zone" (post "Caution, World-Changers Being Built" signs), "Boot Camp" (post "Future Members of God's Army" signs), "Kingdom Kids" (pre-school area), "Little Lambs" (nursery), "Jungle of Joy" (children's church on a jungle theme).

4. Children's Ministry Facility Posters: These are large, glossy, full-color posters that are displayed in lighted, permanent displays on the exterior walls of the children's ministry facilities. Placed in high traffic areas, they clearly communicate the ministry purpose through simple, eye-catching photographs and powerful words. These posters communicate that this is a professionally run organization. The people

in charge here know where they are going and how to get there. Parents will begin to say, "I trust those who serve in the children's ministry with my child. I'm glad I'm at this church. I wonder if I can be a part of this team" or "I'm proud to be a part of this healthy children's ministry team. I want to do all I can to serve the Lord here by being more focused on such a great ministry purpose."

5. Church Foyer Poster: Similar to the above poster, but the placement becomes an advertisement for the children's ministry. (Other ministries would have similar posters on display). Those who visit Crossroads would be drawn to the poster by the graphic appeal, and then would become interested in involving their children in the children's ministry. These poster communicate that this church cares for children. Parents will begin to think, "Maybe I can trust them to help me with the awesome responsibility of developing my child's emotions and character. I'll look into it more carefully next time I come."

6. Freeway Billboards: Catchy advertisement billboards with a great picture of a child and a powerful word or words which expresses the purpose of Crossroads and the children's ministry. If you can accomplish this elaborate kind of signage, you will reach both new and currently attending parents who may say, "I've been looking for a church that really cares for children and wants to help me as a parent. I'll go there this Sunday, and see what I think" or "Hey, that's my church. Wow, how cool that I already go there, and that my children and I are already involved in such a great church. I can use that billboard as a tool to invite my friends to church!"

Step #8: Implement and Broadcast a Child-Safety System.

Assure your congregation that teachers are screened and well-trained in emergency responses. (For a complete treatment of the "church safety" topic, see chapter 9.) Be sure that each member of your children's ministry team wears a security name badge. These are identification badges for all who have been cleared to serve in our children's ministry.

No one is permitted to be with the children without this badge. The badge has a picture of the person on it, a clear church or ministry logo, a ministry position or title, and the person's name. The badge may also have a ministry purpose statement or slogan as well. Parents will say, "They really take my child's safety seriously. I feel safe leaving my child here with this person who has been screened and trained to serve in this ministry. Maybe I can be a part of this great team some day" or "I feel good being an identified member of this great team of qualified people. I feel more accepted by the parents to care for their children."

Step #9: Community Awareness

Heighten community awareness by designing children's ministry community-wide programs. (For details about how to operate these programs, see chapter 11.)

Halloween Alternatives

"Trunk or Treat": Children get treats from the trunks of church member cars on the church parking lot.

"Hallelujah Party": Children dress as Bible characters and come to church with parents to experience games, dramas, etc. while getting treats from classrooms.

Kids Kamp

A summer day-camp program in which the children come to the church for brief activities, then travel to local sites for fun or tours. Children return to church for more fun and brief Bible studies on the daily theme.

S.W.A.T. Teams

A children's "special forces" team composed of specially-trained older children who perform service and outreaches to the community. These "Students With A Testimony" are well-known and respected!

Neighborhood Bible Clubs

A tried-and-true program for involving neighborhood children in after-school church-sponsored study and activity. Children meet in a local home for fun, refreshments, and Bible study. Tutoring or homework assistance may also be offered.

Step #10: Ten Ways to Advertise to the Church and to the Community

Use every form of church and community advertising available to you. Here are some suggestions:

1. Include a children's ministry section on your church's web site. (Go to www.trinity-on-the-hill.org or www.cc-ob.org for some good examples!)

2. Have a section in your weekly church bulletin that is dedicated to Children's Ministry.

3. Create a marquee outside your children's ministry area, the path parents take to drop off their kids, so that they can see what's happening in children's church today, or what special guests will be ministering to the children today.

4. Post eye-catching posters in stores.

5. Contact your local newspaper and ask them to cover one of your children's ministry events.

6. Write news releases that communicate the basic information of your children's ministry events.

7. Use creative door-to-door flyers.

8. Involve the children's ministry in community events and service projects.

9. Invite local television or cable coverage.

10. Create and advertise children's ministry-sponsored community events.

Image Inventory
How Attractive Is Your Image?

Directions: Below is a questionnaire based on the "Ten Steps to Creating an Attractive Image." Place a check beside each statement that is true; then decide just how attractive your children's ministry is to members of your congregation and to your community. Hopefully, you will be encouraged at all that you could do, and never discouraged by what you have yet to do. Remember the words of Jesus, "But I, when I am lifted up from the earth, will draw all men to myself" *(John 12:32).*

1. An Attractive Image at Church
❏ We share children's ministry testimonies in the services.
❏ We involve the senior pastor in our ministry.
❏ We advertise our ministry openings positively.
❏ We include ministry stories and testimonies in the bulletin.
❏ We create children's ministry displays in our foyer.
❏ We have fun events located in our children's ministry area.
❏ We include our children in the adult service.
❏ We have changed the words we use to describe our children's ministry.
❏ We regularly show off our children by having them perform for adults.
❏ We share our children's ministry vision and programs with the board.

2. Attractive Media
❏ We show inspirational video clips during the service.
❏ We summarize and highlight children's ministry events.
❏ We present "You Are There" video clips of Sunday School moments.

3. Attractive Printed Material
❏ We have created a Parent Handbook.
❏ We have created Program Brochures.
❏ We have created a "How to Get Involved in Children's Ministry" Pamphlet.
❏ We develop creative event flyers.
❏ We use the highest quality graphics, designers, and paper possible.

4. An Attractive Team
❏ We have developed rotational teaching teams.
❏ We provide apprenticeship periods for new team members.

5. An Attractive Environment.
❏ We have cleaned up and painted the children's ministry area.
❏ We have added some art to the exterior of the buildings.
❏ We have added some art to the inside of the buildings.
❏ We have improved our landscaping around our buildings.
❏ We have improved our children's play area.
❏ We have added some music to our children's ministry areas.
❏ We have solved the smell problems in the nursery area.

6. An Attractive Identity
❏ We have a children's ministry slogan.
❏ We have a children's ministry logo.
❏ We use our logo on publications, clothing, name badges, publications, etc.

7. Attractive Posters, Murals, and Identifying Signs
❏ We have added some pictures of our ministry team to the hallways.
❏ We have added some pictures of our children to the hallways.
❏ We have vision-reinforcing art in the church foyer.

8. A Safe Environment that Attracts Teachers
❏ We have implemented the "Safety Checklist in Chapter 9.

9. Attractive to the Community
❏ We create community-wide events.
❏ We are involved in community events.
❏ We involve our children in community service projects.

10. Attract People Through Advertising Opportunities
❏ We do printed advertising in our community.
❏ We invite the local newspaper to cover our ministry.
❏ We invite the local cable station to cover our ministry.
❏ We have a "Children's Ministry Marquee" to advertise our weekly events.
❏ We have developed a "Children's Ministry Link" on our church website.

chapter 13
The Fruit Stand:
Recruit With Your Image

Something heavenly happens when the gardener sets aside time to enjoy the fruit of the garden. Whether it is savoring the sweetness of fresh vegetables at dinner, or simply displaying the fruit in a basket, this is a critical time for the gardener, and others, to say, "It is good."

Have you ever walked by a fruit stand during the height of the season when all the delicious fruits and vegetables are on display? It is impossible not to stop, isn't it? At that moment you are tempted to stop everything you are doing and become a farmer yourself, just so you could arrange a stand like that and have people walk by and marvel. At that moment, you don't realize all the hard work that went into making that display; you are just overcome by the results. Bingo! That's what you have been doing in children's ministry also: arranging a "fruit stand" of vision-casting slogans, logos, facilities, budgets, relationships, surveys, and endless hours of praying and planning. Now it all comes to fruition. (The root word of "fruition" is fruit.) This entire book has dealt with the work of preparing a garden in which fruit can grow. You've worked hard to have people stop by the fruit stand of Children's Ministry and admire the plump, delicious fruit of your labors.

"THE LORD OF THE HARVEST"

Your work is never in vain; no matter how few teachers you have or how little money you have, you are displaying a fruit that is the sweetest on the Lord's table: little children who love him! Your work will turn heads; people will stop; they will want to join you. You need to enjoy the process of recruiting in the same way a farmer enjoys selling his fruit. Don't become anxious when it seems like not enough people are stopping to admire the fruit. The

Lord brings the people, remember? All you have to do is get ready. Listen to the Lord when he says: "The harvest is plentiful, but the workers are few. Ask the Lord of the harvest field to send out workers, therefore, into his harvest" *(Luke 10:2)*.

It's God who is at work here, and he has enlisted you as a partner in preparing a field in which the new workers will labor. He wants you to ask him to send the workers. Never be discouraged! You are in outstanding company, and he has promised to "never forsake you."

Of course, you could fuss and fret over recruiting. You could make the choice to take this all onto your own shoulders. That's a bad choice. You can't make these people join your team anymore than you could turn a dog into a cat. Have you ever though about what it would take to get a dog to be a cat? Really now, think of the possibilities! They both have tails, four legs, fur, and whiskers. The only thing that could give us some gray hairs is getting the dog to be independent and moody. I suppose we could set the dog in a fresh cat box with some well-done cat videos playing in front of him, or have him go on a retreat with some key leader cats. The thought of trying to get a dog to be a cat seems a bit absurd. He was created to be a dog. He enjoys being a dog. No matter what we do his fur will always tingle at the sight of a U.P.S. truck! Trying to get someone to be a teacher or some other form of children's volunteer shares the same category as changing the quality of beastly creation:

179

near impossible. This doesn't mean that we are free from any and all responsibility of recruiting new volunteers. Quite the contrary is true. Think about it. If the implication is that people are somehow cut out to be children's volunteers by the Lord, what does that say about the organization we set up for them? What would the Lord say to us if he had spent all those years developing that new volunteer, and we permitted an environment to exist in which this new volunteer soon became another burned-out, bitter Christian casualty? These are eye-opening thoughts. Let's do some digging to find out exactly what the Lord wants us to do about recruiting and discipling new volunteers.

FIVE STEPS TO THE RECRUITING AND TRAINING PROCESS
Step #1: Prepare

Do you think Uncle Sam did his homework before he shot that picture of the Marine with his white gloves and his sword? You bet he did! The Military knows just how to project an image, and it knows just how to make it look good on you. Again, let's take a lesson here. Chapter 12 gave a host of extensive advice on how to develop a strong, attractive children's ministry image. Once you work through the checklist and get to work on some of these image projects, people will sit up and take notice. You will have people appear, seemingly out of nowhere, asking you if you need help. Believe me, people who offer to help in children's ministry don't just want a free T-shirt with that totally cool logo on it. Most of the folks who volunteer really want to be there. They are gifts to you, but the question is, "Are you ready for them?"

In the next chapter, we will discuss in greater detail the importance of building a "Nest" for children's ministry as your leadership teams learns to link hands and administer a system that is volunteer-friendly. However, this illustration gives you a preview into "nest-thinking": "Developing and Working with Volunteers" underscores the fact that we have to attract the people God has prepared to the children's ministry.

Work on a teacher friendly reputation that widely advertises the rotation and teaming of teachers. If you have any bad reps out there, change their minds! Here's a brief review of terminology as was mentioned in chapter 12. Work on these reputation warning signs:

1. Change the terminology from children's "workers" to "children's ministry team members."

2. Change your recruiting language from "we need more help" to "we have some openings."

3. Change the learning perception from instant placement in a room alone to an "apprenticeship period."

4. Change the teaching perception from "you're on your own" to team teaching.

5. Change the term of service from an endless term of commitment to rotation options.

6. Change the training perception from "self-learning and survival" to teacher training.

7. Change the "word on the street" from hearing "horror stories" to "life-changing testimonies."

8. Change the teaching experience from the "lone teacher" to "teacher's meetings and fellowship."

Step #2: Advertise

In chapter 5, and again in chapter 12, I stated that the senior pastor is your most powerful ally. Ask him to preach on the importance of children's ministry on a Sunday morning; if he agrees, ask him to specifically challenge the congregation to get involved in children's ministry.

1. Pulpit Support. Ask the pastor to preach on the importance of children's ministry on a Sunday morning. When the pastor speaks, people listen. Ask him to endorse the importance of the children's ministry publicly.

2. Feature the Children in the Service. Children are your best recruiters! Hearts will melt and eyes will water when you bring in the children. (See chapters 12 and 13 for ideas.)

3. Advertise the Fruit of Your Ministry. Feed your congregation a steady diet of children's ministry fruit. At least once each month, show a video of a great event involving children or have a child give a testimony. (See chapter 12 for more vision-sharing ideas.)

4. Distribute Bulletin Inserts and Flyers. Hopefully your pastor will designate one Sunday every six months (twice each year) as Children's Day. On this day he will preach on the importance of children's ministry, feature the children's choir, or use children in the service, and pat you on the back (of course). Then he will ask you to address the congregation and encourage them to fill out the response insert they have found in their bulletins. It is critically important that you put something in their hands on the day you ask people to join the Children's Ministry Team. If you simply tell them to drop it by the church office, they will forget. Have them put the responses into the offering plate or into brightly-colored containers as they leave.

5. Enlist Your Current Team as Recruiters. The greatest advertisers are your children, but the greatest recruiters are your current teaching staff. If they are happy, they will bring their friends. We want the supervisors and teachers on our children's ministry team to say, "I want my friends and neighbors to join this team."

You've heard it said, "Healthy sheep reproduce healthy sheep." If you haven't heard that said, it's still true. They do! When teachers are blessed in their work, inviting friends to serve them should be a natural thing to do. After all, friends serving together is the best way to develop relationships. Every person has a circle of friends who need to be invited to join the team, and hundreds of recruiters are better than just one!

• Create a "minister with a friend" crusade to encourage team members to invite friends to join the team.

• Thank those who recruit new team members during area meetings.

• Create a recruiting contest, with a great prize, to raise the awareness of the need for more adults.

6. Develop a Youth Leadership Program. The Youth Leadership Program is designed to provide the high school youth of the church with an arena in which they can learn while serving. This program of guided

experiences through serving in the children's ministry is based on 3 principles:

1. All learning is enhanced with involvement.

2. Character development is strengthened through experience and mentoring.

3. Spiritual growth comes through serving.

The Youth Leadership Program invites Christian youth (ages 14-18) to join the children's ministry team as apprentices. Those who choose to commit to this 3-month program will be trained in ministry procedures, supervised by qualified adult mentors, and evaluated regularly. Depending on the youth's character and performance, opportunities for advanced involvement in the children's ministry will be offered. At the successful completion of the 3 months, the youth will be given a certificate and a letter of recommendation from the children's pastor. The program goes as follows:

1. Interested youth apply to the program through an application form.

2. Once accepted, the youth will attend a brief orientation meeting with a children's ministry coordinator. At this meeting, the following occurs:

  a. Basic ministry policies are reviewed.

  b. Apprenticeship-related procedures are reviewed.

  c. Ministry apprenticeship supervisors are introduced.

  d. Apprenticeship evaluation criteria is reviewed.

  e. Apprenticeship schedule and start date reviewed.

  f. An apprenticeship name badge is created.

3. Once the apprenticeship is begun, the apprenticeship supervisor monitors, mentors, and evaluates the youth.

4. Weekly evaluations are filled out and signed by both the supervisor and the youth. A copy of the evaluation is given to the youth, and the original is kept on file at the church office.

5. Upon successful completion of the 3-month apprenticeship, the youth is awarded with a certificate of completion and a letter of recommendation signed by the supervisor and the children's pastor.

6. Upon successful completion of the apprenticeship, the youth will be invited to continue to serve in the children's ministry in one of the 3 capacities below:

    a. Continue serving in the same capacity as a full member of the children's ministry team without the apprentice classification.

    b. Advance to an "Apprenticeship Supervisor's Assistant" position. As a supervisor's assistant, the youth will assist the supervisor in overseeing and monitoring the incoming youth apprentices. This may also include assisting in the evaluation and training of the youth apprentices.

    c. Transfer to another area of the children's ministry. This may include assisting, or teaching, in another age group.

Step #3: Pray

The central issue around which our programs and strategies of recruitment seem to rotate is the question of our role in the process. Do we really have the power to get someone to be a children's volunteer? Our lives are not comprised of splintered, unrelated scenes of life which somehow all go together to make us who we are. We are not some cosmic blend of experiences destined for an untimely demise. God has created and molded our lives to become something from which he can receive praise and worship. Basically, he wants to be proud of his work through us. *Psalm 139* tells us that he is intimately involved with us.

The difference between a Christian and a non-Christian is that the Christian recognizes his Creator and that recognition affects his life. If we realize what God has done for us, the only reaction we can have is that we become driven to serve him with a never-ending fervor. John, possibly the closest person to Jesus, knew of this drive. You can feel the effects of knowing Jesus as you read *1 John 1*.

Service is indeed a natural side-effect of becoming acquainted with Jesus. Followers of Jesus were told to do something with their faith *(Matthew 7:24-27; James 2:14-26)*. If this is true, this tells us much about the first prerequisite for someone who works in the children's ministry. He or she must have a servant's heart. That's something you can't teach a person to have; it is a natural result of a committed spirit.

The question of where, or in what capacity, a person serves the Lord is another issue with which we must deal. Just like that dog has a certain purpose to perform with that noise he makes at night, we, too, have a similar function in which to use the gifts, abilities, and experiences that God has let us have. Is it safe to say that Paul was actually trained for apostleship prior to his conversion? Did his experiences with the religious and governmental systems lend anything at all to his ministry? Without a doubt, we would have to agree that Paul's entire life was focused in on his role as an apostle. It is the same with every person who gives his life to the Lord. The Lord now has the right, given him by the person's will, to focus all the training of his past experiences into a specific area of ministry. This process is known as a calling. Paul recognized this scenario, and he revealed this knowledge in his letter to the Romans *(Romans 1:1, 2)* and to Timothy *(2 Timothy 1:8-11)*.

It must be clear by now that we cannot get people to be volunteers in the church. It is also clear that we do not train or create teachers. Our role is one of assisting the person in seeing the Lord's presence in his or her life, and to help focus past experiences into a ministry. He or she may or may not be called to the children's ministry.

Step #4: Plan

Do your homework when it comes to recruiting. Set your goals, design the process, and contact all the personnel you will need to carry it out. Here are some suggestions:

Plan the Orientation Session. Very soon after the Children's Ministry Sunday and your request to have new people join your team, offer an Informational Orientation Session. People need immediate response to their offer to join your team. Don't let more than two days go by before the orientation process begins. Here's the procedure:

1. Call within two days and thank them for their interest. Tell them of two orientation dates and times and ask which one would be convenient for them to attend.

2. Set a time to plan the orientation sessions.

3. Introduce the coordinators. These are critical moments! Be sure the coordinator is present to welcome the new recruits to the division of children's ministry. This is when you match up the interested people with the age group he or she would like to work in. This is a golden time of "PR" (that's personal respect; see chapter 5).

4. Invite them to visit a classroom. Make an appointment for them visit a classroom right away. Don't let time go by and their enthusiasm grow cold. Each new volunteer should be an honored guest in some Sunday school class on the Sunday after the orientation day.

5. Explain the teacher training program and its options. Be sure you have several different kinds of teacher training options to accommodate their busy schedules. Explain the apprentice program and the team-teaching policy. (See chapter 15.)

6. Show a short, inspirational video clip on children's ministry. This is a "thank you" from children for joining the team.

7. Distribute the children's ministry packet. In this packet should be the application, an explanation of the screening process, a welcome brochure that contains the most often asked questions (including why you have to screen them), an explanation of the rotation plans, and a welcome letter from you. (For more information on screening volunteers, see chapter 8.)

Plan the Training Session

1. Reserve the room at the church.

2. Arrange the food.

3. Invite the senior pastor.

4. Arrange for coordinators to have an integral part of the program.

5. Duplicate materials.

6. Make name tags.

7. Arrange for fun.

8. Prepare a stirring presentation of your vision.

9. Arrange for age-group training led by coordinators.

10. Devise a boiled down presentation of your policies and procedures.

11. Offer "success in the classroom" strategies.

12. Collect the curriculum for review.

13. Have some child interaction.

Step #5: Do the Training

Planning isn't worth the paper it's written on without follow through. Here is a list of question to ask yourself as you get ready to do the teacher training. After you answer them, you will know if you are ready to welcome these new "workers into the harvest field of the Lord."

1. Am I ready to disciple these new team members? Even though we would like to think that only those whom the Lord has prepared have risen to the challenge, it's not always so. You need to give every person the same beginning point: a challenge to service, and the basic components of being a minister:

• A servant's heart.
• Consideration of personal gifts, calling.
• Sacrifice for others.
• Continued personal spiritual growth.

2. Am I ready to provide them with the tools they need. All too often we concern ourselves with the person's heart attitude only, and we fail to provide him with the necessary tools with which to reproduce that attitude in the lives of his learners. The tools we should provide are:

• Identification of age-group characteristics.
• Awareness of how the age-groups learn.
• How to develop a lesson.

3. Am I ready to teach these people how to change lives? There's more to being a teacher than knowing

Garden Pest:
Spiritual Dry Rot

Evidence

This is a disease that permeates the whole person and will spread to other team members quickly. The obvious signs of this Spiritual Dry Rot is negative comments. You cannot see this disease; you can only hear it.

Sources of Infestation

Spiritual dryness. A twisted view of God that makes him impersonal, unloving, and harsh. Service on the team that is driven by guilt or fear. Anger that has not been properly dealt with.

Treatment

1. Direct, immediate, face-to-face reaction from you about the comment.
2. Clarify the reason for your reaction (related to Scriptures, the vision, or image to others).
3. Give clear, written and signed, warnings with clear consequences.
4. Involve the person in a team with other spiritually-strong team members.
5. Support correct behavior if corrections are made.
6. If necessary, remove the person from the team.

---

how to teach a lesson, and successfully completing the lesson before the first parent arrives to recall his or her child. A teacher, in order to be considered successful, must affect the learners in such a way as to produce a change in character evidenced by how they live. Teaching doesn't stop when the class is over or when you go out for a restroom excursion. Teaching, like authentic Spanish food, must remain with you and show some visible signs of its presence. Here are some ways to train teachers to apply this principle:

- A two month apprenticeship program.
- "Big brother/sister" teacher program.
- Visit other exemplary teachers (other churches?).
- Attend conventions/workshops.

4. Am I ready to commit to the well being of these people? No matter what anyone tells you, the hardest part of the recruiting and discipleship process is the on-going maintenance of the complex personality structure that exists when "two or more gather together." If not done carefully, with much prayer and humility before the Lord, all your time and investment

in these volunteers can very easily end in someone's hurt feelings. There are no tried-and-true methods to keep a staff happy, but there are some principles.

- Acknowledge the Lord in your ministry.
- Pray for volunteers with servants' hearts.
- Devote yourself to as many volunteers as possible (coordinators?).
- Train, retrain, expect servants' hearts.
- Deal with any "Vision Blight Fungus" removing them if necessary. (See chapter 3.)
- Do all you can to ensure happy volunteers (facilities, repairs, etc.; see chapter 4).
- Hold regular, fun, all-teacher events.
- Publicize the good fruit of the children's ministry.
- Remain a servant yourself.

Your role is not to make someone a volunteer who does not already have a servant's heart and a love for children. There are people who don't know they have these qualifications. They simply know that they want to help. Give a person like that the tools he needs, and you've got a powerful leader of children!

## chapter 14

Sharing the Dream:
Leading the Team

*W*hen the garden develops and grows in size over the years, one of the greatest challenges for the gardener is to let others share in the joy of the work. The gardener's original joy of creating the garden must now give way to a deeper joy of seeing others enjoy the fruit.

THE PLIGHT OF THE "LONE GARDENER"

Sometimes the blessings of serving at a growing church play "can't find me" behind the challenges that come right beside them. Our "mid-sized" church of 1,000 people moved to a new 42 acre site and put up a tent! Church attendance exploded! In four years, this "mid-sized" church was nearing "mega church" status of 4,000 people! Needless to say, we experienced some growing pains that came along with the blessings.

Our community was growing along with our church. There were 8,000 new homes built within a two mile radius of the church. Our new church congregation included a majority of new Christians or young married "seekers" who found more affordable housing in our city. This new congregation wasn't very willing to volunteer to serve in the children's ministry. We had nearly tripled the size of our children's ministry, and yet the size of the children's ministry team had only grown slightly. I was hired to replace the outgoing children's director who became exhausted, and resigned.

The challenge of recruiting and developing the team was immense. I had some good people who were serving as coordinators. They were basically teachers who took on the role of coordinators as a service to the Lord, and because I needed them. I was praying for God to lead people to the children's ministry who were called to be

leaders. My wife came across a married couple who were in the drama ministry at the church, and suggested I contact them about a new children's church program that we were planning to create. They said they would be happy to work with the new program.

Within a matter of months, the new children's church program was so healthy that we considered repeating it on Sunday night. I was also given permission to hire some part-time assistance for the Sunday night programming. I had lunch with the married couple who were overseeing the children's church program to offer them a paid position that would expand their area of service to include the Sunday night programming as well. During the lunch, I discovered some eternal background information. They had, until only recently, supervised a children's ministry at another church nearby. Now, they were once again praying for the Lord to use them in children's ministry. When I offered them an involvement in a larger portion of the children's ministry, I could see an instant reaction in them. They both looked at each other, and their eyes began to well up with tears. This was before I even mentioned anything about being paid. After a few minutes of talking, I asked them to pray about the offer for a few days. They both said, "We don't have to; the answer is 'yes.'"

Today, these two wonderful people are the backbone of our children's ministry. She is my full-time assistant, and continues to be a visionary who builds both people and programs. He is paid part-time for

The "Nest" of Children's Ministry
A *warm, safe place where people flourish*

his assistance in children's church and leads the children's worship team. They are excellent examples of God's hand in team development. God prepares just the right people for the right positions at the right time. All we have to do is be faithful to him, and continue to prayerfully swing the doors of leadership opportunities open to those who are able and willing.

Ministry leadership can potentially be a dangerous thing. It is very ego gratifying to be the "keeper of the knowledge." It is also very destructive when the ministry starts to grow and you begin to see your life being totally consumed by the work. At some point, we all have to make the decision to share the dream with others, or lose other significant relationships along the way. There is little hope for Lone Gardeners in ministry!

We all want our children's ministries to grow! I'm sure you have been on your knees praying for the Lord of the harvest to send more workers into the harvest field. We all dream about waiting lists of people anticipating an opening on the children's ministry team....WAKE UP! You were snoring! Have you ever wondered why God doesn't just speak a healthy, super-fruitful children's ministry team into existence at your church into existence? There's no doubt he could do that if he wanted. Why doesn't he? I believe he showed me an answer to that question.

In the early years of my children's ministry, I was a bit frustrated at the challenge of recruiting. We had a good curriculum. I had done some pretty impressive recruiting campaigns, but there was just a meager little trickle of new volunteers coming into the ministry. This concerned me. I tried everything. I even began praying the exact words of Jesus: "The harvest is plentiful but the workers are few. Ask the Lord of the harvest, therefore, to send out workers into his harvest field" *(Matthew 9:37)*.

Nothing was working. This went on for nearly two years! Finally, God caught my attention, sat me down, and opened my eyes to what was going on. Here's a synopsis of what he told me.

Let's pretend for a moment that you are God. You have worked hard on a person (we'll call her Tricia) for 21 years. You have been with her through her growing up years. You have cried with her, laughed with her, forgiven her, and corrected her. She became a believer and committed her life to you several years ago, and is now finally ready to serve you in the children's ministry! She is a priceless joy to you. You have big plans for her in your kingdom! With all you have done for her and all you have been through with her, are you going to place her in a ministry that will burn her out or frustrate her to the point of damaging her faith or discouraging her from service? Absolutely not!

God began to show me that he was more than willing to send great, priceless volunteers, like Tricia, once I got ready for them! I needed to create a nest in which they would flourish! He would help me, but it was my responsibility as the children's pastor. I began to work on the various parts of the nest with God's help and wisdom. Soon, I was blessed with volunteers, pressed down and overflowing into my lap. This was a time in which God was waiting on me! Once the children's ministry organization was a safe, warm place for his precious people, they came!

Look carefully at the sticks in the illustration. These aspects of the children's ministry nest are discussed throughout this book. There are probably hundreds of other labels we can put on the sticks that make up our children's ministry nest. It might be safe to say that everyone on your team comes to your team with their own definition of what a comfortable nest contains. If you don't fulfill that expectation, they may leave the team, or serve with a chip on their shoulder.

Notice what the larger, supportive branches are labeled. Rotation and training are critical factors in the success and security of your ministry nest. We'll talk more about both of those later.

How does your children's ministry nest look? Are your volunteers warm and safe? Will they tell their friends about their great experiences on the team, and be your best recruiters? At the end of the chapter, I'll give you an evaluation tool that might help you add some strong sticks to your nest, and line it with warm feathers.

As you build your nest, you must also ask the Lord to help you see the big picture of developing a team of people. I think people are the most complex creatures with which to work. I was raised with dogs all my young life. No, I'm not the "wolf boy" you've read about. My parents raised German Shepherds. Taking care of dogs, cats, horses, or pet snails is pretty simple. You just give them some food, water, a few pats on the head every now and then, and keep the snails away from salt. That's it. No problem. (I can hear my parents groaning with disagreement.) People, on the other hand, have to be motivated, encouraged, challenged, rewarded, and given plenty of rest and strawberry pie! The big picture is that we have to attract adults to the team, and then keep them happy by making sure they feel prepared, equipped, and successful.

In today's busy world, people don't have time to feel trapped or stuck in one place. People become discouraged if they aren't progressing! Learning new ways to do what they feel they are called to do is important. If they stop learning, or cease feeling challenged, they lose interest.

Throughout the rest of this chapter, as in previous chapters, I'll refer back to the "Great Commission Children's Ministry Vision" that was outlined in chapter 7. Remember: Your efforts in developing your team must be based, not only in the fulfillment of your ministry vision, but also in the fulfillment of the Great Commission. Without this as your focus, your efforts could become just nice things done for people instead of efforts that effect eternity in the lives of children.

The Joy of Serving

These strategies relate to vision category #1: "GO." "We will GO into the world of today's children with trained, well-organized, passionate, godly adults who carry the message of the Gospel."

Goal 1.2 We want the supervisors and teachers on our children's ministry team to say, "I enjoy serving the Lord here."

We all like to feel qualified no matter what. I wouldn't enjoy paying the bills at home because I know that I'm not qualified to do it. If I paid the bills, we would soon live in a nice place with bars on the windows and be dressed in matching striped outfits. Enjoyment is something that gives us keen satisfaction. I want those who serve on the children's ministry team to find keen satisfaction in all they do for the children. A vital first step toward that goal is to place the new team members correctly into the team. It is our responsibility, as children's ministry leaders, to assist the volunteers in discerning their spiritual gifts and personality types, and then to place them in areas of service that suit those interests and abilities. When a person is placed correctly, the roots of personal ministry joy go deep into the soil to produce eternal fruit.

To Reach This Goal:

1. Encourage the coordinators to become aware of their team members' happiness.

2. Continue to develop a placement process which targets a team member's gifts and personality.

3. Continue to develop the initial orientation process.

4. Continue to develop the training process which includes on-the-job apprenticeship training

5. Develop a supply system and supply coordinator.

6. Continue to recruit actively to develop a team teaching environment ministry-wide.

Many Parts, One Body

Nobody likes to stay where they sense they aren't needed, or they don't fit. There's nothing more significant than to be missed if you aren't around. Paul's teaching on the body of Christ in *1 Corinthians 12* is all about working together in our gifted and called areas of service toward a common goal. In ministry, there is no excuse for comparison or competition; we are all valuable and valued.

Goal 1.3 We want the supervisors and teachers on our children's ministry team to say, "I feel a part of a team effort here."

The concept of team doesn't just happen. It flows from God and through the leaders. Equality and value for each team member must be an obvious value in everything we do. Coordinators and other leaders in the team must be strong, sensitive, and dedicated to the work and vision of the ministry. Team members will be inspired by what the leaders do far more than what they say. We must create master teachers within the team who will assist in training and influencing the team. Vision and fruit of a team mindset can be shared and enhanced during periodic team meetings. Belief in a strong team produces a stronger team!

To Reach This Goal:

1. Pray for and seek out master teachers in each area and service.

2. Pray for and seek out supervisors for each area and service.

3. Continue to develop the ministry vision in the entire team.

4. Continue to develop a one team mindset throughout the entire ministry team.

5. Continue to develop the individual area's uniqueness (nursery, preschool, elementary).

6. Continue to develop the all-team meetings with area small group meetings afterward.

7. Continue to enhance communications within the team (email, newsletters, letters, etc.).

Once you have all these happy team members, you can begin to develop others within your team to take some of the load off of your shoulders. It's not fun or healthy to do everything yourself! I like to think about delegation with these thoughts: "If I'm doing it all, I am robbing others of the blessings that God has for them if they were helping" or "Delegation is a very selfish endeavor. I do it to protect myself and my family." God doesn't want you to become some miserable, grumpy, old person who is so exhausted that nobody can stand you. That's not what pleases him. He says that he "loves a cheerful giver" *(2 Corinthians 9:7)*.

Delegation is a complex process. Delegation is not just about getting others to do what you don't want to do. I'll have to admit, that has been my motive at times. That's OK if others want to do those things, but that is not the best motive. The correct motive for delegation is to increase the ministry to children and to increase your satisfactory advance toward your ministry vision. It's all about building a better nest and producing more fruit in your garden!

To get you thinking about the concept of delegation, read through the master list of the tasks that are included in the big picture of children's ministry (page 189). I created this for my own use, so you will have to adjust it to suit your own ministry and leadership positions. This might help you in deciding to whom you should delegate.

There are tasks that should and shouldn't be delegated by you. There are some things that you, and only you, should do because of who you are or because of your position on the team. There are

Children's Ministry Jobs *and the Best People to Do Them*

	Children's Pastor	Dir. of Child. Min.	Nursery Coord.	Preschool Coord.	Elementary Coord.	Sun. Eve. Coord.	"Ministry Care" Coord.	Child. Min. Secretary
1. Seek God's wisdom and guidance for vision of ministry.	x	x	x	x	x	x	x	x
2. Determine vision and purpose based on counsel.	x							
3. Recruit new team members.	x	x	x	x	x	x	x	x
4. Design recruitment "campaigns."	x	x						
5. Facilitate recruitment "campaigns."	x	x						x
6. Oversee the application process.		x						
7. Facilitate the application/approval process.		x						x
8. Design orientation process.	x	x						
9. Facilitate orientation process.	x	x	x	x	x	x		x
10. Recruit coordinators.	x	x						
11. Recruit supervisors.			x	x	x			
12. Train, equip coordinators.	x	x						
13. Communicate with, nurture coordinators.		x						
14. Train supervisors.			x	x	x			
15. Communicate with, nurture supervisors.			x	x	x			
16. Appoint "master teachers."			x	x	x			
17. Design on-going team training.	x	x						
18. Facilitate on-going team training.	x	x	x	x	x	x	x	x
19. Oversee curriculum design/choice.	x	x						
20. Purchase curriculum.		x						x
21. Distribute curriculum.			x	x	x	x		x
22. Evaluate curriculum.			x	x	x	x		
23. Oversee the use of non-curricular supplies.			x	x	x	x		
24. Request supplies.			x	x	x	x		
25. Purchase supplies.		x						x
26. Distribute supplies.			x	x	x	x		
27. Oversee children's ministry budget.	x							
28. Design budget figures, changes.	x	x						
29. Oversee the "substitute teacher" process.		x						
30. Facilitate the "substitute teacher" process.			x	x	x	x		
31. Oversee the team-development process.	x	x						
32. Facilitate the team-development process.	x	x	x	x	x	x	x	x
33. Oversee the "teacher appreciation" process.	x	x						
34. Facilitate the "teacher appreciation" process.	x	x	x	x	x	x	x	x
35. Oversee the "Ministry Care" process.	x	x					x	
36. Facilitate the "Ministry Care" process.							x	
37. Oversee all children's events.	x	x						
38. Facilitate camps, VBS, special programs.		x						x
39. Oversee all missions programs.	x	x						
40. Facilitate missions/service training and experiences.	x	x	x	x	x	x		x
41. Oversee all policies.	x							
42. Facilitate the carrying out of all policies.	x	x	x	x	x	x	x	x

The Delegation Grid

Directions: You will go through this grid three times. Follow the directions carefully.

1. For each quality, mark either the "I'm Good At It," or "I'm Not Good At It" columns only.

2. For each of the qualities you marked "Not Good At It," check either the "I Need To Do It," or the "I Can Delegate It" columns. (*Remember that just because you are not good at something, doesn't free you from your responsibility in that area. Sometimes God lets us "enjoy" learning in these areas!*)

3. Re-think your "I'm Good At It" markings. (*Remember, even though you are good at these things, it doesn't mean you should be doing them!*) Pray for others who would feel good at doing your "I Can Delegate It" qualities to be a part of your team.

Columns: I'm Good at It | I'm Not Good at It | I Need to Do It | I Can Delegate It

PEOPLE SKILLS

1. Speaking in front of crowds
2. Speaking one-to-one
3. Correcting others
4. Encouraging others
5. Teaching others a new skill
6. Interacting with others on a social level
7. Being interested with others' lives apart from the job
8. Counseling
9. Teaching a class
10. Leading a small group Bible study
11. Delegating
12. Mediating differences between people
13. Visiting sick people
14. Following up with visitors
15. Recruiting new workers
16. "Firing" people

PLANNING AND PREPARATION

17. Making long-range plans
18. Making short-range plans

Columns: I'm Good at It | I'm Not Good at It | I Need to Do It | I Can Delegate It

19. Setting calendar dates for events
20. Setting weekly or daily deadlines
21. Keeping track of the "details" of upcoming events
22. Making lists of supplies needed for events, etc.
23. Purchasing supplies
24. Organizing and distributing supplies
25. Making phone calls
26. Doing research about how other churches operate
27. Evaluating the success of programs, etc.
28. Setting goals
29. Proposing changes

BUDGET MATTERS

30. Keeping detailed records
31. Shopping for bargains
32. Projecting future growth
33. Working with money
34. Saying "No" to people regarding spending
35. Paying bills

other things that you can, and should, let others on the team enjoy doing. The "Delegation Grid" on page 190 is a tool that will help you discern what can or can't be delegated.

When you begin to divide the team's responsibilities up among more people, you could find yourself having to deal with problems in communication. Never do anything that may compromise or water down your vision. If delegation produces some communication confusion, here are some ways to counteract it.

Four Steps to Staying Connected While Delegating

Depicting the flow of leadership and supervision in your ministry team is critical to all on your team. The flow chart is an expression of your ministry vision and personal philosophy about leadership. See the two sample flow charts on this page and page 192. Some churches put the leaders at the bottom of the flow chart, and the team members at the top to depict their opinion that the leaders are servants first, and leaders second. Some churches have no flow charts. They don't believe in them because, as they say, "There is only one Master, and that is Jesus." Some flow charts are complex, multiple-level corporate structures while others are simple pictures with two or three levels. There is no right or wrong way to visualize your ministry structure. You will create and refurbish your flow chart until it feels right to you and your church.

1. Establish team leaders prior to delegating smaller responsibilities. Know who supervises whom, and to whom everyone reports. (For instance, the lady who will do your nursery laundry needs supervision and communication. Who does this? How does it happen?)

2. Communicate the overall ministry vision and the purpose for leadership to the leaders. (This shouldn't be a one-time communication. Your leaders should have weekly or monthly meetings with you to reinforce or apply the vision and leadership purpose to their weekly tasks.)

3. Create clear operation expectations and guidelines for every team member. The leadership person over that team member supervises those guidelines.

4. Encourage the leadership and team members regularly. Thank-you cards, phone calls, and personal thanks from you during the service time keep those who serve satisfied.

Children's Ministry Team Flowchart #1

CHILDREN'S PASTOR
Director of Children's Ministry
Nursery Coordinator
    First Service Supervisor
      Area Ministry Team
    Second Service Supervisor
      Area Ministry Team
    Evening Service Supervisor
      Area Ministry Team
Pre-school Coordinator
    First Service Supervisor
      Area Ministry Team
    Second Service Supervisor
      Area Ministry Team
    Evening Service Supervisor
      Area Ministry Team
Elementary Coordinator
    First Service Supervisor
      Area Ministry Team
    Second Service Supervisor
      Area Ministry Team
    Evening Service Supervisor
      Area Ministry Team
Special Programs Coordinator
    Children's Church coordinator
      Music Leader
      Drama Leader
    Camps Coordinator
      Winter Camp Team
      Summer Camp Team
    Youth Leadership Coordinator
    Service Project Coordinator
    VBS Coordinator
      VBS Ministry Team

Children's Ministry Team Flowchart #2

CHILDREN'S PASTOR
Director of Children's Ministry

Nursery Coordinator
Preschool Coordinator
Elementary Coordinator
- Recruit new volunteers
- Train, rotate, apprentice volunteers
- Oversee curriculum use
- Oversee supplies use
- Organize facilities use
- Facilitate volunteer appreciation
- Integrate service/missions plans
- Facilitate communication
- Facilitate youth volunteers
- Assist in budget plans

Team Development Coordinator
- Coordinate recruiting
- Coordinate training process
- Coordinate volunteer support
- Coordinate communication
- Coordinate image/marketing

"MinistryCare" Coordinator
- Recruit new employees
- Train new employees
- Oversee curriculum use
- Oversee supplies use
- Organize facilities use
- Coordinate substitutes
- Facilitate employee appreciation
- Facilitate communication
- Assist in budget plans
- Oversee policies/procedures

Program Coordinator
- Oversee children's church
- Oversee VBS
- Facilitate misc. programs
- Assist in budget plans

Ministry Scheduler
- Place team members
- Make monthly schedule
- Coordinate substitutes

DEPARTMENTAL ORGANIZATION

As you can see in the first flowchart, there are several levels in this traditional format. The bosses are at the top with volunteers at the bottom. In this model, the volunteers work through supervisors, the supervisors work through the coordinator, and the coordinator works through the Director of Children's Ministry. As with any model, there are pros and cons. I'll discuss them later, and give you another option.

The first leadership position to ask the Lord to develop is that of a department coordinator. When I first came to my present church, the children's ministry team had no coordinators. There was a children's pastor (who just retired), a director of children's ministry, and a part-time, shared secretary. I knew the first positions I needed to create were the department coordinators. How do you decide which positions need to be created or filled first? How do you determine which area of ministry should come first in terms of budget, staff, and attention? Here's my formula for deciding all the important stuff in leadership. First, decide on the most important program (is it Sunday morning?). Then, determine what would make the program more efficient and fruitful for God. Then decide how to accomplish that. (The addition of people, resources, or organization?)

When I realized that, at that time, Sunday morning programs were the most important, I applied the above formula. I saw that the director of children's ministry and the secretary were spending up to eight hours on the phone each week just trying to staff the Sunday morning programs. I knew this wasn't the best use of these people's time and energy. I also realized there was no reason to have to spend so much time getting those who had volunteered to serve to fulfill their service commitments! I decided to develop three department coordinators (nursery, preschool, and elementary) who would supervise the teams in those areas. These coordinators would deal with only those team members who served in their areas. Let me tell you, these three coordinators were a breath of fresh air and hope for the whole team! Team members were encouraged, supervised, and we had less needs for substitutes than ever before!

The department coordinator's primary responsibility is to supervise the team, curriculum, and team members in that particular area. Before the coordinators were placed, I had the frightening responsibility of overseeing over 100 team members. Once I placed the coordinators, I still was ultimately responsible for the entire team, but I actually placed all my attention on developing and supervising three leaders.

ADMINISTRATIVE ORGANIZATION

I have filled up the hard drive on my computer with the various stages of administrative evolution expressed by different flow charts. It's a constant challenge for me. How can I best organize people so the ministry functions at peak performance? I know one thing for sure, the larger your children's ministry, the more people you need to run it! If you are serving at a church that has grown quickly, bless you! Fast growth means more piles on your desk and a full voicemail box. In order to keep moving toward your ministry vision, you must develop specialists on your team who will assist you in the supervision of the ministry. Two of the team leadership positions that are valuable to a growing team are the Team Development Coordinator, who supervises the recruiting, screening, and training process, and the Program Coordinator, who supervises the overall program development and evaluation process.

Children's Ministry Program Coordinator
Brief Overview of Responsibilities for the Program Coordinator

• Attend conferences in your ministry field.

• Further your education through reading.

• Network with other churches and children's ministry coordinators.

• Design and staff new children's ministry programs.

• Design and direct the various children's church sessions.

• Design and direct Vacation Bible School type programs.

• Recruit and train all program personnel.

• Attend children's ministry team meetings (Wednesday mornings).

Detailed Description of Responsibilities for the Program Coordinator
Personal

1. Continue being a faithful servant of Jesus through regular personal devotion and attendance in weekly worship services.

2. Be a peacemaker who is at peace with the Lord, his/her calling, and the ministry purpose.

3. Be teachable, and be willing to learn from books, tapes, articles, seminars or conferences which are offered as part of the on-going training process.

4. Be willing to encourage, correct, and challenge those under his/her leadership.

Training

1. Attend all conferences or seminars which are paid for by the children's ministry unless exempted by the children's pastor. Conferences or seminars which aren't paid for by the children's ministry will be considered optional.

2. Read one book, related to the field of programming, per quarter. These books will be the choice of the coordinator and will be paid for by the children's ministry.

Networking

1. Visit one other children's ministry per quarter. These visits may either be chosen by the coordinator or suggested by the children's pastor. These visits may be combined with the visits of another coordinator for fellowship or fun. These visits must be scheduled at least one month in advance to assure that the responsibilities of the church are covered as well as being respectful to the ministries visited.

2. Be connected with other churches' children's ministry coordinators via phone or email. These connections are made at the coordinator's own discretion, and the conversations will remain confidential unless the coordinator wishes them to be shared.

Ministry Leadership

1. Assist in creating new programs. These programs will be conceptualized by the entire children's

ministry administrative team. The Program Coordinator will work with the Team Development Coordinator to seek a director for the new program, and then will assist the director in the creation, launch, and evaluation of the new program.

2. Oversee all the children's church sessions (Sunday morning, Sunday evening, Saturday evening, etc.).

3. Oversee Vacation Bible School-type programs. The Program Coordinator will most likely work together with the Team Development Coordinator in creating a team of volunteers and a director for these programs as well. The Program Coordinator may, at his or her own discretion, choose to personally direct these programs.

Team Development

1. Work together with the Team Development Coordinator in recruiting and training those who serve in the program. For the safety of the children, the adult-child ratios stated in the Children's Ministry Policy Handbook must be guaranteed before the program can be approved. Carry out the training process of the program personnel.

2. Supervise the nurture and support of those ministering in the various programs. The director of the program will carry out this support through personal contacts, phone calls, notes of encouragement, etc. Financial support for gifts is available through the children's ministry budget. The Team Development Coordinator may assist in ideas and support.

Budget

1. The Program Coordinator will assist the director of the program in submitting a budget for the program, or will submit a budget personally. This budget will include all costs included in the creation, and operation of the program as well as any team development costs.

2. In addition to the program budget, the Program Coordinator will submit projections for the number of children involved in the program and the cost charged per child (if applicable).

Weekly Hours

1. Since this is a part-time position, the number of hours which will be devoted to this job is limited to 20 hours per week. The children's pastor must approve any additional hours.

2. Office hours will be required on Mondays and Thursdays only. On Wednesdays, children's ministry team meetings will be held from 9 a.m. to noon.

Children's Ministry Team Development Coordinator

Brief Overview of Responsibilities for the Team Development Coordinator

• Attend conferences in your ministry field.

• Further your education through reading.

• Network with other churches and children's ministry coordinators.

• Assist the children's pastor in limited administrative duties.

• Coordinate ministry image development and marketing.

• Coordinate team member support efforts.

• Coordinate the recruiting process.

• Coordinate the application/screening process.

• Coordinate the orientation, apprenticeship, and training process.

• Attend children's ministry team meetings on Wednesday mornings.

• Be present in office on Wednesday mornings and another morning.

Detailed Description of Responsibilities for the Team Development Coordinator

Personal

1. Continue being a faithful servant of Jesus through regular personal devotion and attendance in weekly worship services.

2. Be a peacemaker who is at peace with the Lord, his/her calling, and the ministry purpose.

3. Be teachable, and be willing to learn from books, tapes, articles, seminars or conferences which are offered as part of the on-going training process.

4. Be willing to encourage, correct, and challenge those under his/her leadership.

Training

1. Attend all conferences or seminars which are paid for by the children's ministry unless exempted by the children's pastor. Conferences or seminars which aren't paid for by the children's ministry will be considered optional.

2. Read one book, related to the field of team development, per quarter. These books will be the choice of the coordinator, and will be paid for by the children's ministry.

Networking

1. Visit one other children's ministry per quarter. These visits may either be chosen by the coordinator, or suggested by the children's pastor. These visits may be combined with the visits of another coordinator for fellowship or fun. These visits must be scheduled at least one month in advance to assure that the Sunday morning responsibilities are covered as well as being respectful to the ministries visited.

2. Be connected with other churches' children's ministry coordinators via phone or email. These connections are made at the coordinator's own discretion, and the conversations will remain confidential unless the coordinator wishes them to be shared.

Ministry Leadership

1. Oversee the youth leadership program. The Team Development Coordinator may choose to remain as director of the youth leadership program, or empower others to direct it under the direct supervision of the Team Development Coordinator.

2. Assist the children's pastor in limited administrative duties (phone calls, schedules, letters, etc.).

Team Development

1. Coordinate the process of creating, establishing, and marketing our children's ministry purpose and image.

2. Coordinate the team member support efforts.

3. Coordinate team communications within the team (newsletters, emails, cards, letters, etc.), and from the children's ministry to the rest of the church.

4. Coordinate the recruitment process.

5. Coordinate the application/screening process.

6. Coordinate the orientation/apprenticeship/training process using Department Coordinators, master teachers, and the Program Coordinator.

Weekly Hours

1. Since this is a part-time position, the number of hours which will be devoted to this job is limited to 20 hours per week. The children's pastor must approve any additional hours.

2. Office hours will be required from 9 a.m. to 3 p.m. on Wednesday only. Team meetings will be held on Wednesday mornings from 9 a.m. to noon.

Department Coordinators

Placing the correct people in the positions of department coordinators is critical. This is not just about filling organizational holes in your flow chart! Remember you are about spiritual matters and significant people-development goals! The characters of those you place in these critical leadership positions must match your vision. Here are some thoughts on the type of people that fit this position.

Qualifications of a Department Coordinator

1. A person with a strong, growing, active walk with the Lord.

2. A person with a compassionate love for the spiritual and physical condition of children.

3. A person who can patiently nurture adults through example and encouragement.

4. A person who is a team leader and cheerleader.

5. A person who has the gift of teaching.

6. A person who has taught in the children's ministry for at least a year (in the age group he or she will coordinate).

7. A person whose family and personal life permit this additional responsibility.

8. A person who is willing to support the policies and leadership of this church.

Job Description The department coordinator is designed to be a person who will increase the team's effectiveness though greater personal contact and communication. The department coordinator will also serve as an ambassador to the children's pastor. The coordinator will:

1. Be the children's pastor's EYES

    a. To provide eye-to-eye contact to the team members in his/her area.

    b. To provide eye-to-eye contact to the parents of the children in his/her area.

    c. To provide eye-to-eye contact to the children in his/her area classes.

    d. To see areas of need or repair in his/her area.

    e. To check curriculum and supply requests for his/her area.

    f. To check the personnel needs prior to rotation for his/her area.

2. Be the children's pastor's HANDS

    a. To supportively touch the team members in his/her area.

    b. To hold the hands of new volunteers as they are introduced to their master teacher for their apprenticeship.

    c. To prepare the rooms in his/her area for the teacher (unlock cabinets, prepare check-in materials, check tables and chairs).

    d. To pick up trash, clean up, and close the class (lock cabinets, collect check-in materials, collect offering, etc.).

    e. To take class materials (offering, sign-in sheets, etc.) to the office after the service.

3. Be the children's pastor's VOICE

    a. To speak words of encouragement to the team members in his/her area.

    b. To pray with the team members in his/her area.

    c. To carry the vision for the ministry to the team members in his/her area.

    d. To relay information from the children's pastor to the team members in his/her area.

    e. To speak with the parents of children in his/her area. This is an initial point of contact; the children's pastor will always join if needed.

    f. To reinforce ministry standards or policies to team members, parents, or children in his/her area.

    g. To be available during orientation meetings to talk with prospective volunteers for his/her area.

4. Be the children's pastor's EARS

    a. To be a sensitive ear and good listener to the team members in his/her area.

    b. To be a sensitive ear and good listener to the parents of the children in his/her area.

    c. To listen to comments, not directly spoken to him/her, from team members, parents, or children in his/her area which might indicate areas of need or improvement.

    d. To listen to news stories, etc. which might effect the entire children's ministry or just the ministry in his/her area.

    e. To listen to the Lord's voice regarding the ministry in his/her area.

5. Be the children's pastor's FEET

    a. To be in his/her area during service times.

    b. To be available to go to the supply area to get supplies needed in his/her area.

    c. To be present in team meetings for his/her area.

    d. To be available to be with a child outside the classroom who is causing disruption.

Brief Overview of Responsibilities for the Department Coordinator

1. Attend conferences in your ministry field.

2. Further your education through reading.

3. Network with other churches and children's ministry coordinators.

4. Assist in forging and carrying out the overall ministry purpose.

5. Assist in carrying out the children's ministry policies within the department.

6. Nurture and support those ministering in the department.

7. Empower and nurture service supervisors within the department.

8. Oversee the placing of substitutes each week (by the ministry scheduler).

9. Assist in the recruiting of new team members.

10. Supervise the apprenticing of new team members in the department.

11. Assist in the training of team members.

12. Assist in dealing with difficult team member situations.

13. Oversee the curriculum design and use (with supervisor assistance).

14. Prepare and distribute new curriculum each quarter.

15. Oversee the supply needs and purchases (with supervisor assistance).

16. Supervise the distribution of supplies (with supervisor assistance).

17. Oversee the cleanliness of classrooms (with supervisor assistance).

18. Assist the children's pastor in dealing with difficult parent or child situations.

19. Oversee the check-in process (with check-in personnel).

20. Oversee the fulfillment of approved adult/child ratios (with check-in personnel).

21. Attend children's ministry team meetings.

Detailed Responsibilities for the Department Coordinator

Personal

1. Continue being a faithful servant of Jesus through regular personal devotion and attendance in weekly worship services.

2. Be a peacemaker who is at peace with the Lord, his/her calling, and the ministry purpose.

3. Be teachable, and be willing to learn from books, tapes, articles, seminars or conferences which are offered as part of the on-going training process.

4. Be willing to encourage, correct, and challenge those under his/her leadership.

Training

1. Attend all conferences or seminars which are paid for by the children's ministry unless exempted by the children's pastor. Conferences or seminars which aren't paid for by the children's ministry will be considered optional.

2. Read one book, related to the coordinator's department, per quarter. These books will be the choice of the coordinator, and will be paid for by the children's ministry.

Networking

1. Visit one other children's ministry per quarter. These visits may either be chosen by the coordinator, or suggested by the children's pastor. These visits may be combined with the visits of another coordinator for fellowship or fun. These visits must be scheduled at least one month in advance to assure that the responsibilities of your area are covered as well as being respectful to the ministries visited.

2. Be connected with other churches' children's ministry coordinators via phone or email. These connections are made at the coordinator's own discretion, and the conversations will remain confidential unless the coordinator wishes them to be shared.

Ministry Leadership

1. Assist in forging and carrying out the specific ministry purpose for the department.

2. Assist in carrying out the children's ministry policies within the department.

Team Development

1. Nurture and support those ministering in the department. This will be done through personal contacts, phone calls, notes of encouragement, etc. The ministry scheduler will play a major role in this vital responsibility. The service supervisors will assist in this effort as well. Financial support for gifts is available through the children's ministry budget.

2. Seek out and empower service supervisors for the department. Oversee these supervisors' support and communications with those who serve in the department during that service hour.

3. Meet jointly with the service supervisors of the department at least once per quarter for support, communication, and fun.

4. Organize all substitute teacher needs for the department. This can and should be eventually handled by the team member his or herself via the team roster. If the team member has difficulty in covering his or her absence, he or she will then call the ministry scheduler. The coordinator will be called if the service ministry scheduler cannot fill his or her individual service needs.

5. Supervise the recruiting of new team members for the department. This responsibility must be shared by all who serve in the department. Recruitment efforts will be carried out in partnership with the entire children's ministry leadership team.

6. Supervise the apprenticing of new team members in the department. This can and should be done by the service supervisors.

7. Supervise the training of new team members as well as the on-going process of training the veteran team members.

8. Assist the children's pastor in dealing with difficult team member situations. The coordinator may deal directly with the team member if the children's pastor is not available and the situation requires immediate attention. All difficult team member situations will be dealt with in partnership with the children's pastor, unless the children's pastor is not available, or unless the children's pastor directs otherwise. If the coordinator is not present, the children's pastor will deal with the situation in partnership with the service supervisor.

9. Create, stuff, and mail the monthly packet of information to the team members in the department. This packet will include: a personal letter from the coordinator; a memo which highlights business items (changes, dates, etc.); a team roster with names of phone numbers; a monthly schedule of service responsibilities for the entire department

Curriculum

1. Communicate with the children's pastor regarding curriculum needs or changes.

2. Prepare and distribute new curriculum to the team members in the department. This preparation can be accomplished during a departmental social gathering with financial support coming from the children's ministry budget.

Supplies

1. Communicate with the children's pastor regarding supply needs. This communication will be accomplished during weekly staff meetings. Purchases will be made by the coordinator as directed in the "How to Spend Money" procedure sheet.

2. Distribute supplies to the appropriate team member or service supervisor.

3. Oversee the organization and cleanliness of the classroom cabinets. This can and should be done by the service supervisors.

Service Supervision

1. Assist the children's pastor in dealing with difficult parent or child situations. The coordinator may deal directly with the child or parent if the children's pastor is not available and the situation requires immediate attention. All difficult parent or child situations will be dealt with in partnership with the children's pastor unless the children's pastor is not available, or unless he directs otherwise. If the coordinator is not present, the children's pastor will deal with the situation in partnership with the service supervisor.

2. Oversee the fulfillment of the adult/child ratios in the department classrooms. This will be done by the check-in personnel. Classroom ratios and sizes are all monitored at the check-in counter. If problems occur at the check-in counter, the coordinator or supervisor will contact the children's pastor for assistance.

Weekly Hours

1. Since this is a part-time position, the number of hours which will be devoted to this job is limited to 20 hours per week. The children's pastor must approve any additional hours.

2. Office hours will be required on the morning of the leadership team meeting only. The meeting will be held on a given weekday morning and consist of an all-team meeting and an individual meeting with each coordinator.

Weekly and Monthly Reports

1. During the individual meeting with the children's pastor the Department Coordinator will be given a Task Sheet for the coming week. These tasks will be determined as a result of the meeting, and will be agreed-upon by those in the meeting. These tasks will be worked on during the coming week, and progress will be reported at the next individual meeting.

2. At the end of the month, the Department Coordinator will be asked to submit a Monthly Report which reviews the ministry for the month and

lists specific plans for team development for the coming month.

Children's Ministry Department Coordinator Priorities

I have found that it is very easy for the department coordinators to slip into the "it's all about me" pit. This is understandable, but not acceptable. Your team must be about the vision and about the people on your team. If you don't plan ahead now, you will have big problems when the cute little eight piglets grow to adult pigs! Ministry is about prayer, preparation, plans, and priorities.

The challenge to us all is to remain focused on the vision and the priorities while still caring for the hundreds of surprises and details of the work. To help us all stay focused, here is a list of priorities in order of importance. How we care for these priorities varies, but we cannot focus on the lower ones and neglect the higher ones.

1. Your own personal, intimate, growing relationship with Jesus. If you aren't growing and learning, it will show in your treatment of others and in your lack of fruit in your life and ministry.

2. Care for the existing people on your team. People are the highest priority! If the people God leads to you are happy, organized, and nurtured, they will serve deeper and more consistently. Casting your vision, offering increased levels of expectation or responsibilities, and empowering others for leadership are all top priorities in ministry. Caring for your weekly/monthly schedule and weekly communications with your team must never take a second seat to anything else. If you have trouble getting your teachers to meetings, try adding some of these ideas to your meeting:

• Go on shopping trips with a 99 cent meal afterward.

• Have a barbecue at the park.

• Have cookouts at the beach.

• Arrange a group trip to a sporting event.

• Arrange a group trip to a concert.

• See a movie together and go out for pie afterward.

• Go on a surprise "drive-by desserting" to a team member's home.

• Go to a parade.

• Take a train trip to a nearby town for a meal.

• Saturday sidewalk chalk art at church.

• Go miniature golfing.

• Have a team pot luck dinner and variety show at church.

• Go on a fishing trip.

• Have a Super Bowl party at church or at home.

3. Your weekly program or supply needs. Compared to the people needs, your program or supply needs are less critical. If you are lacking supplies or your program is not as impressive as you would like, but your people are happy and are sure of their ministry, you will still have great fruit. If your program is great and you have all the supplies you need, but your people are not happy or are not secure in their ministry, you will not see the fruit.

As you develop your team, your program will grow and expand as well. As you develop your team, your own personal stress and to do list will reduce. As you develop your team, your ability to dream and facilitate the ministry vision increases. As you develop your team, the number of children who are impacted for the Lord will increase. As you develop your team, your team will multiply in number. As you develop your team, you will please the Lord. What you are about here is spiritual and eternal! It is the work of the Creator himself.

No matter how gifted, called, or qualified your coordinators are, they are still people who need supervision and periodic challenges. If you are an "I just want us all to enjoy each other" sort of person, and not a "let's get it done" sort of person, you may have difficulty supervising the coordinators and expecting a certain level of performance from them. I am blessed to have an assistant who is stronger in the "let's get it done" area than I am. The following is an overview of the expectations for your coordinators. Keep in mind, your coordinators are people, not merely those who perform a function (see, that's my "I just want us all to enjoy each other" side coming out).

Service Supervisors

Once your coordinators are in place and functioning, you can begin to think about developing service supervisors. A service supervisor is a person whose responsibilities are to directly support the children's ministry area coordinator by focusing on the details and needs of a specific service hour. This person is basically the department coordinator's ambassador for that service. He or she will make sure the service runs according to the department coordinator's plans. The service supervisor is a volunteer who has been a faithful, consistent team member within the department. This division of responsibility is designed to enhance communication and support in the entire children's ministry team. Here is a description of the responsibilities of a service supervisor.

Service Supervisor Qualifications

1. A person who has faithfully served as a teacher on the children's ministry team for at least 6 months.

2. A person who has an obvious, growing relationship with Jesus.

3. A person who has a passion for service.

4. A person who has a compassion for children.

5. A person who exhibits exemplary qualities in the classroom (creativity, classroom management, lesson design/execution, etc.).

6. A person who is able to minister to the parents and fellow children's ministry team members in a supportive, gentle, understanding manner.

7. A person who is teachable.

Responsibilities

A supervisor's primary responsibility is to the Lord. The responsibility of supporting the area coordinator is secondary. The bottom line of the following list of responsibilities is to be a contact person for the specific service hour. It is the supervisor's responsibility to serve as a communication bridge between the area coordinator and the ministry team members who serve during that service, and vice-versa. The specific responsibilities are:

1. To assist the area coordinator in the apprenticeship of new volunteers.

2. To be on call if a situation arises in which a team member needs help during the service hour. If the area coordinator is not present, the supervisor will act on the coordinator's behalf.

3. To personally greet the team members who serve during the service hour (either before or after the hour's service).

4. To be aware of the needs of the team members who serve during the particular service hour.

5. To communicate the needs of the particular service hour to the area coordinator.

6. To communicate messages from the area coordinator to the team members who serve during the particular service hour.

7. To attend all children's ministry team meetings.

8. To assist the coordinator in distributing the curriculum (if applicable) at the beginning of a new quarter.

9. To be the first person called if team members, who serve during the supervisor's specific service hour cannot find a replacement for themselves when not able to serve. The supervisor will do whatever is necessary to guarantee that the children are cared for. If the supervisor has difficulty, then the coordinator is contacted.

Term of Service

The supervisor will continue serving in that capacity unless the area coordinator suggests/requests that he or she step down, or until the supervisor desires to step down.

The appointing of a team member to a supervisor position is a ministry advancement that should be carried out with a planned process. If a service supervisor is not placed correctly, the other team members may have difficulty submitting to the person's authority. Here is a process by which you can promote a team member to the supervisor position.

Children's Ministry Supervisor Recruitment and Development Process

Process goal: To empower and develop those people who will become service supervisors under the leadership of the department coordinator.

1. Prayer & Seeking. The entire leadership team prays for the Lord's direction in choosing supervisors. The department coordinator watches for people in the department who fit the qualities of a supervisor.

2: Offer & Prayer. The department coordinator offers the position to *one person per service at a time.* The coordinator compliments the supervisor-candidate on his/her faithfulness and qualities, gives him/her a copy of the *Service Supervisor Job Description*, and encourages the person to prayerfully consider this critical leadership position for one week.

3. Apprenticeship. Prior to an official introduction, the new supervisor will spend at least two weeks listening to another supervisor or the department coordinator making phone calls in preparation for the week's service. During those two weeks, the new supervisor will also walk beside the department coordinator as the coordinator greets team members prior to the service, deals with situations during the service, and then thanks team members after the service.

4. Introduction & Prayer. After a successful apprenticeship period, the department coordinator will officially introduce the new service supervisor at the next department meeting or social gathering. The new supervisor's responsibilities will be reviewed, and any changes in procedures will be clarified. The entire department will pray for God's blessing on the supervisor.

5. On-going Support. The department coordinator will continue to remain close to the service supervisors. These supervisors will be the coordinator's leadership team for the department. Weekly phone calls, letters of encouragement, periodic visits during services, etc. will insure clear, positive communication.

6. On-going Training. The department coordinator will continue to pass on tapes, books, articles, or conference opportunities to the service supervisors. The children's pastor will offer many of these same materials to the department coordinators themselves.

A supervisor or coordinator's primary responsibility is to assure that the direct ministry to the children runs smoothly and efficiently. As has been stated before, happy, secure team members will most likely affect the children more positively than confused team members. Clearly defining the various functions that a team member performs is a very healthy thing to do. Whether these functions occur in a Sunday school, a children's church, or at a camp doesn't matter. Setting clear expectations for every position or post is needed.

Security Monitors and Posts

This position is perhaps one of the most important in terms of child safety, parental approval, and child happiness. The monitors are those people who focus on what is going on in the program as well as around the program. They are the eyes and ears of the supervisors, teachers, or leaders who are directly involved in program functions. The monitors have specific duties that are performed at specific locations ("posts") in your ministry program area.

Responsibilities

1. Monitor the doors. With one eye and ear, pay attention to what is going on around you, and with the other eye and ear, monitor the doors around you. The enemy would love to destroy what the Lord is doing by having us be convicted of negligence in the safety of the children! We must all take this threat very seriously!

2. Monitor the safety and peace of all the children. We must all look and listen to hear or see any signs of a child not feeling good or not at peace. We must all invade and intervene into every situation that needs us!

3. Serve the parents. We must all make eye contact with, and smile at, every parent who comes within our area. The parents are the most critical factor in the children returning!

4. Pray for and compliment the fellow team members. This is not just the responsibility of the Director, a supervisor, or a coordinator! We are the body of Christ! If we all pray for, compliment, and touch each other, the strength of our ministry will multiply accordingly!

Monitor Posts

1. Check-in door: The goal of this post is to ensure that the parents and children are greeted with smiles and assisted in getting into the service quickly and efficiently. An outside person assists parents with filling out name stickers, registration forms, paging system tags, hand stamps, etc., and identifying the children with the appropriate stickers, tags, hand stamps, etc. An inside person confirms that the children are identified, blocks any non-team adults from entering the room, and keeps children from leaving through the door. As each child comes through the door, the child's name is announced to the "Pre-worship activities" personnel (until the worship has begun).

2. Pre-worship activities: The goal of this post is to make the child's first experience in children's church enjoyable! The monitors here should smile and make eye contact with each child and then welcome each child into one of the available activities. The use of the child's name at this point is critical.

3. Transition door: The goal of this post is to welcome late-arriving children and to make sure they feel welcome. This person directs the child to the worship area. If possible, make eye-contact with a "worship support" person who can wave to the child to come sit by him or her.

4. Worship support: The goal of this post is to support the worship leader/teacher by modeling the desired behavior. This person exudes extreme energy in touching, smiling, and being with the children around him or her. If necessary, due to the size of the group, this person may need to move around after a couple of minutes to assure that all the children have been blessed by his or her presence! Passive sitting or standing is not permitted at this post!

5. Worship area: The goal of this post is to be an environment that enables the children to worship and experience God through the direction of the worship leader/teacher. The worship leader/teacher must become the vessel through which the Spirit of God flows into the children. This person plays with the children through his or her eyes, voice, and body movements. This person draws the children into worship and introduces the concepts or story for the day. This person must become a child, to win the children with the power of the Spirit. This person determines when to move the children to the centers and prepares them for the next phase of the program.

6. Activity centers: The goal of this post is to ensure that the objectives of the centers are achieved. This person makes sure the centers are supplied, organized, and ready for the children prior to the children's arrival. While the children are involved with the center, this person helps the children feel successful. This person compliments and encourages the children. This person listens for the signal to move the children to the next center, and then assists in the movement.

7. Incoming door: The goal of this post is to greet the parents as they come to pick up their children. This person must smile constantly and be courteous, even in the face of upset parents. This person moves the parents through the door and tells them to walk straight across the front of the room to attract their children to them, and then to the exit door.

8. Outgoing door: The goal of this post is to control the secure exit of the children. This person checks to assure that parents and children are matched up correctly. This is a two-person post to assure security! If the crowd of adults and children gets too large to guarantee the security of this post, the monitors have the authority to stop the process, and ask the parents to slow down. The security of the children must never be compromised to speed up the exit process! If a parent does not have the correct tag, label, key ring, hand stamp, or whatever device that indicates he is the correct parent to pick up a child, he must be asked to step aside, and one of the outgoing support personnel will be called to assist while the check-out process continues safely. Never engage an angry parent at this door! Get assistance, refer the parent to the proper personnel, and return to your duties.

If a parent takes a child without the proper identification device, both of the outgoing support personnel must be told immediately; they must notify the supervisor in charge and set into motion whatever policy and procedure addresses improper pick-up, whether it involves chasing down a parent or initiating a lockdown procedure.

9. Outgoing support: The goal of this post is to assist in the efficient, secure flow of parents and children out of the room. These monitors watch, just like a Secret Service agent, as the parents enter the room, connect with the children, and then proceed to the outgoing door. This person watches for any unusual movement to control a child or any signs of fear from the children. If anything catches the attention of the monitors, they must approach the parent with a smile and ask if the parent needs assistance with the procedure. The support monitor must verify that the correct parent and child have been matched up; the monitor can then smile and welcome them back next week. If there is any threat to the security of the children, this person must deal with it directly with the assistance of the another outgoing support person, and if needed, with the help of the supervisor or coordinator.

TEAM BUILDING

When people work together, things happen. When good people work together better things happen. When good people work together with God, eternal things happen! God didn't make any perfect people. He didn't make any one person with all the gifts, abilities, or talents needed to operate a children's ministry (sorry to disappoint you). We need each other! We have to work together toward a common vision. Remember what Paul said about the body: "There are different kinds of gifts, but the same Spirit. There are different kinds of service, but the same Lord. There are different kinds of working, but the same God works all of them in all men.... All these are the work of one and the same Spirit, and he gives them to each one, just as he determines. The body is a unit, though it is made up of many parts; and though all its parts are many, they form

one body. So it is with Christ.... Now you are the body of Christ, and each one of you is a part of it" *(1 Corinthians 12:4-27)*.

The Process of Building Teams

The best team is built on the best leaders. The best leaders in church ministry are those whose hearts are totally God's. They are those whose walks with the Lord are intimate, growing, and obvious. They are those people who attract others to serve alongside them. They are those people whose blessing from the Lord overflows into their team.

Principles to Protect

1. Don't ask someone to do something you haven't already done.

2. Don't give away too much too soon.

3. Don't give away your calling.

4. Invest in one leader at a time.

5. Recycle your leaders.

Be an example. Let others see your willingness to serve, compassion for others, and passion for the "cause." Be an example in your attitude, speech, and actions. Do everything!

Invite others to join you. As you serve joyously, others will be interested in serving alongside you. Invite them to join you and share fellowship and companionship as you also enjoy the fruit of your service for the Lord. Be nice!

Give others opportunities. As others serve alongside you, let them have various opportunities to express themselves, or test their abilities. Don't be afraid to ask them to do more. Those who are willing to do more need more to do. Increase the challenges.

Watch, encourage others. As others take on the various challenges, watch their performance. Encourage those who try new things because of their willingness to try! Be very vocal about your support and thank them for what they attempt regardless of the "success" of their good efforts. Compliment them in front of others.

Let others "fail" then succeed. If they appear to

"fail," or view their efforts as such, encourage them to try again. Help them learn from their last effort, and apply what they learned to the next effort. Be there to encourage them, and celebrate with them afterward. Each attempt brings them closer to success.

Challenge others with leadership. Those who have succeeded in failing and trying again, and who are good with people, can be encouraged to consider leading others. Offer them small leadership roles and evaluate their abilities.

Support others' leadership. When you decide to let others direct an area; introduce them to the rest of the team and publically support their character and leadership position. Challenge others to view them as their leader and prayerfully support them. Continue to encourage them in their leadership role.

Let your leaders reproduce. Challenge your leaders to lead others. Create a plan by which the leaders can repeat the process that they have been trained through in others and let them supervise them. Leadership recycling is the style of Jesus!

Goal 8.2 We want the supervisors and teachers on our children's ministry team to say, "I feel supported and appreciated here."

A healthy team begins with healthy people being given the support and encouragement they need to do their jobs. It is our responsibility to offer everyone service options within the team, and then to place them where their particular personalities or spiritual gifts apply the best. People who serve in either a volunteer or paid basis need regular encouragement and personal support.

To Reach This Goal:

1. Develop a plan for regular team appreciation events.

2. Continue to develop regular communication, including email communication.

3. Send coordinators to other churches and conferences to learn techniques in team-development.

4. Create area team fun events (bowling, pot lucks, variety shows, etc.)

To build a team, you need to have a clear process through which people are recruited, supervised, empowered to higher levels of responsibility, and then appointed to leadership positions. Every coordinator is a team-builder! We all have the beautiful challenge of searching for those within our team who could be cultivated to become leaders.

Team building is not just in the overall children's ministry team. Each coordinator is faced with the challenge of building a team within his or her department. Those who serve in a particular area should feel a sense of team among the others in that area. Building a team within a department is sort of like building a family. You will care for each other, cry for each other, and sacrifice for each other. You, as the parent, need to be careful not to offend another family member. Here are some thoughts on team building from this perspective.

The Building of the Ministry Family

1. The Courtship. During this phase, the attentions, respect, and love of the ministry team members is earned. This can be accomplished through personal attention, compliments, encouragement, sacrifice, and prayer. (This is the first phase of the process, but this courtship should never end. Once it does, the family will fall apart.)

2. Dating. During this phase, the members of the team and the coordinator enjoy being together. Having fun, apart from the Sunday school or church setting, is the goal. Getting to know each other through these off-duty moments is critical. This continues the courtship and prepares the members for the next phase.

3. The Engagement. During this phase, intentions and beliefs of the coordinator and team members are disclosed and discussed. The coordinator's vision, mission, passion, and philosophy of ministry becomes clear to the entire ministry team. Each team member is challenged to consider his or her own commitment and passion. If severe differences in these areas are discovered, compromises may be considered, or the relationship may need to be broken off. The future growth of the family and ministry takes priority over feelings.

4. The Marriage. At this point, there is a depth of honesty, companionship, and trust that cannot be easily broken. The dedication to the ministry and to each other is visible to all. Respect and professionalism are natural results of this relationship. The children and parents in the ministry are the real recipients of the blessings of this healthy marriage.

5. The Family. At this time, the team members naturally desire to reproduce. They can't help telling others about the joys of service and the fulfilling companionship they are experiencing. The children who are brought into the family are nurtured and taught by example. The family grows. Others who

20 Ideas for an Effective Team Meeting

1. Set a regular date for the meetings.
2. Limit the meetings to 1 hour.
3. Require attendance.
4. Coordinators remind teams of meeting.
5. Rotate refreshments responsibility.
6. Publicize a fun theme for the meeting.
7. Start on time, end on time.
8. Appoint an official greeter.
9. Begin with a fun ministry story.
10. Spend a significant time in worship.
11. Share a time of prayer together.
12. Reserve 25 to 30 minutes for business.
13. Praise new (and old) team members.
14. Print business, mention highlights.
15. Welcome limited discussion of topics.
16. Invite team member praise stories.
17. Share an inspirational challenge.
18. Close with a good time of prayer.
19. Encourage fellowship after the meeting.
20. Always invite your senior pastor.

"Well done, my good and faithful teachers!"

Get better at boasting in the Lord! Advertise what God is doing in and through the lives of the team members and the children in our ministry. How can you tell the stories that you all talk about in your team meetings to the rest of the church family? Don't be selfish and keep these stories to yourselves! God loves to be proclaimed and praised for his mighty works! Some ideas for boasting in the Lord and celebrating the awesome ministry of your teachers might be:

1. Permanent displays outside the 3 department areas in which we place beautifully-created "Team Member of the Month" posters.

2. Monthly "Stories from the Ministry" cards handed out to parents (stories involving both children and team members).

3. Newspaper stories in the city paper.

4. Parent gift bags containing a goodie, some thanks, and a story given out at check-in.

TEACHER APPRECIATION IDEAS

1. Paint trophies (Golden Glue Bottle Award)
2. Movie passes to teachers who need a break
3. A surprise limousine ride to church
4. "Just thinking of you" notes in mailboxes
5. Restaurant coupons for dinner with spouse
6. Surprise standing ovation from students
7. Their picture and story on Wall of Fame
8. Candies or notes in their room as they arrive
9. Included in a "great teachers" song
10. Coupons for supplies at local bookstore
11. Cards, notes
12. Gifts

Garden Pest:
Six-Hour Cutworms

Evidence

These pests only work for a short period of time. They may be seen in your garden from time to time, but they don't last long. There is an "I can't do that" attitude that shows up at different stages. The "can't" attitude effects all they do and those around them. This worm is mostly found in volunteers. The visible evidence of the Six-Hour Cutworms is unfinished jobs or unmet expectations. The other sign of this pest is a finely developed talent for making excuses.

Sources of Infestation

A weak spiritual life. No intimate relationship with God. Lack of understanding regarding the Great Commission. Selfishness. Laziness. Too many other responsibilities.

Treatment

1. Spray on liberal amounts of children's ministry vision.
2. Clearly state the need for faithfulness and commitment.
3. Team with other faithful, committed team members.
4. Reinforce corrected behavior and completed tasks.
5. Give clear, defined, written and signed, warnings of consequences.
6. If necessary, remove the person from the team.

---

come in contact with the family desire to be a part of the family themselves, or to model their own family after this one.

Goal 1.6 We want the Lord to say, "Well done, my good and faithful servants."

We are told that God looks at the heart, not at the outward appearances. We want the Lord to see straight through our outward appearances and right into our faithful, sacrificial hearts. The mark of a growing spirit is a lack of complaining. The moment we begin complaining is the moment we shift our eyes from him to the problems. If we want to become a big ministry, the only way to do that is to be made up of individual team members who are faithful in the

small things and serve God no matter what.

To Reach This Goal:

1. Continue emphasizing the Great Commission in everything you do (written communications, meetings, etc.).

2. Continue publicly encouraging faithful behavior in your team members.

3. Continue bringing specific prayer requests to your team.

4. Continue teaching your team members what faithful service means through Bible studies, tapes, meetings, printed communications, etc.

5. Continue growing in your own personal, intimate relationship with God.

## chapter 15

Sharing Your Tools:
Equipping the Team

Your tools are precious possessions. When you share your tools, you are telling the person with whom you are sharing them, "I trust you; you're important to me." You're also giving that person the ability to become what you are.

TEACHER TRAINING: THE KEY TO A DYNAMIC TEAM

In chapter 12, I mentioned the effectiveness of the military in recruiting with their strong image of smartly clad, capable men and women. Do you remember the posters with the awesome fighting jet in the background? Now, imagine that the military simply gave the keys to those smartly clad soldiers and said, "Here you go; take her for a spin!" I don't think their uniforms would remain neatly pressed for very long because, inevitably, they would crash and burn! Every fighting force needs to be trained, so again let's take another lesson from Uncle Sam and train our soldiers in the Lord's army to wage the eternal battle for the souls of our precious little children who grace the doors of our ministries. Let's explore what it means to train teachers in church ministry as well as examine some sample strategies to help you accomplish this all-important task.

Principles of Effective Teacher Training

1. Levels of Training: Develop levels of training to include those who first join the team and those who need regular on-the-job training.

2. Face-to-face Initial Training: The initial training for those who are just joining the team cannot simply be a tape. In the initial packet of information given, there should be a letter and a video that invites them to their first training session. This session is critical. It must connect them with real people who will welcome them to the ministry. Subsequent training sessions can be on tape, but not the first one!

3. Include Variety: The training process should include variety. Some training can be done via tapes, other training can be linked to socials or fun outings (bowling, skating, potlucks, etc.), and others can be meetings held at church during Sunday morning.

4. The All-Important Human Connection: The ultimate challenge in training is to connect those who are being trained with real people whose passion, character, or abilities can be incentives or examples. People aspire to greatness only to the degree that greatness is connected to another person.

5. Build Servant Leaders! The primary goal in our training process must be in how to build relationships. This critical principle applies to children, parents, and other team members. The phrases "public relations" and "customer service" apply loosely here. Without this foundation of focusing on the needs of people, training in lesson design or lesson delivery is wasted. Public relations training should include greeting, assisting with directions or instructions, policy/procedure support, check-in/pick-up, problem-solving, and "GOOYWATS" (Going Out Of Your Way Always To Serve).

6. Specific Procedure Training: Training must also include specific training in procedures that are common to all areas or unique for a department. Procedure training should include check-in/pick-up, classroom procedures (especially nursery procedures), post responsibilities, bathroom trips, "problem children," emergency situations, child abuse prevention and reporting, and an overview of the safety policies and procedures in the children's ministry personnel manual.

7. *Instruction in the Art of Teaching:* Training for ministry areas must be given. This training is vision-related training. Ministry training should include lesson design and preparation, worship leading, prayer times, directed conversations, using teachable moments, relationship building, out-of-class experiences (sports events, home visits, etc.), making phone calls, and writing letters.

8. *Offer Training Completion Incentives:* The training process must include incentives for completion of the training and rewards for completion. Each training session or tool must also include an evaluation tool that will verify the successful completion of the training as well as evaluating how well the information was learned.

Vision Casting

We need to saturate our ministry team with our vision so they can become conduits for it. We can only do this by creating strategic plans to do so. Here are some ideas.

1. *Vision Tapes.* Vision-related tapes mailed out to the team members from the director and/or the coordinators. These tapes (both video and audio with sound effects) must be created in harmony with a unified plan. They can't be sporadic or impulsive. They must be planned. These tapes can include:

- Stories from the ministry.
- The value of spiritual nutrition (prayer, Bible study, worship).
- The reason and value of the components of our vision.
- Relationship building.
- Bringing hope to the children.
- Child-focused vs. lesson-focused ministry.
- Using teachable moments.
- Leaving a legacy.

- Seeing the big picture (God's Kingdom, history of the church, carrying on Jesus' work, touching children's future, being stepping stones of a child's spiritual development)
- Serving Jesus vs. serving us.
- The potential of passion.
- Our shared responsibility of team support.
- Faithfulness.
- The challenge of discipleship for ourselves and others.
- Followers first, then leaders.
- Being a mentor.
- Ministering beyond Sunday.

2. *Vary the Setting of the Tapes.* The setting for these tapes (both audio and video) can and should be varied. The possibilities for settings include:

- Shopping in a mall or grocery store.
- Doing housework or yard work.
- Driving in a car.
- At an amusement park.
- While paying bills.
- Picking up children at school.
- At a movie.
- During black-out (battery low).
- While working on the car.
- While waiting at car repair shop.
- While playing (bowling, golf, skating, etc.).
- At a job (lawn care, cook, dishwasher, engine repair, etc.).
- While exercising.
- At a restaurant.
- While visiting a jail.
- At a sports event (soccer, hockey, etc.).
- Late at night and can't sleep.
- On a tour of your town (housing areas, parks, malls, schools, etc.).
- At the doctor's office.
- While on vacation (world sites).
- At unusual places on the church campus.
- Backstage after a concert.
- During surgery (on someone else of course!).

3. *Vision Showcases.* These are locked, wall-mounted display cases that display glossy, four-color posters depicting the children's ministry team. These posters can be pictures of children or team members carrying out the vision with bold, powerful slogans or words on them.

Building Team Members Who Can Build Relationships

1. Integrate small-group options in every large-group gathering. Build into each children's ministry gathering options for large and small group experiences, while not sacrificing the tremendous value of worship and prayer. It is necessary to offer both a worship/prayer time and a small group time during the same service session.

2. Put natural talents into leadership positions. Those who serve on our ministry team must be trained in the principles of relationship-building. The best way to do that is to look for someone who is naturally gifted in this area and use that person as a master teacher. This master teacher will then be placed in positions of influence for both the children and the team members.

3. Train the team to go beyond the classroom. We need to plan for, train for, and provide opportunities for team members to encounter children outside of the church property. Of course, these adults must be carefully screened and never involve themselves with the children without parental permission. Service projects, trips, camps, fun events, etc. have an accelerated effect on relationship-building, such as:

• School lunch visits (with parent approval).

• After school chat room on the church web site.

• "Come and see me" cards (child invites team member to sports event, recital, etc.).

• "Come to my child's birthday party" cards (parent invites team member to child's birthday party).

• Phone appointments with children after school.

Components of a Teacher Training Workshop

As you can see from the previous lists, there are may places and many ways in which teacher training can be done, but the most frequently organized trainings go something like this.

Friday Night & Saturday Morning. Friday evening, after dinner, is a time for the inspirational cheer-leading. The senior pastor speaks to the new recruits, then leads a round-robin of "getting to know you" along with "who is who" among the children's ministry leadership team. All the coordinators and service supervisors attend this event!

During this inspiration evening, include the following:

1. Refreshments.

2. Greeting/get acquainted time (ice breakers).

3. Testimonies and praise stories from current teachers.

4. Worship.

5. Teaching on personal spiritual preparedness before ministry.

6. Introduction to the children's ministry goals.

7. Introduction to the child's world and conditions.

Saturday morning from 8:30 to 12:30 is a mad attempt at equipping these dear recruits with only the basics that they need to know in order to survive their initial entrance into the classroom. Remember you are teaming them up with seasoned teachers, so you do not need to tell them everything they need to know down to every last detail. You will overwhelm them, and they will suddenly become "too busy."

The components of your Saturday session should come from the list below:

1. Components of a good lesson.

2. Overview of the curriculum.

3 Teaching on leading small group discussions.

4. Teaching on facilitating lesson-related, student activities.

5. Teaching on basic counseling (listening) skills.

6. Teaching on classroom control and discipline.

7. Teaching on legal issues, liability, and safety.

8. "What to do when . . ." (policy overview relating to classroom situations).

9. Teaching on how to mentor a child and connect outside the classroom.

10. Teaching on how to relate to and minister to parents.

11. Overview of the rotation plan.

Children's Ministry Team Training Plan

TRAINING COMPONENTS

Orientations

Monthly meetings, either during or after services on Sunday morning, for new volunteers. Orientation will include:

- Vision-casting.
- Review of policies / procedures.
- Finger printing.
- ID badges given.
- Connection with "mentors."

Team Rallies

Quarterly gatherings of the entire children's ministry team after Sunday services. The rallies will include:

- Vision-casting.
- "Fruit displays" (stories, etc.).
- Worship.
- Prayer (large group and small group).
- Review of policies / procedures (limited).
- New ideas or "advanced training."
- Review of calendar events.
- Small group interaction (depts.).

Apprenticeships

Four week training under "master teacher" mentors.

ON-GOING TEAM DEVELOPMENT

Leadership Newsletter

A monthly communication to our leadership team which includes *The Flame*.

Department Packet

A monthly communication to the department team which includes a letter from the coordinator, a business "memo," lesson info., and schedules.

Department Social Gathering

Monthly gatherings of the department team for fun and fellowship.

TRAINING / TEAM DEVELOPMENT MEDIA

Overall Ministry Vision Video

A video introducing the overall ministry vision and welcoming the new volunteers to our team.

Department Vision Video

A video introducing the goals for the department and how the vision is developed at this age group.

"Refresher" Audio Tapes

These tapes will be light "refreshers" of policies, procedures, or the ministry vision.

---

12. Explanation of apprentice period.

13. Overview of supply system.

All Day Saturday. Some churches prefer to do the "baptism by fire" approach and do all of this in one Sensational Saturday! If that is your choice, end the day with a Welcome Banquet with children as waiters!

One Month Sunday School Class. Other churches prefer to spread out the training over a month in a new teacher Sunday school class. They divide the above list up into four parts and deliver one part each Sunday for a month. Various topics are taught by different age-group coordinators. This works out well, especially if the coordinators take their respective teachers out for lunch afterwards.

A Three-step Training Process. The ideal teacher-training plan incorporates an extended apprenticeship under master teachers in your ministry, and an on-going, in-service training plan. The "Children's Ministry Team Training Plan" shown above sketches out this ideal process.

The process of equipping teachers to become part of your Great Commission army is a delightful one if it is done on a quarterly basis, with glittering publicity, and with strong pulpit support. Of course, we are imagining a perfect world, but why not talk in ideals? Without sketching out the optimum scenario, how will we know when we have arrived, right? The "Children's Ministry Team Training Plan" illustration explains the sequencing of the optimum teacher-training schedule.

The Teacher Rotation Plan. There are two fears that stand guard in front of the "volunteer gate," keeping many new volunteers away from your ministry. They are the fear of failure and the fear of being trapped. People are convinced that they will make so many mistakes as a teacher that the children they teach will not pass "GO," but go directly to...well...you know. Your teacher-training program will reduce this fear.

The other fear is one of equal dread, that of being trapped in the ministry until Jesus comes back. This second fear is actually quite valid, I'm sad to say. We need to do all we can to protect our teachers from burnout. Today's busy culture produces people who are hesitant to commit to any long-term service. We are always challenged to attract people with just the right schedule of service. Most people will volunteer for a once-a-month commitment. It is our hope that the once-a-month people will move into a longer regular commitment. You might consider a 3- to 6-month rotation plan.

The bottom line of this plan is that the new volunteers are apprenticed (we apprentice new workers just about everywhere, except the church) for six months or less, then they serve for six months and then are guaranteed a six month break from the ministry. They can choose to stay in for another six months, but after a year, they must take a six month break. Those who are on rotation can become valuable to you as substitute teachers if they wish, or be transferred to another age group.

This plan is perhaps the best thing that happened to my children's ministry. I hope you try it out for yourself. It may take a while to get your staff up to a six month commitment, but when you do, you will enjoy the fruit it produces!

First Six Month Period
• New teachers recruited.
• New teachers begin apprenticeship under "master teachers."
• Old teachers are given options for rotation.
• Teachers returning from rotation begin teaching again.

Second Six Month Period
• New teachers recruited.
• New teachers begin apprenticeship under "master teachers."
• Young teachers who have completed their

Children's Ministry Training Process

ORIENTATION
• Application received 1 week prior
• Overall ministry vision video viewed
• Basic policies/procedures reviewed
• Ministry handbook given
• "Agreement to Serve" given
• Finger prints taken
• ID pictures taken, badges given
• Connection with department mentors
• Ministry schedule confirmed
• Apprenticeship period reviewed

APPRENTICESHIP
• Procedures observed
• Curriculum learned
• Relationships begun
• Fears removed

EMPOWERING
• Newsletters received
• Team rallies attended
• Packets received
• Leadership options considered
• Social gatherings attended
• "Refresher" media received

apprenticeship are given options for rotation.

• Old teachers are given options for rotation.

• Teachers returning from rotation begin teaching again.

Third Six Month Period

• New teachers recruited.

• New teachers begin apprenticeship under "master teachers."

• Young teachers who have completed their apprenticeship are given options for rotation.

• Old teachers are given options for rotation.

• Teachers returning from rotation begin teaching again.

Options for Rotating Teachers

1. Remain in ministry for one more six-month period before mandatory rotation.

2. Rotate out of ministry completely for six months.

3. Rotate into the substitute list and be available to assist in upcoming teacher training.

Options for Returning Teachers

1. Return to the position they left when rotating.

2. Move to another position in the same age group.

3. Move to another age group.

Training for Teamwork

Working with and within a team is much like a marriage. For a marriage to last and grow in strength, both partners must believe that the other person is looking out for their best interests. This concept is a blend of both faith and trust. When disagreements or differences come, and they will, they can be dealt with positively when such faith and trust are protected. Working together on a team is just as challenging. If the team members share a common goal and mutual trust, challenges will only strengthen the bonds of the team.

Here are some guidelines for establishing and protecting the team's trust and communication. These require a certain degree of commitment and discipline on the part of every team member.

1. Share a common goal—Each team member will be challenged to understand and adopt the team's

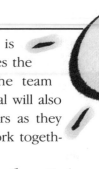

goal. Once the goal is agreed upon, it becomes the focus of everything the team does. This common goal will also unify the team members as they invest, sacrifice, and work together.

2. Get to know each other—Each team member must make concerted efforts to understand each team member's personality. As with the courtship phase (which never ends with a strong marriage), the engaged couple spends time and effort in understanding their future mate. Team members must spend time with other team members outside of the team meetings and work time. Each team member has feelings, drives, and passions that comprise their personality. Without knowing the person, we only can react to the words or actions of the person. Reacting to the words or actions without knowing the person can cause division and eventually destroy the team.

3. Communicate and listen—One of the most important things a married couple can do to strengthen the marriage is to talk to each other. Another critical thing to do is to listen. Team members must have passion and feel strongly about their own area of service. Those strong feelings must be communicated without possessiveness or defensiveness. Each team member must talk about his or her passions and feelings. The goal is to help the other team members understand, without trying to change their minds. The natural effect of trying to get your spouse to change is usually a deeper gap in communication. Successful team members talk and listen without trying to force their views on others. Listening is a critical step toward understanding. Understanding is a critical step toward unity. Unity is a critical step toward effectiveness. Talking about feelings and listening to views are never wrong.

4. Think the best—As with a marriage, when a team member appears to have purposefully spoken or acted unfaithfully or outside of the guidelines of the team, the other team members must think the best of that team member and seek to understand the team member's motives and reasons for the action. Humans all too often jump to the worst conclusions without first consulting the person in doubt. Team members must take the time to patiently ask, "Tell us why..." or "Help us understand..." or "What prompted you to..." and then listen with ears of understanding to the answers. When a team member has indeed veered from the guidelines, chances are good that he or she will be more apt to admit it or accept criticism if he or she has had an opportunity to be heard.

5. Sacrifice/compromise—When marriage partners are willing to sacrifice or compromise for the sake of the other person, that other person usually is more willing to compromise and sacrifice as well. This is the cycle that is described in *Ephesians 5*. Team members must also be willing to give up for the good of the team as well. This can only be accomplished if there is trust among the team members. Without trust and understanding, sacrifice or compromise becomes almost impossible. In order for a team to work together, the team members cannot be possessive of ideas. All ideas become team ideas. There may be point persons for certain ideas, but those team members must be more sensitive to other team members' views, not less.

6. Shared successes—Team successes may be more felt by a team member who had more involvement in the program or idea, but all team members should feel a sense of gratification in each success. If only one team member feels the joy of a success, that may be an indicator that the other team members weren't as involved in the development of the program or idea. As with a marriage, when one partner experiences joy or a success, the other partner rejoices too. Jealousy or competition can destroy both a marriage and a team.

TRAINING CHILD-FOCUSED TEACHERS

We continue now with a format to which you have become quite accustomed: Examining the strategies by which we will be able to reach all of our "Great Commission Vision Goals." The remainder of this chapter will focus on the goals for successful teaching and for establishing positive relationships with the children in our ministries.

"GO" Strategies

These strategies relate to vision category "GO." "We will GO into the world of today's children with trained, well-organized, passionate, godly adults who carry the message of the Gospel.

Goal 1.1 Before they come to an event, we want the children of our ministry to say, "I want to go there because I feel safe, welcomed, and valued."

Those of us who work with children know that children feel emotionally safe when their fragile self-concepts are protected, and their feelings and opinions are valued. Children return to where they are personally greeted and not made to feel guilty if absent. Children will return to the place where their presence and ideas are valued equally. Teaching new teachers to become child-focused is a critically important component of your teacher training.

To Reach This Goal:

• Train all team members in affirmation techniques.

• Expose all team members to positive examples of child-focused behavior.

• Reward team members for excellence in child-focused behavior.

• Instruct teachers to handle all classroom situations that might cause them to lose their cool and thereby become less than child-focused.

Goal 1.5 We want every children's ministry team member to say, "I am so glad I get to make the contribution I make with my talents."

No matter what part a person plays on the team, he or she must feel valued and vital to the success of the process. Not everyone needs to be a teacher. We need greeters, restroom helpers, craft experts, etc. to balance our team. Teachers need to focus on the process of teaching. People will want to continue doing what makes them comfortable and fulfilled. People like to be a part of something big. There are people who don't want to be "in front of the curtain,"

Twenty "Small Jobs" with a Big Impact

1. Hallway assistants/greeters
2. Classroom greeters
3. Arts and crafts assistants
4. Supply room volunteers
5. Information booth volunteers
6. Worship team members
7. Field trip team members
8. Video team members
9. Sports team members
10. Puppet team members
11. Camp team members
12. Infant rockers
13. Storytellers
14. Drama team members
15. Phone callers
16. Letter and card writers
17. Data keepers
18. Supply shoppers/gatherers
19. Teachers' aides
20. Musicians

but would rather be behind the scenes and let others get the applause. We need every member of the body.

To Reach This Goal:

1. Create a list of small jobs and publicize in adult worship.

2. Create a promotional video of people serving in small jobs.

3. Plan a behind the scenes person appreciation party.

4. Create a behind the scenes award.

5. Create a list of the entire team according to each person's function. Use this list to aid in supporting and appreciating each person.

6. Match each team member with another team member's name for prayer and support (verbally, via email, etc.).

Goal 12.3 We want the supervisors and teachers on our children's ministry team to say, "I enjoy being a partner with the home."

Parents need support and help today. If we can influence and support the parents, we can double the influence on the children! Phone calls to the children's home or personal notes and letters draw the parents closer and closer.

To Reach This Goal:

1. Encourage team members who do successfully communicate with the home to share those stories during team meetings.

2. Provide team members with note cards printed with the children's ministry logo to be used for parent communication.

"TEACHING" Strategies

These strategies relate to vision category "TEACHING." "We will train our team members in effective TEACHING methods based on the interests and needs of today's children.

Goal 8.3 We want the supervisors and teachers on our children's ministry team to say, "I want to try new approaches to learning."

Every teacher needs to add personal touches to the lesson experience. These additions to the curriculum don't need to be approved unless they are major variations of the lesson topic or activities that might be unsafe or risky. Team members need to share success stories with each other. These will be done via email or during ministry team rallies. People like to feel like they are advancing in their abilities. Trying new things is risky. A healthy all-team mentality of "Try It," with no fear of criticism if things don't work out as planned, is good.

To Reach This Goal:

1. Develop a rotational plan for sending team members to local children's ministry conferences

2. Let team members who supplement the curriculum successfully share their techniques during area meetings (or even during all-team meetings).

3. Highlight team members who "Try It" in the newsletters, emails, etc.

4. Provide subscriptions to children's ministry magazines for team leaders.

Teachers must be allowed to be both unique and creative; however, they do need a firm understanding of what children need at each level of their development. Following is a listing of the basics of what each age-level of teacher-training should contain.

Review of Children's Needs by Department

Each department coordinator was asked to describe the needs of the children in their department, as well as what the coordinator wanted to accomplish in those children in preparation for their graduation to the next department. Here are some of the answers.

Nursery Department

1. The children in this age-group experience separation anxiety when they are dropped off in the classroom or nursery by their parents. It is our primary challenge to help the children adjust and get through this fear. Those who have been regulars in the nursery do adjust to being separated from their parents, and by the time they get to be 3 year-olds, they are ready for the preschool classrooms. It is the first-time children who have the most difficulty with the situation.

2. The children need to be loved.

3. The children need a fun environment.

4. The children need to feel secure and not scared.

5. Be sensitive not only to the children, but also to their parents. The parents have the same concerns as the children. Develop a First-time Parent Packet.

6. The adults who serve in the nursery areas need to be trained to be sensitive to both the children and parents.

7. The environment needs to be visually stimulating and inviting. First-time children must be interested in coming into the room because of what they see or hear.

8. There need to be fun things to do. There needs to be variety to suit the individual children (play areas, soft touch areas, cushion areas, etc.). Half-walls to divide areas. Children can wander and choose based on preference or mood.

9. We want the children to learn or feel, "Church is good." The overall theme is: "Others will care for me."

Preschool Department

The preschool child needs all of the above, and more.

1. The children need appropriate tasks to do.

2. They need comfortable surroundings and furniture.

3. They need to learn the foundational character traits of respect, kindness, and the hows and whys of things.

4. The children have expectations for the adults who serve in the classroom. The parents, as in the nursery, share those expectations. The adults who serve in the preschool area must be gentle, yet sometimes firm, kind, patient, sensitive to the needs of the child, and fun.

5. The children need to begin learning basic Bible truths. The emphasis needs to be on the principles, not on the facts of the Bible story. The major Bible stories need to be covered.

6. The children are beginning to understand the difference between good and bad.

7. The children need to be shown the conflicts in the stories. They are interested in good guy/bad guy aspects of stories.

8. Bible stories must be applicable and familiar to the children, or at least contain applicable and familiar aspects to them.

9. The children need to learn how to share.

10. They need to learn the value of getting along with others.

11. The children need to learn the value of an orderly classroom.

12. The children need to learn the value of waiting their turn.

13. Lessons and classroom environment must be visually stimulating.

14. Adults who serve these children must give their primary attention to the children, not the subject of the lesson, or the schedule of the session. The overall theme: "Others have needs too."

Elementary Department

The elementary child needs everything an infant and a preschooler needs plus the following.

1. They need to feel loved personally, not just as a member of the corporate class.

2. The children need to learn how to follow directions.

3. The children need to learn how to share.

4. Correct choices and behavior must be rewarded.

5. The children need to be shown (or be inspired to discover) personal applications to the basic Bible truths.

6. The children need to know that God cares for them personally.

7. Bible memorization is valued only as much as it can be shown to assist in personal choice-making skills.

8. The children need to take responsibility for their own actions and maturity.

9. The children need to learn how to discern between right and wrong choices (both for themselves and for others).

10. The children must learn that they need to care for others.

11. Adults who serve these children must teach through being role-models.

12. Adults who serve these children must become involved in the lives of the children apart from just teaching a Bible lesson. The overall theme is: "I need to care for others."

Goal 9.1 These strategies relate to vision category "TEACHING." "We will TEACH THEM with relevant curriculum which emphasizes both biblical content and fun!" Before they come to an event, we want the children of our ministry to say, "I want to go there because it's fun."

Nobody likes to sit and listen to a lecture; children need activity and challenges. Many excellent resources exist for jazzing up any lesson. Be sure your teacher-training includes a large library of those.

To Reach This Goal:

1. Make CD's & split-track tapes of music, game books, dramas, stories, and object lesson books available to your teachers in a resource lending library.

2. Train all team members in supplementing the curriculum, in activity-based education, and in how to evaluate the curriculum based on activity and application.

3. Train all team members in classroom management.

4. Do all we can to reduce class size or to increase times of interaction and guided conversation.

5. Train the teachers in the teaching methods of Jesus, and help them model his style.

No matter what your teacher training sessions include, you must make your children's ministry team members keenly aware of how sacred their task is. Help them understand that, as teachers, they are walking in the footsteps of the Master Teacher—Jesus—and there is no higher call than to serve in his Great Commission.

WHAT TO DO WHEN...

This is a fun part of my teacher training program; it underscores how fragile some moments can become and how easy it is to become so situation-focused that it becomes impossible to be student-focused. I have this little pet peeve. I think most of our efforts in teacher training are great, and to be truthful with you, very little can be done to hurt the thrill a new volunteer brings into the ministry for the first time. Having said that, I think there is one thing we neglect to tell these brave new recruits before they go out to the trenches. We don't tell them how to clean up after a child has lost his or her breakfast on the carpet. (If you're reading this during a meal, I'm sorry.) The poor teacher has stayed up all night cutting out camels and studying her lesson. She got to her room early enough to lay out the crafts and arrange the tables "just so." She is totally prepared for everything—but this! All of her preparation and planning goes out the door when the child becomes sick. The other children all scream and move to the walls. They all look at her for direction. She has none.

Whew, scary, huh? That is not the only situation that can come up during a class session. I knew I wanted my teachers to be able to handle just about anything because these unplanned situations are teachable moments in the children's lives. If I really believed that the teachers are the living Bible curriculum, then I had to prepare them for these moments so they could continue teaching while the children watched their reactions. So, I created this list. Obviously, you have to tailor-fit the list to your own church setting. Fill in the blanks with the names of people to contact for that situation. If your name goes into all the lines, God bless you. This may also let you see that you need help during the services. I hope this list will bless your smooth-running program.

Guidelines for Some Unexpected Surprises

1. You need supplies that aren't included in your curriculum.
- Buy the supplies you need, turn in receipts to ____ for refund.

2. You can't teach your class (due to sickness or family emergency).
- Call your coordinator. Do not leave your teaching partner alone with the class.

3. A child in your class gets sick or injured during class.
- Ask your teaching partner to take the child to the children's ministry office, or, if the child cannot be moved, go get help or call for an ambulance. Have the child's parent or guardian brought to him/her as soon as possible. DO NOT LEAVE YOUR CLASS UNATTENDED!

4. A child throws up during class.
- Contact your coordinator.
- Remember the "never alone" policy. Care for the sick child as best you can in the room until help arrives.
- If you can, take the children elsewhere while the room is cleaned.
- Contact parent as soon as possible.
- Fill out an incident report.
- Clean the classroom with a good-smelling cleanser/deodorizer available in your classroom cabinet or in room # ____ .

- Open all windows and doors to ventilate the smell out of the room. If at all possible, complete your class in another area. Remember to either return to the room before parents come to pick up their children, or put a note on the door telling them where their children are.

5. A child is dropped off in the wrong room.
- Be looking for the child's parent at the end of the class. You'll need to take the parent to the correct class.
- Note: For safety and liability reasons, you should have a check-in system that doesn't permit parents from sending their children alone to class.

6. A child is a discipline problem, and you've tried everything you've been trained to do.
- Ask your teaching partner to find ____ or your coordinator for consultation.
- Remember the "never alone" rule.
- Separate the disruptive child from the rest of the class. DO NOT PLACE THE CHILD OUTSIDE THE CLASSROOM!
- Remain in visual contact with the child at all times.
- Place a member of your teaching team next to the child for the rest of the class.
- Talk with the parent, or whoever brought the child regarding the child's behavior, regarding our discipline policy, or refer the parent to ____ .

7. There is an earthquake.
- Instruct the children to get under their tables until the shaking stops. If the building is damaged, evacuate the building as soon as shaking stops. MAKE CERTAIN ALL CHILDREN ARE ACCOUNTED FOR.

8. There is a fire.
- Know the location of the nearest fire extinguisher and alarm station.
- Instruct the children to line up and follow you as you walk out rapidly. Do not run! Leave the building according to the escape plan, or through the nearest exit. Your teaching partner should follow the class

and MAKE SURE ALL YOUR CHILDREN ARE OUT SAFELY.

• Once your class is safely outside and away from the building, your teaching partner should go offer assistance to the nursery team.

• Nursery: place babies in cribs and wheel out, or on blankets and carry out. If you have enough volunteers, hand carry babies out. MAKE SURE ALL BABIES ARE ACCOUNTED FOR!

• Make sure ____ has been notified and the fire department has been called.

• If you are unable to return to the classroom before the parents arrive to pick up their children, appoint someone to greet the parents and direct them to the area where their children can be found.

9. A parent is angry with you.

• Never engage an angry parent during class. Politely ask the parent to return after class (for the sake of the children).

• Request assistance from your coordinator or another team member. If the parent cannot be satisfied, refer them to ____ or the church office.

10. A child isn't picked up after class.

• After all the other children have been picked up, leave a note on your door to the parents, and together with another team member, take the child to the children's ministry office.

• If the child is not picked up after the service is over, attempt to contact the parent at home, or together with another team member, check the child back into class for the next service.

• If the child is not picked up after the final service, contact ____ or the senior minister.

11. Your curriculum is lost or misplaced.

• Let your coordinator or ____ know, or use the extra teacher's manual stored in the supply room.

12. You need more curriculum.

• Let your coordinator or ____ know.

13. You would like to deviate from the curriculum

• Let your coordinator or ____ know.

## chapter 16

The Gardener's Peace:
Protecting Your Passion

A gardener creates a place for others to enjoy, but he owes himself a little reward for his hard work by sitting down and enjoying the garden himself.

The first garden was created just for those who would live in it. God, the first gardener, had it all planned. He created an amazing, peaceful, self-maintaining garden with everything the two people needed. He designed everything just for them. Then, to make a long story short, he had to kick them out and eventually destroy everything he made. Can you imagine his sadness?

Now he invites us to join him for a walk in the garden. His new garden is a spiritual place. It is a place of peace, joy, and his presence. There are places to reflect, dream, and sleep there. The garden has been planted in our soul. Jesus' death on the cross is the garden gate, and we who accept his death enter in and find rest.

The beauty of this garden of God is that it goes with us! Wherever we are, there is rest and peace available to us. God has given us only one job to perform in this garden: to bring others with us. The work of children's ministry is about rescuing children from the weeds, rocks, gnats, and gophers of the world. God offers the children true peace and purpose, but he gives us and the parents the tools that will draw them into the garden. The tools God gives us are designed to plant human souls in God's garden. He lets us plant, but he causes the growth. He lets us enjoy the fruit and the joy of our planting.

We are now at the end of this book. We've covered much ground. We have one more topic to deal with here: protecting your passion and your peace. Your passion, vision, and faithfulness to God will produce a healthy garden! If you seek the Lord first, you will be blessed, and your garden will grow. With that growth come challenges. It may seem strange, but a successful garden may be more challenging than one that doesn't produce much fruit. A struggling garden drives you to your knees regularly. A successful garden tempts you to stand up and be recognized for your great accomplishments. Be careful.

In order to remain in God's perfect peace, we have to keep our minds on him. The moment we forget who produced the growth of our garden is the moment the weeds start to choke out our plants! It takes a lot of concentration to handle a successful garden and to keep your focus correct. It is the same concentration that Peter had, and then lost, when Jesus asked him to come out and walk around on the waves with him. Let's look at how to handle a growing garden!

HOW TO WALK ON WATER
Remain focused on your Lord and purpose

Sometimes the greatest threat to our ministry is success. When the Lord gets us to climb out of the boat and we begin being blessed, we are tempted to take our eyes off of him and either focus on our success or be consumed by worry about the details. Our constant challenge is to keep our eyes and our attention on Jesus and the purpose for our ministry.

The First Stepping Stone:
Protect Your Passion "First Love"

Continually deepen your intimacy with Jesus. Remember

Garden Pest:
Swarming Aphids

Evidence

These unusual forms of the common aphid get their name from the strange behavior for which they are known: swarming the plant all at once. A person that is the victim of this condition has little or no hope, short of being severely pruned back at work. The aphids come slowly over weeks. Late night meetings, extended hours on Sundays with no family time at church, or phone calls at home are all forms of the Swarming Aphids. Soon the family's priority is lost under a thick layer of aphids. Evidence that the aphids are present is an angry spouse, or undisciplined children. Personal signs are statements such as, "I can't be home, they need me at church."

Sources of Infestation

Finding personal value in the work of the ministry instead of the relationships at home.

Treatment

1. Be aware of the problem, and be afraid of losing your family.
2. Inform your supervisor at church that you cannot sacrifice your family for the ministry, and that you will not be working past normal office hours any longer.
3. Protect your days off. Spend them doing things with your spouse or children.
4. Kindly ask people not to call you at home after hours unless it is an emergency.
5. Take walks with your spouse or family.
6. Say "no" to expectations that will draw you away from home outside of office hours.

Revelation 2:4: "I hold this against you: You have forsaken your first love." Be careful about becoming so busy with your success that you forget the Lord and your ministry vision. God is the source of your strength and success. Grow in your relationship with God through:

1. Your own personal reading, studying, and memorization of Scripture.
2. Regular worship.
3. Constant prayer (practice stillness, and listening to him).
4. Listening to worship music.

The Second Stepping Stone: Protect Your Family

So many godly pastors and ministries have fallen because they neglected their family or marriage. In order to have peace in your ministry, you must have peace at home! Make your family's needs critical. Say "no" to work often. Come home early. Take back-to-back days off (shift your normal days off around periodically).

God will not bless a ministry led by a person whose home is out of order. If you want to have a successful ministry, invest in your family!

The Third Stepping Stone: Return to Your "Gilgal"

Remember how far you have come. When you are backpacking, it's a good idea to stop and look behind you and see how far you have come rather than always keeping your eyes on the trail or on the summit ahead of you. When the climb gets especially hard, you need the pat on the back that looking back can give. You also need to keep your eyes on the compass or landmark to make sure your are traveling in the right direction. That's why the Lord commanded that his people build a place of remembrance—a Gilgal altar—so they could remember what the Lord had done.

In Joshua chapter 4, God tells the Israelites to build a pile of stones at the place in which they crossed over the Jordan River into the promised land. This pile of stones was at a place called Gilgal. God told the people to come back to this pile of stones periodically and to remember what God had done to get them out of Egypt and bring them into the promised land. They were to tell their children the whole story whenever they returned there! If you read the Old Testament, you will see references to them returning to Gilgal before important battles, and after victories. Gilgal became a place of remembering! Remembering is a critical practice to God. He wants us to remember what he has done and where we are going!

Return to Gilgal and remember your vision. Remember your passion. Remember your children's ministry vision. Remember who you are (your past, your faults, the lessons you learned, the forgiveness and mercy you received from God, etc.). Remember your calling and your first day in ministry. Remember, and give God the glory he deserves!

Return to Gilgal and remember your goals. Remember the plans and dreams for children's ministry that made you weep at one time. Remember the things you wanted to accomplish when you first started this ministry. Remember the hope you had. Remember the possibilities based on God's leading and power. Remember, and give God glory for the calling and wisdom he gave you.

Return to Gilgal and remember your policies and procedures. Remember what you want to accomplish, and how to make it happen while protecting the children. Remember God's wisdom about being careful and safe.

Return to Gilgal and remember your programs. Remember your original design of the programs. Remember your vision for the programs. Remember what God told you about the part those programs play in your ministry vision.

Return to Gilgal and remember your image. Remember what you want people to think or feel when they think of the children's ministry. Remember that God creates and gives the vision; he must also lead you in creating the image of that vision.

Return to Gilgal and remember your team. Remember that these are people who need real hugs, encouragement, and direction. Remember that God created all of them and that he can give you insight and ideas for developing a team that you never even considered!

The Fourth Stepping Stone: God's Formulas for Success and Failure

God's formula for success could be stated as follows: Reverence of God + Willingness to sacrifice for him and others = Success. God's formula for failure is just the opposite: Reverence of self - Willingness to sacrifice for God or others = Failure

Be Humble

Confidence is a critical factor in becoming a fruitful children's minister. You must be confident to set goals, determine objectives, create programs, and attract the kind of people who will empower you to accomplish your goals. Confidence can also be your worst nightmare. Have you ever met a person who is overly confident? Too much confidence, or misplaced confidence, can drive others away and even prevent you or your ministry from receiving God's blessing. What makes the difference between good confidence and bad confidence? The difference is in the source of your confidence.

God has more than likely given you all you need to do what he has called you to do in ministry. He has saved you through Jesus, given you his Holy Spirit to teach you and empower you, led you in and out of experiences that teach you, and provided you with certain gifts to help you do what he has called you to do more effectively. You have all you need. The only thing he won't do for you is to make you decide to follow, honor, obey, and worship him with all your heart, soul, and mind. That is your decision.

God's Church is filled with people who say they serve God, but who really are serving themselves. They like "the ministry" for what it does for them. They really love the adoration, respect, and feeling of spiritual power. These "ministers" flourish for a while, but as *Psalm 37:2* says, "they will soon wither." In the book of Malachi, God clearly expresses his opinions about those ministers of the Lord who show contempt for his name. God is serious about your motives, passion, and purpose. "Humble yourselves, therefore, under God's mighty hand, that he may lift you up in due time" *(1 Peter 5:6)*.

Self-Confidence vs. God-Confidence

Self-confidence (Pride)	God-confidence (Humility)
"I can do this, no problem!"	"Thank you, God, for the gifts and abilities."
"I don't need any help."	"Whatever help God sends me, I'll use."
"Look what I did!"	"It's a privilege to be a part of God's work."

The Fifth Stepping Stone:
Handling Blessings and Worries

When dealing with blessings, don't take the blessing personally; it's not because you are a super pastor! (See *Deuteronomy 8:17, 18*.) Don't take the blessing for granted. Thank God for it and remain humble. Consider the source of the blessing. It didn't come from you or your actions! (See *Exodus 20:5*.) Remember Who you serve, and what he has done to get you here. Receive the encouragement for correct perspective and keep going.

When faced with worries, don't look down! Don't focus on the lack or need. (See *Colossians 3:2*.) Keep focused on God, your ministry vision, and the Great Commission. God will take care of the needs of your ministry if you are faithful in following him.

The Sixth Stepping Stone:
Purify Your Mind

Your mind is the battleground of your spirit. In your mind dwells the control center for your thoughts, actions, words, and motives. There are so many Scriptures that clearly challenge us to give God full control of our minds. The goal of a pure mind is to better hear and see God. Look at these references in the Bible to our thoughts, and also the results of a pure mind:

1. "Set your mind on things above" *(Colossians 3:1, 2)*.

2. "The peace of God...will guard your hearts and your minds" *(Philippians 4:4-7)*.

3. "Whatever is true...whatever is pure...think about such things" *(Philippians 4:8)*.

4. "Take captive every thought" *(2 Corinthians 10:5, 6)*.

5. "Blessed are the pure in heart, for they will see God" *(Matthew 5:8)*.

6. "My sheep listen to my voice; I know them, and they follow me" *(John 10:27)*.

7. "The prayer of a righteous man is powerful and effective" *(James 5:16)*.

As you take control of your thoughts, you will be amazed at how much easier it is to flee from temptation. A pure mind is like a systemic insecticide (an insecticide that works from within the plant) against the evil, sinful, temptations that act like insects in your garden. With a pure mind, the enemy won't even be able to tempt you. With a pure mind, God will be able to draw you closer to himself and multiply the blessings in your own life and in the ministry he has given you.

Ten Ways to Purify Your Mind:

1. Control your negative self-talk, and replace it with memorized Scripture.
2. Limit your time with negative people.
3. Remove swearing from your life.
4. Walk out of offensive movies (violence, swearing, nudity, amoral behavior, etc.).
5. Listen to worship music.
6. Change the channel during offensive radio or television programs.
7. Think good thoughts about people.
8. Remove offensive reading materials.
9. Memorize Scripture.
10. Pray at all times.

The Seventh Stepping Stone: Keep Learning

I believe children's ministers must be in a constant state of learning. Paul was a very wise man who never stopped learning. He knew the value of learning, and he encouraged all of us to be perpetual students: "This is my prayer: that your love may abound more and more in knowledge and depth of insight, so that you may be able to discern what is best and may be pure and blameless until the day of Christ, filled with the fruit of righteousness that comes through Jesus Christ—to the glory and praise of God" *(Philippians 1:9-11).*

If your heart becomes old or tired you will be of no use to God or the church. The greatest vaccination for pride is forcing yourself to be a student. In so doing, you willfully humble yourself under an author (by reading a book), teacher (by attending a seminar), and under God (by cultivating your relationship with him). That is what *Proverbs 3:5-7* is all about. When you acknowledge him in all your ways, he promises to "make your paths straight" with wisdom and insight that you could never even dream of!

Eleven ways to keep learning:

1. Be a daily student of God's Word.
2. Avidly read new books (non-fiction, ministry-related).
3. Subscribe to, and read, ministry magazines.
4. Listen to recorded messages in your car and at home.
5. Watch children's programs on television.
6. Network with other children's pastors.
7. Attend ministry conferences.
8. Interview school principals often.
9. Walk through a shopping mall and observe trends, people, etc.
10. Interview children.
11. Interview parents.

The Eighth Stepping Stone: Protect Your Ministry Purpose

Throughout this book we have journeyed along with the goals of our "Great Commission Vision" serving as signposts along the way; they have reminded us of where we are going and how far we have yet to travel before we reach our destination. As we come to end of our trek together, I want to present these goals to you with a slightly different spin. Instead of reading the goals again, just listen to what people will say as you complete each one of the fifteen goals in the "Great Commission Vision."

Children will say:

"I want to go there because I feel safe, welcomed, and valued."

"I want to go there because I have friends there."

"I'm sad it's over."

"I want to sing to God because I love him."

"Praying is fun!"

"I can't wait to come back again."

"I want to go there because it's fun."

"I want to go there because I learn more about God there."

"I learned how to be a better friend," or "I learned how to be a better student," etc.

"I want to help others."

"I am not ashamed to take a stand for God at school."

Parents will say:

"They really understand what I'm looking for in a children's ministry."

"I feel safe leaving my child there."

"My child sings these songs at home. Where can I buy the music?"

"I know the teachers care for my child."

"The children's ministry gives us valuable tools in raising our children."

"I feel like my church is a partner with me in raising my child."

Children's Ministry Team Members Will Say:

"I enjoy serving the Lord here."

"I feel a part of a team effort here."

"I want my friends and neighbors to join this team."

"I am so glad I get to make the contribution I make with my talents."

"These children are praying for each other without being told to do so!"

"I enjoy learning right along with the children."

"I cherish the process of preparing, planting, watering, and harvesting."

"I feel supported and appreciated here."

"I want to try new approaches to learning."

"I want to connect with the children beyond the classroom."

"I enjoy being a partner with the home."

The Congregation will say:

"These people look like a team with a purpose."

"The children's ministry inspires me."

The Lord will say:

"Well done, my good and faithful servants."

"Because you are faithful in the small things, I will lead you to large things."

It has been a pleasure writing this book. It has taken me through over 25 years of ministry experience. The experiences, stories, and wisdom contained in this book come from a fine blend of successes and failures. The difference between a success and a failure is purely in the application of that knowledge. A failure is when something goes differently than you expected, and you don't learn from the experience. A success is when you have applied what God has taught you to a new experience, regardless of the outcome of that application. God is just as interested in the application of successes as he is of the failures.

If I could leave you with one parting comment, it would be that with which Solomon ended his book of Ecclesiastes: "Now all has been heard; here is the conclusion of the matter: Fear God and keep his commandments, for this is the whole duty of man" *(Ecclesiastes 12:13)*.

What you are about is a deeply spiritual experience. Treat it that way. The moment you find yourself focusing on the money or other desk clutter that tends to pile up over the week, stop. Return to Gilgal, and remember. Remember the special children God has given you to love. Remember those children and parents who exist without hope outside your program walls. Remember Jesus' command to "Go." Your budget, programs, curriculum, personnel problems, and political challenges are all about those children! If you can keep them in mind, you will be fine.

Now, if you'll excuse me, I have to go enjoy some juicy peaches....